Kantoor van die Staatspresident
State President's Office

STAATSPRESIDENTSMINUUT NO:

Kragtens die bevoegdheid my verleen by artikel 69(1) van die Wet op Gevangenisse, 1959 (Wet no 8 van 1959) soos gewysig keur ek goed dat spesiale afslag van vonnis aan die ondergenoemde gevangene toegestaan word en dat hy op 11 Februarie 1990 vrygelaat is nadat ingevolge artikel 69(2) van genoemde Wet gehandel is:

NELSON ROLIHLAHLA MANDELA

STAATSPRESIDENT
Datum:

MINISTER VAN DIE KABINET

19.1025.DK

Note: Approval of 'special remission' of sentence of 'undermentioned prisoner' Nelson Rolihlahla Mandela, awaiting signature by the State President. Stamped by Minister H.J. (Kobie) Coetsee. Source: Coetsee Collection, ARCA.

NELSON MANDELA'S number on Robben Island was 466/64 – prisoner number 466, who arrived in 1964. In later years, it was used to brand a global HIV/AIDS awareness campaign, with Mandela as patron. However, in the broader prison system, he had another number which spanned the entire period of his incarceration. That number was 913.

RIAAN DE VILLIERS
and JAN-AD STEMMET

PRISONER 913

THE RELEASE OF NELSON MANDELA

TAFELBERG

Tafelberg,
an imprint of NB Publishers,
a division of Media24 Boeke (Pty.) Ltd.,
40 Heerengracht, Cape Town, South Africa 8000
www.tafelberg.com

© 2020 Riaan de Villiers, Jan-Ad Stemmet

All rights reserved.
No part of this book may be reproduced or transmitted in any form or
by any electronic or mechanical means, including photocopying and recording,
or by any other information storage or retrieval system,
without written permission from the publisher.

Set in Candida
Cover design by Nudge Studio
Book design by Nazli Jacobs
Edited by Russell Martin
Proofread by Riaan Wolmarans
Index by George Claassen

Printed by **novus print**, a division of Novus Holdings

First edition, first impression 2020
ISBN: 978-0-624-07632-2
Epub: 978-0-624-07633-9
Mobi: 978-0-624-07634-6

*Dedicated to
all those who worked to
resolve the South African
political conflict.*

Contents

About this book – *Riaan de Villiers*	ix
My journey with the Coetsee archive – *Jan-Ad Stemmet*	1
Who was Kobie Coetsee? – *Riaan de Villiers*	8
Eavesdropping on Mandela	28

1.	Let the games begin . . .	33
2.	The missing letter to P.W. Botha	41
3.	Tardy ministers and the State Security Council	46
4.	Brothers in arms	57
5.	The birth of an idea	66
6.	A meeting with Kobie Coetsee	79
7.	Mandela's 'political testament'	90
8.	Botha crosses the Rubicon, and then tries to swim back	97
9.	'A conjuncture of circumstances'	106
10.	'A large piece of bitterness . . .'	114
11.	The management of Nelson Mandela	117
12.	The release of the 'eight'	122
13.	'You are to blame . . .'	137
14.	'A grain of sand in an oyster . . .'	154
15.	The men from COSATU	163
16.	A long-distance phone call	165
17.	The ANC takes stock	169
18.	Things hot up in Lusaka	172
19.	A tale of two statements	185
20.	Things go south	191
21.	Two notable documents . . .	197
22.	. . . And an enduring mystery	213

23.	At the last minute	220
24.	'Reform in a stable climate . . .'	228
25.	A visit from Winnie	238
26.	Pressures in Paarl	242
27.	Snacks, drinks and lunch for 22	245
28.	Panic stations	251
29.	The last report	259

A note about the references	264
Endnotes	265
Index	273
About the authors	279

About this book
Riaan de Villiers

THIS VOLUME is based on largely secret records about Nelson Mandela kept by Kobie Coetsee, Minister of Justice and Prisons, in the last phase of the apartheid regime. In this position, Coetsee presided over the last eight years of Mandela's incarceration and his eventual release. The records effectively comprise Coetsee's file on Mandela – 'Prisoner 913' – kept in his ministry.

Coetsee removed the archive – probably illegally – when he vacated his ministry shortly before the transition to democracy. He was about to hand it to the co-author of this volume, the historian Jan-Ad Stemmet, when he died suddenly in 2000. The extraordinary story of Jan-Ad's brief interaction with Coetsee and the rediscovery of the archive some 13 years later is told in the next essay.

The fact that Coetsee kept a file on Mandela (and other 'security prisoners') is not remarkable in itself – given his portfolio and Mandela's growing prominence, this would have been routine. However, the archive helps to reveal that Coetsee's records far exceeded the bounds of any conventional administrative function.

As is widely known, from 1985 onwards Coetsee took a special interest in Mandela, and eventually started secret talks with him that presaged his eventual release. This interest, and the way it played itself out, is reflected in the archive's extraordinary scope; the vast 913 file contains a wealth of material about every conceivable aspect of Mandela's incarceration, ranging from secret government memorandums and other documents through medical reports, letters, press cuttings, and handwritten notes to a plethora of other material.

Rather sensationally, the archive also contains transcripts of clandestine recordings of many of Mandela's conversations with a growing stream of visitors while in prison, ranging from foreign dignitaries and the Commonwealth Eminent Persons Group to government ministers, his lawyers, family members, fellow 'security prisoners', and other political role players.

As explained elsewhere, prison warders at that time routinely made notes of visits to certain categories of prisoners, notably 'security prisoners'. However, the archive discloses that Coetsee introduced what amounted to a second-track intelligence operation, aimed at monitoring everything Mandela and some other prisoners said or did, and utilising this knowledge to inform his own agenda as well as government strategy.

Put differently, Coetsee used his position to become Mandela's 'gatekeeper', jealously guarding access to his 'star prisoner', and placing himself in a position to control or influence the entire process surrounding Mandela's incarceration and eventual release. As such, these transcripts provide a unique window on Mandela's beliefs, motivations, strategic decisions, and the course of events at that time.

////

If the archive presents researchers with a unique resource, it also presents them with a formidable challenge. It comprises hundreds of files totalling some 13 000 pages, filed in a sprawling and untidy range of categories. Over the years, some items have become misplaced, resulting in some key documents turning up in unexpected places. Documents are typed, telexed, handwritten and photocopied, and some are very difficult to decipher.

The archive is equally vast in scope, reflecting a range of dimensions – administrative, legal, political, diplomatic, medical and personal – surrounding Mandela's incarceration, moving through several stages from his 'deep' incarceration which still held in the early 1980s through renewed prominence sparked by growing international pressure and internal unrest, to his eventual 'open imprisonment' and release.

Notably, the Mandela file – simply labelled '913' – is just one such composite file in the Coetsee archive. Similar, albeit less extensive, records were kept on other 'security prisoners', notably Walter Sisulu (Prisoner 916). (Also, while our narrative ends when Mandela walks out of prison on 11 February 1990, the secret surveillance of leading ANC figures continued for a significant period, and some of these records also appear in the archive.)

The entire archive – or, more accurately, the whole 913 file – tells a sweeping and multifaceted story, far too big to capture in a single volume. Given this, we decided to focus on a single theme, namely the light cast by the archive on the hidden process surrounding Mandela's impending release in the last years of his imprisonment.

As noted by my co-author, the Coetsee archive is not complete enough to allow the development of a continuous and comprehensive narrative. Therefore, we have juxtaposed our selected material with standard accounts by two key role players, namely Mandela himself – in his autobiography *Long Walk to Freedom* (1994), and former President F.W. de Klerk, in *The Last Trek: A New Beginning* (1998), who released Mandela and set in motion the transition to democracy. Put differently, we use the disclosures in the archive to amplify their accounts, plugging the gaps where indicated. In line with these accounts, our narrative moves forward chronologically.

In the course of developing our narrative, we also found that *Secret Revolution: Memoirs of a Spy Boss* (2015) by Dr Niël Barnard, head of the National Intelligence Service (NIS) at that time, became directly relevant.

////

Against this background, the archive yields some notable new insights. Without wishing to pre-empt the detailed disclosures as they arrive at their proper time in the course of our story, it reveals:

That Mandela repeatedly offered to act as 'facilitator' between the NP government and the ANC, and that some of his proposals for a negotiated settlement cut across accepted ANC policy;

That Mandela, with the collaboration of Coetsee and the Department of Prisons, launched an extensive campaign, while installed in a cottage at Victor Verster Prison, to meet as many released prisoners and other political leaders as possible, with a view to moderating their political views and strategies;

That, from December 1989 onwards, again with the government's knowledge and approval, Mandela began to talk to the ANC leadership in Lusaka, conveying various requests and proposals, including the terms of a proposed negotiated settlement;

That the ANC responded by moderating some of its public statements – notably its 8 January statement in January 1990 – at Mandela's (and effectively the government's) request, and potentially also some of the decisions taken at a key meeting between released 'security prisoners' and other internal leaders of the broad resistance movement and the ANC in exile in Lusaka in late January 1990; and

That talks between Mandela and the government about the terms of his release and a negotiated settlement continued up to De Klerk's address on 2 February.

Lastly, it casts light on one of the most puzzling themes in the story of Mandela's release, which perplexed various other role players – ranging from Margaret Thatcher to diplomats active in South Africa to the ANC's leadership in exile – for some time, namely his apparent reluctance to leave prison. This was partly due, the archive discloses, to his strategic efforts to bargain for a 'package he could take to Lusaka'. However, it also reveals that Mandela was greatly discomfited when De Klerk abruptly told him, on 9 February 1990, that he would be thrust back into the outside world two days later.

////

In the process, the archive reveals that both Mandela's and De Klerk's accounts of events are highly selective, to the point of being misleading. While, in *Long Walk to Freedom*, Mandela writes quite openly about his decision to start talking to the government, as well his interaction with Coetsee and other government role players, highly complex and contentious aspects of this process are dealt with in a deceptively simple way. Moreover, in a now glaring anomaly, he jumps straight from his meeting with De Klerk on 13 December 1989 to the latter's famous address in parliament on 2 February 1990. The archive discloses that a great deal happened in between.

For his part, De Klerk writes – in typically rational and measured fashion – about being unaware of the second-track process involving Coetsee, being informed about it after becoming leader of the National Party prior to rising to the presidency, lending this process his tacit approval, and his first meeting with Mandela in December 1989. He goes on to record that they largely swopped generalities, and 'concluded that they could do business with one another'.

However, the archive reveals that their meeting went far further – that they began to discuss the terms of Mandela's release as well as the terms of the transition, and arranged that Mandela would start relaying some of these proposals to Lusaka. Moreover, an offer was made to Mandela that might have changed the course of South African political history, only to disappear mysteriously just before 2 February 1990.

////

Early readers of this manuscript have responded in positive and encouraging terms, but have also asked several probing questions. One issue they have raised is why we don't make more of the series of meetings between the secret committee appointed under President P.W. Botha and including Dr Barnard, aimed at exploring – and moderating – Mandela's political beliefs.

The answer is twofold. In his memoirs, Barnard writes extensively about these meetings which ranged from mid-1988 to some point in 1989.[1] According to him, the committee comprised himself; S.S. (Fanie) van der Merwe, director-general of Justice; Mike Louw, deputy director general of NIS, and General Willie Willemse, Commissioner of Prisons, who had come to know Mandela in earlier years on Robben Island. (In *Long Walk to Freedom*, Mandela writes that the committee was headed by Kobie Coetsee, and included Willemse, Van der Merwe and Barnard.)[2]

Barnard states explicitly that the meetings were recorded by NIS, and seems to draw on what may well be a complete set of transcripts in the course of his discussion. However, the Coetsee archive contains only one such transcript, dated early in 1989, and only Barnard and Willemse were present. While the source is not stated, this transcript probably came from NIS, and seems to confirm that these meetings were not recorded by the Department of Prisons as well.

This single transcript paints an unflattering picture of Barnard's interaction with Mandela. However, we eventually decided to omit it from our narrative, first because reflecting only one of this lengthy series of meetings might have painted a distorted picture of the discussions as a whole, and second, because, given its probable source, it might have caused legal difficulties.

Another issue raised by readers is why we have not included more material about Mandela's interactions with Winnie Madikizela-Mandela, his children, and other members of his family.

The archive confirms that Madikizela-Mandela visited her husband in prison very regularly, sometimes under extremely difficult circumstances. In earlier years, besides his lawyers, she was effectively Mandela's only link with the outside world. This role gradually faded as Mandela's global stature grew, the terms of his imprisonment improved, his interaction with the government intensified, and he was allowed greater contact with a range of political role players. At the same time, the transcripts in this period attest to growing tensions between Mandela and Winnie, much of it centred on her conduct and those of his children. In the last phase, Mandela was reluctantly forced to come to terms with more serious allegations about Winnie's conduct. However, he still seemed to gain comfort from her visits.

Among other things, Mandela was a patriarch, and the transcripts tell a moving story of his attempts to continue playing a role as husband and father from behind prison bars, and his anguish at his inability to protect his family against the ravages wrought by his absence as well as sustained brutalisation by the security police. This is a moving, often disconcerting, story which, for space and other reasons, we have left to other researchers to explore. Doing justice to this material will require a separate study. For ethical and other reasons, it would need to be approached with great care and circumspection.

A few of these conversations have been included, due to their direct relevance to our theme as well as their public interest. This includes some startling revelations in a conversation between Mandela and two family members about the background to his arrest. Even then, some names and a single sentence have been withheld.

A third issue is why we don't draw more explicit conclusions about the revelations in the archive, notably what they imply about the central figure of Mandela, and formulate an overarching thesis.

The disclosures and their implications are complex and contentious. For that reason, we have concentrated on placing the material relevant to our theme in the public domain and drawing out some immediate implications, leaving readers to reach their more general conclusions themselves.

In the course of a particularly trenchant report, one early reader asked what our study really said about Mandela, suggesting a formulation of his own, namely that, while in prison, Mandela had trodden a 'fine line between compromise and capitulation'.

While acknowledging the elegance of this formulation, we would hesitate to draw such a generalised conclusion. During his incarceration, Mandela was faced with a formidable array of challenges, under overwhelmingly difficult circumstances, and over a very long period. The archive reveals how – and then, only over the last part his 27 years in prison – he sought to deal with these pressures – from the government, the ANC in exile, his fellow prisoners, the growing internal resistance movements, as well as his family – while struggling to keep abreast of political events in South Africa as well as internationally. It's a monumental story.

In this setting, readers may be surprised, and perhaps even taken aback, by some of the disclosures involving Mandela. However, for us – having lived with the archive, including aspects which remain undisclosed, for several years – he has grown rather than diminished in stature, and become more human in the process. It also makes his eventual ascent to the leadership of the ANC and the South African presidency all the more remarkable. Perhaps, then, the archive is also valuable because it reminds us – as Mandela himself was wont to remark in later years – that he was no saint, but a (flawed and fallible) human being.

My journey with the Coetsee archive
Jan-Ad Stemmet

IN 2013, I received a call from Huibré Lombard, head of the Archive for Contemporary Affairs (ARCA) at the University of the Free State. ARCA staff were busy cataloguing a new collection, and she thought I might be interested.

ARCA is a gem. It began life in 1970 as the Institute for Contemporary History, or Instituut vir Eietydse Geskiedenis. Its formal mission was to collect and preserve documents that would record South African political history after 1902. It initially consisted of three divisions, namely a documentation division, a press cutting division and a research division. In 1998 the documentation division became the Archive for Contemporary Affairs. More informally, ARCA was (and remains) the archive of choice for National Party politicians and other role players in Afrikaner public life. As such, it's a political and historical treasure trove.

It's also a black box – partly housed underground, it's an immense catacomb of interleading fireproof chambers, locked vaults, and safes-within-safes. Some material is subject to moratoriums, some proscribed by law and some imposed by donors themselves. The route from my office to ARCA's front end is a short walk across the campus, one I had taken many times previously, but which after the phone call I now took with a renewed sense of excitement.

Huibré had placed a single grey archival box on top of a desk in the main reading room – a tranquil space where historians and other researchers are surrounded by books, antiques, and busts of apartheid-era heads of state and government. Inside, I found a delectable wad of yellowing documents, all stamped 'UITERS GEHEIM / TOP SECRET'. The apartheid-era government stamp still retained its forbidding magenta colour. I looked more closely at a single document, and read: 'Transkripsie van gesprek tussen 913 en Winnie Mandela . . .' (transcription of conversation between 913 and Winnie Mandela). For a moment, the room around me faded. I realised a wheel had turned full circle, and I was looking at material from the secret archive of apartheid minister Kobie Coetsee.

////

IN JULY 2000, as wide-eyed young historian, I conducted a series of interviews with government role players in the South African transition. I also decided to interview Kobie Coetsee, Minister of Justice and Correctional Services from the early 1980s to the early 1990s, who was known to have played a central (if shadowy) role in the process surrounding Mandela's release. People who knew him said he had become disillusioned, and would probably not agree to an interview.

I contacted him in July 2000. Speaking on the phone, he was brusque, and reluctant to see me. But he eventually agreed, and we met at his home in Bloemfontein on Thursday, 27 July 2000. While cordial, he was initially reserved. But when he began to talk about the 1980s, he became animated, and eventually quite agitated. He seemed to feel his contribution to the process resulting in Mandela's release had not been adequately recognised. I sat in silence, listening to a steadily mounting monologue.

Coetsee told me he had previously intended to write his memoirs, but had given up on the idea. To my amazement, he jumped up and insisted that I redirect my research to focus exclusively on his professional life. This, he assured me, could be published and become a bestseller. If I undertook to do this, he would make me the heir to his knowledge and his entire private archive.

'I will give you all of it,' he said, and added: 'What I will give you are bombs, bloody bombs, my friend. And when I say bombs, you'd better believe it. I mean, atom bombs. We – you and I – will blow everything open. Everything!' We agreed that I would return the next week so that we could discuss a plan of action, and he left for his farm outside Bloemfontein.

Two days later, on Saturday, 29 July, I switched on the television to watch the evening newscast. In a lead item, the SABC reported that Coetsee had died earlier that day of a heart attack. Shocked and dismayed, I thought I would never learn what Coetsee had been so agitated about, and would never gain insight into his archive. I continued my research, and was privileged to gain access to some of South Africa's most important political mandarins, power brokers, and other political heavyweights. Coetsee featured mainly in negative brushstrokes and sharply critical anecdotes. Years passed, and despite the fact that I drove past his home on my way to the university every working day, my encounter with Coetsee gradually passed to the back of my mind.

////

AT ARCA, this process was put in rapid reverse. As I pulled out more documents from vaguely labelled boxes, it began to dawn on me that, 14 years after my encounter with Kobie Coetsee, I had finally come face to face with his archive. While I was unaware of this, it had been donated to ARCA by his widow, Ena, several years previously. She had also passed away since. I also soon realised that, despite Coetsee's second-tier status, this was one of the greatest single discoveries in recent South African political history.

A large part of the archive comprised a series of files simply named '913'. Many were stamped 'SECRET' or 'TOP SECRET'. I soon established that '913' was the permanent number assigned to Nelson Mandela by the Department of Correctional Services, over which, in addition to the Justice portfolio, Coetsee had presided from 1980 to 1994. This was used to tag the extended file on Mandela that Coetsee kept in his ministry, which had grown to huge proportions over the years. Spanning more than a decade, the file dealt with almost every aspect of the elaborate government process that had developed around Mandela's incarceration, up to his release in February 1990 and beyond. Whether legally or illegally, Coetsee must have removed these documents together with the rest of his archive when he vacated his ministry in the Union Buildings just before the first inclusive elections in 1994.

I was awed by the sheer size of the 913 file, which took many months to assimilate. It comprised thousands of documents, collected in various folders, and including government reports, memorandums, letters, informal notes, press cuttings, and other documents. Perhaps most startlingly, it also contained transcripts of hundreds of meetings between Mandela and his visitors in prison, ranging from Winnie Mandela, his children and other members of his family, and his legal advisers and fellow 'security prisoners', to domestic and foreign journalists, politicians, government officials and other role players in the lead-up to the transition.

Some of these transcripts were handwritten by prison officials who, as prescribed by prison regulations, had sat in on these visits. However, it also became clear that many had been transcribed from clandestine recordings which had formed part of a massive covert surveillance programme instituted in the early 1980s as Mandela gained growing political importance. The transcripts were minutely scrutinised and analysed, in order to extract every possible ounce of intelligence and strategic advantage. Covering letters and scribbled annotations revealed that some of these transcripts had, upon request, landed on the desks of Coetsee and other selected government role players within a day.

Added to these were a raft of reports, thick and thin, summarising and analysing every possible aspect of 913's existence – his medical condition, his psychological make-up, his emotional well-being, his view of whites, blacks and the South African situation, the ANC in exile, the mass political and labour movements – as well as lengthy analyses of what would happen if he died in prison, or were to be released under various conditions. The gradual development of the global 'Release Mandela' movement was chronicled in startling detail, down to the very last municipality issuing a statement or renaming a street in far-flung corners of the world.

The person at the centre of this process – amounting to a full-blown, second-track intelligence operation – was Kobie Coetsee. The first recordings appear in 1984, four years into his term, and the archive reveals how he actively used his dual portfolios and his privileged stream of information to become the gatekeeper to the world's most famous prisoner. While other 'security prisoners' were also monitored, it is clear that Coetsee developed an almost obsessive preoccupation with Mandela, resulting in a staggering amount of information. For about a decade, he knew more about Mandela than anyone else, and used this knowledge to control and manipulate the complex situation surrounding Mandela to his and the government's perceived advantage.

All this presented me with a massively exciting opportunity – but also a massive challenge. As a result, in the same year, I invited Professor Willie Esterhuyse of the University of Stellenbosch to join me in studying the archive, and we spent months sifting through the material. Our paths eventually diverged, and Professor Esterhuyse went on to write about Mandela's and Coetsee's 'leading-edge diplomacy' in a book published in 2015.[1]

In 2017, my friend, the former journalist and specialist editor Riaan de Villiers, joined me as co-author. A visit to Bloemfontein, many emails and many hours of phone conversations followed. Initially, we tried to develop an account of all the themes and the entire period covered by the archive, but remained overwhelmed by its vast scope. Moreover, as our understanding of the material deepened, we began to realise that the archive contained some startling revelations about the latter stages of the process surrounding Mandela's release, and we decided to concentrate on this single theme. Excitedly, we began to reread certain documents and transcriptions, and share some new insights. From then on, the book began to take shape quite rapidly.

////

Two overarching points need to be made. The first concerns the vast scope of the archive, not only in terms of volume but also its multiple dimensions. Almost a decade's worth of secret memorandums and other government documents provides a unique window on the hidden workings of the NP government, as well as the actions of key role players. At that time, insight into this material would have been truly lethal knowledge. Added to this, summaries and transcripts of Mandela's conversations with literally hundreds of visitors illuminate not only his interaction with Coetsee and other government figures, but also his relationships with his captors; his fellow prisoners; his legal representatives; and Winnie Mandela and other members of his family. Some of these revelations are not only political, but also social, as well as intensely personal. Beyond our chosen theme, much of this remains unexplored.

The second, related, point concerns the scope of this book. Perhaps it will be best to say what it doesn't do, before saying what it does. Firstly, it does *not* seek to retell the story of the South African transition, based on revelations in the archive. The transition was a hugely complex process, with many more dimensions, both local and global, than those touched on in this book. All of these worked in concert to end white domination and propel South Africa into a largely peaceful transition to an inclusive constitutional democracy. It has been and would remain a mistake to try to reduce the transition to a single causal driver.

Secondly, this book does not even seek to retell the story of this single strand, namely the largely secret process surrounding Mandela and his interaction with various government and other role players during the last few years of his incarceration. Among other things, the Coetsee archive is not complete or continuous enough to allow for the development of an entire alternative narrative. However, what it does do is to cast new – and sometimes startling – light on aspects of this process, which, we believe, requires the accepted history to be partly revised and rewritten.

Throughout, we have tried, as far as possible, to let the material speak for itself. In some instances, beyond providing essential background and context, we have tentatively drawn out some of the implications; in others, we have left this to the reader.

To conclude, the Coetsee archive forms part of our national heritage. As such, it is bigger than any single researcher or author, and no one should seek to claim any exclusive insight into or ownership of its contents, much of which is extremely sensitive. We tried to deal with the material pertinent to our theme as responsibly as possible, steering clear of conspiracy theory as well as political pulp fiction. We hope other researchers will do so too.

Who was Kobie Coetsee?

Riaan de Villiers

> 'In a sense I had, by the early eighties, already accepted that I
> had this position, it was a very powerful position. History will tell whether
> I have abused this position, or whether I've used this position
> to bring about change.' – Kobie Coetsee,
> interview with Padraig O'Malley, 26 September 1997

WHEN, ON Saturday, 29 July 2000, Kobie Coetsee died of a heart attack at age 69, the reaction in the South African media was curiously muted. Time and events had moved on, and comments came from younger politicians and others who had not been Coetsee's contemporaries. The 'big guns' of the 1980s and 1990s had fallen silent.

In a Sapa report carried on IOL News, Inus Aucamp, New National Party leader in the Free State, described Coetsee as a 'leader of outstanding talent with a brilliant intellect who played a significant role in South African politics', without offering any insight into what that role had been.

A bit closer to home, but still without any real explanation, the NNP's national leader, Marthinus ('Kortbroek') van Schalkwyk, declared that Coetsee had 'broken the ice between then President P.W. Botha and Nelson Mandela, and understood how important it was to release Mandela'. He added that Coetsee was 'very effective in administering his department, and also introduced the first domestic violence legislation in South Africa'.

Paul Setsetse, spokesman for Justice Minister Penuell Maduna, observed that Coetsee had worked closely with Maduna, and that his demise was a 'sad loss for the country'. He added that Maduna and Coetsee had forged a close friendship during the Codesa talks.[1] Tony Leon, leader of the Democratic Party, said he had 'great admiration and considerable affection' for Coetsee. The latter had reformed the institution of law in South Africa, and was a reformer ahead of his own party and era.

The Sapa report then proceeded to a biography which failed to mention the most important feature of Coetsee's political career – his decision, while serving as Minister of Justice and later, Prisons, in the mid-1980s, to start secret talks with Nelson Mandela.[2]

In some ways, Coetsee's death gained greater prominence overseas than in South Africa itself – but to no greater avail. An obituary in *The Telegraph* of London on 31 July 2000 started with the wild assertion that Coetsee had 'guided the National Party in its first tentative steps towards reform, and brokered the first meeting between P.W. Botha, then president of South Africa, and Nelson Mandela'. It went further downhill from there, providing an over-dramatised account riddled with errors of fact and interpretation.[3]

The obituary in *The Guardian* on 5 August 2000 was even more misguided – a surprising failure by a respected newspaper that had covered events in South Africa assiduously and quite accurately for many years. Among other things, after stating that Coetsee had 'decided to take up a challenge' from Winnie Mandela to 'meet his most famous prisoner', it went on to say, absurdly, that Coetsee's first meeting with Mandela at Pollsmoor Prison 'so impressed Coetsee that he soon went back for more'. One can only surmise that this obit was written by a backroom staffer who had never reported from South Africa, and had cobbled it together from files.[4]

Both obituaries declared that C.R. (Blackie) Swart, South Africa's first Republican head of state, was one of Coetsee's grandfathers, leading them to conclude that he had 'learnt politics at his grandfather's knee'. This is a total untruth, seemingly prompted by a clumsy sentence in a stock South African biography which the obit writers must have found online. It does, however, seem that both Coetsee's grandfathers saw active service in the Anglo-Boer War. What can be gleaned with reasonable accuracy from these and other obituaries is the following:

Hendrik Jacobus (Kobie) Coetsee was born in the town of Ladybrand in the eastern Free State on 19 April 1931. His father, Jan, was a printer, who married Josephine van Zyl. Both were active members of the National Party (NP). Kobie was an only son. He went on to study law at the University of the Free State, qualifying with a BA LLB. In that time, he was active in the youth branch of the NP. He then practised as an attorney in Bloemfontein for some 17 years. In this period, he also volunteered for military service, and became an officer in the President Steyn armoured car regiment in Bloemfontein. In 1956, he married Helena (Ena) Malan. They had two sons and three daughters.

In 1968, he became the member of parliament for Bloemfontein West, a seat that fell vacant when J.J. (Jim) Fouché succeeded Blackie Swart as State President. In 1972, Coetsee was admitted to the Bloemfontein Bar, enabling him to practise as an advocate in the higher courts.

In 1978, he was elected as chairman of the Defence Group of the NP caucus. In the same year, shortly after becoming Prime Minister, P.W. Botha appointed Coetsee as Deputy Minister of Defence and National Security. (Botha himself held on to these portfolios until 1980, when he appointed General Magnus Malan as Minister of Defence.). In 1985, Coetsee became leader of the NP in the Orange Free State.

In this period, at Botha's behest, Coetsee reorganised the national intelligence services in the wake of the Information Scandal, which had led to the resignation of the previous Prime Minister, John Vorster. In October 1980, he was appointed as Minister of Justice, which gave him a seat on the State Security Council. Crucially, he became Minister of Correctional Services as well.

Coetsee introduced significant legal reforms, including the small claims court system and the Matrimonial Property Act, which improved the status of married women, as well as the accrual system of sharing property between spouses. He also changed the conscription system to allow conscientious objectors, who had previously been jailed, to perform community service instead.

In April 1986, he appointed a commission to examine the role of the courts in protecting group and individual rights, resulting in a report on human and group rights that, he later believed, influenced the addition of a Bill of Rights to the South African Constitution of 1996.

From 1985 onwards, he played a seminal role in the South African transition by embarking on exploratory talks with Nelson Mandela while the latter was still in prison. In July 1989, he was present at the historic meeting between Mandela – then still a prisoner – and an ailing President P.W. Botha.

In May 1990, he formed part of the government delegation at the talks between representatives of the NP government and the newly unbanned African National Congress (ANC) which resulted in the Groote Schuur Minute. He played a major role in the constitutional negotiations from the early 1990s onwards that led to the adoption of the interim constitution of 1993.

In this period, he piloted the Indemnity Act through parliament, which granted temporary immunity to people who returned to South Africa to take part in the negotiations after the unbanning of the ANC. He also played a major role in the protracted and controversial negotiations around amnesty for people on both sides of the conflict who had committed acts of violence.

From April 1993 until April 1994, he also served as Minister of Defence. After the 1994 elections, he was elected as president of the Senate, with the support of the ANC and other parties, and held this position until 1998. In that year he retired, supposedly to pursue his hobbies of hunting, shooting and fishing, and he died two years later.

This still does little to explain the ambiguities and opacities that perpetually seem to surround Coetsee. For this, we need to turn to comments by some of his contemporaries.

First up is P.W. Botha. 'The Big Crocodile' appointed Coetsee as Deputy Minister of Defence and of National Intelligence, and then to the senior cabinet posts of Minister of Justice and Correctional Services. Coetsee later said they had worked closely together for many years, and he believed they trusted one another. However, following Coetsee's death, Botha was surprisingly equivocal about their relationship.

Following its grandiose opening paragraph, the *Telegraph* obituary referred to earlier went on to say that, by 1985, Botha's government had 'conspicuously failed' to quell black unrest, and the South African economy was under siege. Coetsee's 'damascene conversion' came that year when Winnie Mandela persuaded him to meet her husband, who, while still a prisoner, was in a Cape Town hospital recovering from a prostate operation.

Coetsee was immediately impressed by Mandela, whom he likened to 'an old Roman citizen, with dignitas, gravitas, honestas, simplicitas'. The two men struck up an unlikely friendship, and several further encounters followed in Pollsmoor Prison where Mandela was confined, leading eventually to the meeting between Botha and Mandela in 1989. (Much of this is either incorrect or oversimplified, but that is not directly relevant here.)

According to the obit, Mandela called Coetsee a 'reformer ahead of his time'. Botha, however, was inclined to denigrate Coetsee's contribution to the reform process, calling him a 'funny little man'. 'I always felt after talking to him,' Botha was quoted as saying, 'that it was a case of confusion worse confounded.' The source of this comment was not cited.[5]

While the source of Coetsee's remark about Mandela was also not provided, it was drawn from an interview with Coetsee by John Carlin, South African correspondent for the leading British newspaper *The Independent* from 1990 to 1995. Generally credited with being one of the most capable foreign correspondents to cover the transition to democracy, Carlin distilled his experiences into two books. In *Knowing Mandela* (2013),[6] Carlin offers a personal account of Mandela, based on their relationship which developed in the period from 1990 to 1995 and thereafter, as well as research conducted during his spell in South Africa. This includes in-depth interviews with 24 role players in the South African transition. The interviews have been collected under the theme 'The Long Walk to Freedom of Nelson Mandela', related to a television series Carlin helped to make, and are available online.[7]

This resource shows that *The Telegraph* got the quote by Coetsee about Mandela slightly wrong as well. In the full-length interview, Carlin records Coetsee as saying: 'I have studied the classics, and for me, he [Mandela] is the incarnation of the great Roman virtues of gravitas, honestas, dignitas. Everywhere and anywhere, where people choose people, you can't help but choose Mandela.' In *Knowing Mandela*, Carlin recounts that, while saying this, Coetsee was 'shedding tears'.[8]

Then, however, with surprising rancour, Carlin describes Coetsee as a 'small man whose place as a trusted member of the P.W. Botha court owed more to the fawning obsequiousness he showed the Big Crocodile than to any great intellectual merit or originality of thought. He fancied himself a bit of a classicist, and enjoyed flaunting his knowledge of Ciceronian discourse among his decidedly unlearned cabinet colleagues.'[9] Nothing in his interview with Coetsee seems to justify this snide observation. However, it emerges that Carlin was not the only person whom Coetsee rubbed up the wrong way.

At least the *Telegraph* obit was more accurate about Mandela; indications are that he was well disposed towards Coetsee, and remained so in later years. In *Long Walk to Freedom* (his famous autobiography, revised and partly ghost-written by the American journalist Richard Stengel), Mandela recounts his secret meetings with Coetsee and the process surrounding them in some detail, but without commenting on Coetsee personally. His only remark about

Coetsee appears in a passage where he writes about being moved, in December 1988, to a cottage in the grounds of the Victor Verster Prison outside the Western Cape town of Paarl, a 'halfway house between prison and freedom'.

On his first day there, he writes, he was visited by Coetsee, who brought a case of Cape wine as a housewarming gift. 'He was extremely solicitous, and wanted to make sure that I like my new home . . . He told me the cottage . . . would be my last home before becoming a free man. The reason behind this move, he said, was that I should have a place where I could hold discussions in privacy and comfort.'[10]

(While the cottage might have offered more comfortable surroundings for Mandela's discussions, they certainly weren't going to be private. As recounted in greater detail elsewhere, the house and garden were bugged, and many of Mandela's conversations with his stream of visitors were recorded and transcribed.)

A longer, unedited version of this account appears in *Nelson Mandela: Conversations with Myself* (published in 2010), a selection of items from Mandela's personal archive, including the unedited transcripts of 70 hours of interviews with Stengel. This passage reads:

> The following day, in the afternoon, Kobie Coetsee, the minister of justice, came and . . . wanted to know how this building was – the house – and went from room to room inspecting it. We went outside inspecting the security walls, and he says, 'No, these security must be raised' . . . He was very careful and he . . . wanted to make sure that . . . I was comfortable, and he also brought me some nice, very expensive wines . . . He was very kind, very gentle, and then he told me . . . 'No, we'll move you here. This is a stage between prison and release. We are doing so because we hope you'll appreciate it. We want to introduce some confidentiality in the discussions between ourselves and yourself.' And I appreciated that. That's what happened . . .[11]

At least, even according to the actual interview, Coetsee did not tell Mandela that his 'discussions' with his interlocutors would be private.

Next up is F.W. de Klerk, who succeeded Botha as State President some six weeks after the latter's meeting with Mandela, and eventually released Mandela in February 1990. (Botha had suffered a stroke and, after initially relinquishing the party leadership while holding onto the presidency, was eventually ousted when most of his cabinet turned against him.) In his autobiography, *The Last Trek: A New Beginning* (1998), De Klerk writes intermittently about his interactions with Coetsee, in his characteristically deliberate and measured style.

Soon after becoming leader of the NP in the Transvaal, De Klerk recounts, he attended a cabinet team-building and planning exercise at a remote Defence Force base on the border between Namibia and Angola. At some stage, 'elements within the security establishment' mooted the idea that, if all other options for constitutional reform were exhausted, the government should suspend the existing constitution and rule by decree. 'I vehemently opposed this idea, and was strongly supported by other senior members of the cabinet, including Chris Heunis and Kobie Coetsee.'[12]

He also writes, again with seeming approval, that, as Minister of Justice, Coetsee always insisted that all the government's actions, especially during the states of emergency, should be taken in strict compliance with the law, and he had 'even established a legal centre' to assist them in doing so.[13]

In 1986, he notes, Botha proposed the formation of a National Statutory Council as a forum for negotiations with black South Africans. However, it never got off the ground. Neither Chris Heunis, as Minister of Constitutional Development, nor himself, then leader of the NP in the Transvaal, was informed of the exploratory discussions with Mandela which were being conducted by a few senior officials as well as Coetsee.[14] However, he later writes, again with tacit approval, that Coetsee had cleared the meeting

15

between Mandela and Botha with him beforehand, in his capacity as leader of the NP.[15]

When, in the course of the constitutional negotiations, tensions developed around the release of political prisoners, De Klerk was persuaded 'with the greatest reluctance' to change his initial position. Coetsee was bitterly upset when he learnt about the decision, as he wanted to use this issue as a bargaining chip with the ANC. 'He came to see me, and offered to resign. I assured him that he was a valued member of our team, and that he had an important role to play. He agreed to remain in the cabinet.'[16] Later, in his only personal remark about Coetsee, De Klerk remarks drily that the latter was 'renowned for playing his cards close to his chest'.[17]

In an interview with Carlin, De Klerk reiterated that he did not participate in the behind-the-scenes discussions with Mandela, and was not briefed about this process when it began. Immediately after becoming party leader in February 1989, he was briefed by Kobie Coetsee, and from then onwards he was 'fully part of the whole process'. He had prior knowledge of the meeting between Botha and Mandela. It had his approval, and from the start of his presidency, the release of Mandela and other political prisoners was 'very high' on the agenda.

Seemingly trying to get him to discard his reserve, Carlin asks: 'You say in your book that when Kobie Coetsee did tell you about these talks . . . you weren't critical, but you were surprised . . .'

Holding his line, De Klerk replies: 'Surprised in the sense that I had not been informed, inquisitive and surprised that such a high-profile person would be negotiating from jail, and asking myself to what extent Mandela would have a mandate to do so . . .'

He was eventually told that after initial discussions, some rules had been relaxed and Mandela was allowed to have 'certain interactions' in order to obtain a mandate and keep his power base informed about what he was doing. 'Obviously, I found that acceptable, because you can't just deal with an individual without a mandate. It would have limited advantages, whereas if he were properly mandated, it would have far greater implications, and hold much more promise.'[18]

From 1989 to 2005, Padraig O'Malley, an Irish academic and mediator specialising in the problems of divided societies, notably Northern Ireland and South Africa, amassed many hours of interviews with role players in the South African transition. Entitled 'Heart of Hope', the O'Malley Archive is hosted by the Nelson Mandela Centre of Memory, and is available online.[19]

O'Malley interviewed De Klerk no fewer than six times between 1995 and 1999, and questioned him about Coetsee in their penultimate session, in July 1998. After playing a major role in opening up a dialogue between the government and Mandela, O'Malley suggested, Coetsee seemed to have 'disappeared off the screen', and became 'more of an opponent of some of the elements of the settlement that was reached than a proponent'.

De Klerk said he would not say this. Coetsee was accused of having failed to negotiate a more favourable amnesty situation (presumably for members of the South African security forces). It was true that the amnesty negotiations had stumbled from time to time, which led to certain measures being written into the transitional constitution that should have been negotiated in greater detail. However, the ANC had delayed this deliberately. This was the issue that almost scuttled the peace conference, and triggered the infamous clash between De Klerk and Mandela at Codesa.

Many people, including NP members, blamed Coetsee for the outcome of the negotiations around amnesty, and Coetsee had become a controversial figure. However, De Klerk would not say that Coetsee opposed the eventual agreements. After the elections, Coetsee was made president of the Senate, with the support of the ANC. 'Even now, there's a very good relationship between him and Mandela. He is one of the few NP former high-profile figures that Mandela never said anything negative about.'[20]

But comments about Coetsee by another key role player in the transition enter a different landscape. Besides Coetsee, Dr Niël

Barnard, head of the National Intelligence Service (NIS) from 1979 to 1992, played a major role in the secret talks with Mandela. In an interview with Carlin, he portrayed Coetsee and his role in changing the dynamics around Mandela in a reasonably favourable light. Coetsee, he said, had been 'critically involved' in the view that Mandela had to be prepared for life after prison, and leading the country. 'So Kobie Coetsee was responsible, as far as I can recollect. Let's now move Mr Mandela from Pollsmoor to Victor Verster . . . so that he can live in a normal house, so that he can gradually prepare himself for life after prison.'[21]

In *Secret Revolution: Memoirs of a Spy Boss*, however, the notoriously abrasive Barnard takes a different tack. He now claims that P.W. Botha asked him (Barnard) to head the 'small government team' tasked with undertaking exploratory talks with Mandela. At that time, he and the NIS were 'entirely unaware' that Coetsee had already held numerous conversations with Mandela. He had regularly seen Coetsee, especially at meetings of the State Security Council, but he had 'never uttered a word' about his earlier discussions with Mandela.

Barnard then writes: 'Why he handed over this task – or whether it was taken away from him – we will probably never know. He was often involved in all sorts of plans and schemes which only he understood. Nevertheless, Coetsee was an intelligent man, and I am convinced that he wanted the conversations to continue, but perhaps he did not have the time or the stamina for it himself.'[22]

The gloves really come off in the course of three interviews with Padraig O'Malley. In the second interview, in November 1999, Barnard lambasts Coetsee for his role in the problems surrounding the amnesty process. According to Barnard, during the talks prior to the Pretoria Minute in August 1990, agreement was reached on amnesty across the board. However, at the last minute, Coetsee persuaded F.W. de Klerk that this was the wrong approach, and the issue was then omitted from the final formulation of the Minute.

Barnard then goes on to say: 'To a certain extent . . . all the difficulties that we to this day have with amnesty were the responsibility of one Kobie Coetsee, who thought that he could think about weird and wonderful ideas. I think when you're in a process like this and you get an opportunity, you must have a big mind and move as quickly as possible.'

O'Malley: 'What were his objections [to a blanket amnesty]? This was like wiping the slate clean.'

Barnard: 'I think that's one of the issues which one must ask him. He's a very strange man.'[23]

However, it's in his first interview with O'Malley, in September 1998, that Barnard really puts his cards on the table.

O'Malley: 'You have said that the role Kobie Coetsee played in the process has been greatly over-exaggerated. Could you put that into some context for me?'

Barnard: 'I will. First of all . . . he tried to take the line that he was basically the man who had been orchestrating this whole exercise. I think the answer is no. Secondly, if you would have listened to what Mr Botha has been saying, he certainly didn't command the kind of influence with Mr Botha which he said he did. With a lot of respect, I had to convince Mr Botha, finally, to see Mr Mandela, in person, alone, myself, not Kobie Coetsee, because at the time it was becoming extremely critical and I told Mr Botha in my view if you look at the history of this country you cannot lose if you see Mr Mandela.

'If it's a successful meeting and you can lay the foundation for the future political negotiation of this country, you would always be able to say that historic meeting between me and Mr Mandela paved the way, laid the foundation for the present political dispensation in this country, I opened the doors finally, I saw him, I started the discussion. If it is not successful, quite obviously you would be able to take the line, I saw Mr Mandela, it became clear to me that it was not possible to find a solution, I am telling this to the public, I tried, it doesn't seem to me to be possible, so I cannot help you. So there is only a so-called win-win situation. See the man now so that we can take the process forward . . .'

At the root of Barnard's issue with Coetsee, then, was a rival claim to ownership of the secret conversations which laid the foundation for Mandela's release and, ultimately, his presidency.

Tony Leon, who rose meteorically in white opposition politics from the mid-1980s onwards, and later led the official opposition in parliament for a period of eight years, recalls his experiences of Coetsee in his political biography entitled *On the Contrary: Leading the Opposition in a Democratic South Africa* (2008). Among other things, it contains a brilliant, often disconcerting, account of the confused and brutal political environment of the late 1980s and early 1990s, as well as the often chaotic constitutional negotiations.

He writes: 'In my capacity as DP justice spokesman, I had got to know Coetsee reasonably well. However, no one (not even his wife, I sometimes suspected) really knew him at all. He seldom revealed his true thinking on matters, and managed to literally smile and wink his way out of many tight corners. However, he was certainly a reformist Justice minister and had the trust of De Klerk. He had been P.W. Botha's first line of contact with the imprisoned Nelson Mandela, and his close proximity to Mandela and his then wife, Winnie, had also (in my view) led to her under-prosecution for very serious crimes.'[24]

He then recounts how, to his astonishment, in the course of the constitutional negotiations at Kempton Park, Coetsee leaked to him a draft agreement between Coetsee and the ANC legal negotiator Dullah Omar to the effect that all the Constitutional Court judges would be appointed by the President and cabinet. 'In other words, the lynchpin of the new legal order would be open to blatant political manipulation, at the level of selection at least, and would simply ape the discredited appointment mechanism of the past. However, this court would be entrusted with far greater and more sweeping powers than any other in South Africa's history.

'In terms of the ANC–NP agreement (which I was to learn later, with some stupefaction, had been authored by Coetsee himself), the cabinet, with a likely and hefty ANC majority, and the president, undoubtedly Nelson Mandela, would handpick their own judges! Dumbfounded as I was by the agreement Coetsee had authored and agreed to, I was even more perplexed as to why he was the whistle-blower on his own compact.

'I later learned that certain of Coetsee's cabinet colleagues whom he had not consulted before inking his signature to the agreement were appalled at what he had done. He was clearly looking for an escape hatch, and while he would oscillate in all directions over the next few days, blowing both hot and cold on the document, he had apparently decided that I constituted the best getaway vehicle if he needed to resile from his commitments.'

Leon went on to launch a vigorous campaign to overturn the deal, proposing instead that Constitutional Court judges should be drawn from recommendations submitted to the cabinet by a Judicial Service Commission comprising members of government, the judiciary, and the independent legal profession. A political mini-storm ensued, in which Coetsee continued to play an uncertain role.

'*Die Burger*, normally the staunchest NP press ally, thundered against Coetsee and claimed in a shattering editorial that his proposal amounted to the "castration of the constitution". This, and the undoubled internal pressure mounting against him in his own ranks, led finally to Coetsee dropping his legendary equivocation. We were now, finally, on the same track.'

On Wednesday, 17 November 1993, with the midnight deadline for an agreement approaching, negotiations reached a frantic pitch. Cyril Ramaphosa finally agreed that the judges would be nominated by the Judicial Service Commission, and the President could not add any other candidates. More horse-trading followed; at around midnight on Wednesday, 17 November, the 'much delayed and deeply contested draft constitution was put to the full plenary of the negotiations process, and passed with acclaim'. Leon writes that he felt a sense of relief and accomplishment, and that his 'fifteen minutes of fame' were widely appreciated.

The next day, Thursday, 18 November, provided De Klerk and Roelf Meyer with a 'major hangover' when, at a 7 am cabinet meeting, senior members of De Klerk's cabinet, including Tertius Delport, revolted against the terms of the constitutional agreement. A private discussion followed, in which De Klerk aimed to bring Delport and five or six other cabinet members on board. But things got even worse. Delport grabbed De Klerk's lapels, exclaiming: 'What have you done? You have given South Africa away.' Eventually, De Klerk managed to preserve his cabinet's unity. When parliament met the following week to debate the new constitutional agreement, De Klerk was 'enraged' when Leon suggested that the constitutional talks had finally put the lid on the NP's coffin.

Leon recounts one last, poignant encounter with Coetsee: 'Towards the end of 1999, I was in Bloemfontein when I received a call from Kobie Coetsee, by then retired from politics and again living in the city. He wanted to discuss a matter with me. We arranged to meet in the VIP lounge at the airport, shortly before my departure to Cape Town. I had always found the former minister of Justice elliptical and impenetrable; this meeting was no exception. He expressed deep concern about the ANC's intention to "damage the constitutional settlement". "We" should collaborate in its defence – but there were no specifics.

'I went on to ask him what he had made of the TRC's statement about the "strategic decisions with regard to the prosecution of Madikizela-Mandela" [for her alleged complicity in the killing of the young activist Stompie Seipei] being influenced by the "political sensitivities of this period". He gave no direct response, simply fixing me with his sphinx-like smile. We were never to meet again – a few months later he died, on 29 July 2000.'[25]

It would be untrue, however, to say that Coetsee remains a total enigma. He was also interviewed by O'Malley on four separate occasions, over several years. He seemingly trusted O'Malley, and spoke to him candidly and at some length. It seems safe to say that he probably went some way towards saying the things he intended to record in his memoirs, which he was then working on but later abandoned.

Among other things, those conversations went far deeper than Carlin's single interview, and reveal Carlin's malicious comment about Coetsee to be materially misguided. Specifically, his conclusion that Coetsee was a person of 'limited intelligence with no great capacity for original thought' was quite incorrect.

Over the years, and at a distance, Coetsee emerges from these transcripts as a highly intelligent person who, in the course of a long career in some of the most important portfolios in the NP government from the late 1970s to the early 1990s – including defence, security, justice and prisons – built up a deep knowledge and understanding of the complex political processes that played themselves out in those key state functions in that period.

The interviews provide significant insights into Coetsee's own beliefs and motivations; for instance, he says, he realised in the mid-1970s that separate development was both immoral and unviable. He continued to work in the NP, though, as he realised that 'you can't change anything if you're not there'. He then went on to a sustained effort to 'swap the sword for justice'.

The interviews also provide a fascinating insight into the real drivers of the NP government's impetus towards reform, largely under P.W. Botha, from whom Coetsee took his orders, which have been widely misunderstood and undervalued.

However, in the ebb and flow of Coetsee's conversations with O'Malley, interrupted and resumed over several years, they never got around to talking in detail about his activities in the crucial period from the mid-1980s onwards, when the conversations with Mandela began and the foundation was laid for his eventual release. Whether by accident or design, Coetsee said nothing about his massive, partly secret archive or the fact that it contained transcripts of many conversations between Mandela and his visitors over a period of six years – or that surveillance of ANC negotiators continued well after 1990, into the constitutional negotiations.

Or did he? The transcription of the O'Malley interview on 5 September 1998 contains a tantalising passage. O'Malley asks Coetsee whether he agrees that the NP was a pushover in the constitutional negotiations or, in the journalist Patti Waldmeir's words, 'the Boers gave it all away'.[26] In response, Coetsee says one has to look at areas where the NP negotiators succeeded.

This includes the issue of whether or not the provinces should be retained. He then claims that Cyril Ramaphosa and Roelf Meyer had agreed that there would be no provinces, but that they might be considered at a later stage. Stalwarts in the NP (which seemed to include Coetsee) went to F.W. de Klerk and threatened to walk out if he did not dig in his heels. De Klerk agreed, and the provinces were retained. 'We succeeded also because we read the innards of the ANC correctly, that there were more people that would feel safe within the provincial structure than there were people who would feel safe outside.'

O'Malley: 'How did you come to that conclusion?'

Coetsee: 'That is a different story, my friend, that is a different story, and I'll tell it to you one day.'

He goes on to say that he was a spokesperson on this issue, and by then he had become annoyed by the way in which 'certain things' were lost by the wayside through backroom deals. He was certain the ANC would agree to provinces, even when Ramaphosa and Meyer had agreed that there would be no provinces, but they could be reintroduced at a later stage. 'We pushed and I pushed, knowing that there would be forces inside the ANC that would accept it.'

O'Malley: 'How did you know there were forces within the ANC that would accept [this]?'

Coetsee: 'I'm just saying to you that I knew. I don't think it's necessary for us to record this at this point of time. But I knew. And we pushed and we succeeded.'

Lastly, the O'Malley interviews also go some way towards explaining why people found Coetsee so exasperating. He does indeed talk in an elliptical way, while also switching freely between topics, and moving backwards and forwards in time. At times, O'Malley too is confounded. Amusingly, Coetsee reveals that he is well aware of his trademark style and its power to annoy and confuse, that he derived pleasure from this, and deliberately used it to his political advantage. All this comes together in a single passage. Coetsee tells O'Malley that, at some (typically unspecified) point (but presumably in the early 1980s), he received visits from two opposition luminaries: Helen Suzman, veteran liberal parliamentarian, and Frederik Van Zyl Slabbert, leader of the Progressive Federal Party, then the official opposition in parliament. Suzman spoke to him about releasing Mandela, and Slabbert about releasing dissident Afrikaner poet Breyten Breytenbach. He hints that they influenced his political thinking.

Eventually, he told them that, with the approval of P.W. Botha and the cabinet, he was going to change the policy relating to the release of 'security prisoners', as he called them. He would announce this in an extended committee session of his vote – Justice and Prisons – in the Senate, instead of the more prominent House of Assembly. He would announce that 'there's going to be a change in policy, and I stipulated the conditions which will lead to the release of Mr Mandela, although I'm not going to announce that as such. But the first person to benefit would be Breytenbach . . .'

He contacted Slabbert and told him there was one condition, namely that he and Suzman should not be 'jubilant in the press'. Botha did not want to be embarrassed. And he would always honour them (Slabbert and Suzman) for honouring the agreement – 'they listened to me, they walked out, not a smile on their faces, knowing that this was the beginning. And you must get Hansard of my announcement there, and you will see it was couched in a style which people say belongs to me, you couldn't read it there but it was there. You understand what I'm saying?'

O'Malley (clearly confounded): 'This was on the release of Breytenbach.'

Coetsee: 'Yes, but it was changing just the policy, and the rest followed . . . The press wrote a few lines on it, they didn't realise what they were writing, and I enjoyed the situation . . .'

What is beyond doubt is that Coetsee decided to start talking to Mandela, albeit under a general brief from P.W. Botha to resolve the growing problems surrounding 'security prisoners', comprising mounting legal claims and court cases as well as rapidly escalating international pressure on the one hand, and pressure from the Breytenbach family – who knew Botha – on the other. Added to this, as F.W. de Klerk later remarked, long-term 'security prisoners' were due for some kind of parole in any case. The only sticking point was whether they would continue to advocate political violence after their release.

In this context, the Coetsee archive also reveals, quite startlingly, that Coetsee proposed the unconditional release of Mandela and numerous other 'security prisoners' to the State Security Council in December 1984 – four years before Mandela met P.W. Botha, and five years before he walked out of Victor Verster Prison.

It seems clear that Coetsee (assisted by his prisons management team) took the initiative to move Mandela into separate quarters in Pollsmoor Prison, away from his colleagues, thereby creating space for more uninhibited talks with government representatives, as well as the later decision to move home to a cottage in the grounds of Victor Verster Prison, a 'halfway house between prison and freedom'. While this might have been with Botha's knowledge – and could hardly have happened otherwise – it attests to the autonomy and room to manoeuvre that Coetsee had appropriated. And after those steps, there was no turning back.

Coetsee spoke to O'Malley (and perhaps Patti Waldmeir) more freely than to anyone else. At the same time, there is no record of him disclosing to anyone that he had created an extensive surveillance apparatus around Mandela, and monitored his conversations in prison for a number of years. This remained a secret until 2013 when, as recounted elsewhere in this volume, the historian Jan-Ad Stemmet opened the first of a stack of cardboard boxes containing Coetsee's papers at the Archive for Contemporary Affairs (ARCA) at the University of the Free State.

As noted previously, monitoring conversations with at least some 'security prisoners' was standard practice. Moreover, in the light of Mandela's unique and growing stature, a degree of additional surveillance could have been expected. But why the 913 file (Mandela's real prison number) assumed such massive proportions, and what exactly Coetsee sought to achieve by building it, remains a mystery. Given this, the archive itself – with its startling revelations, unexplained gaps, and remaining mysteries – may well be Kobie Coetsee's most fitting and lasting legacy.

Eavesdropping on Mandela

ALL MANDELA'S conversations were monitored – in other words, they took place in the presence of a warder, who made written notes. This was done on standard printed forms titled 'The monitoring of conversations' (*Gespreksmonitering*), but sometimes also on lined government-issue A4 paper. Indications are that this was standard practice, at least for certain categories of prisoners.

On Robben Island, visitors spoke to Mandela (and other prisoners) through a partition, and this regime also held sway at Pollsmoor Maximum Security Prison. It was only in May 1984 that Mandela was allowed a 'contact visit' with his wife, Winnie Mandela, their eldest daughter, Zenani (Zeni), and one of his grandchildren, which meant they sat in a room with no partition, and he could embrace them for the first time. It can be assumed that visible monitoring continued.

In Mandela's cottage at Victor Verster Prison, his conversations were monitored by a warden who sat in another room, out of sight of his visitors. This often seemed to be Major Charl Marais, who came to know Mandela and his responses to certain issues very well. (Indeed, towards the end of Mandela's sojourn at Victor Verster, Marais skipped writing out certain passages, noting that Mandela's views on these issues were 'well-known' or 'had already been recorded'. As some transcripts show, Mandela also sometimes called him in during conversations with visitors to ask him to attend to some or other issue, such as the issuing of passports for family members and others.)

What was thoroughly unusual was that at least some of Mandela's conversations were also recorded, and more completely transcribed. These were funnelled to Kobie Coetsee, who would decide whether or not to pass them on to the State President or other government role players. They provided Coetsee with an additional instrument for controlling the entire process surrounding Mandela – or at least the perception that he was doing so.

While, to the best of our knowledge, Mandela never said so in writing, indications are that – during his sojourn at Victor Verster at least – he knew his conversations were being recorded. On several occasions – faithfully reflected in the transcripts – he warned his visitors that they were 'not alone', and they would then start whispering. Sometimes, he switched on a noisy overhead fan, or tuned his radio to a music station. As a result, long and presumably vital passages in those conversations are not on record. Whether he ever used this knowledge to try to mislead his captors, or send them implicit messages, is not clear.

The transcripts begin in 1984 – two years after Mandela and his four fellow Rivonia trialists were moved from Robben Island to Pollsmoor Prison on the mainland. This helps to corroborate that, due to mounting international and domestic pressures, the situation surrounding Mandela – and the government's strategic perception of it – had begun to change.

The cottage at Victor Verster Prison was particularly heavily bugged, and there were even bugs in the garden. At that stage, as the Coetsee archive reveals, Mandela was pursuing an extensive campaign to influence the views of other political prisoners, those who had just been released or were about to be released, as well as other internal (and, as it turns out, external) political leaders. Clearly, knowledge of what he was saying to them was meant to provide his captors with ongoing 'feedback' – information to be utilised for adjusting the continuing and increasingly pressured political process.

A mini-industry must have arisen around this activity. Transcribing taped conversations is tedious and time-consuming, and a number of prison staff must have been involved. Sometimes, when a particular conversation or meeting was thought to be politically critical, transcripts were called for and provided to Coetsee and other political role players within a day.

This helps to account for the uneven quality of the transcripts. Some were well recorded and transcribed. Others were poorly recorded, and transcribed by prison officials with a limited knowledge of English. Some deficient transcripts contain handwritten corrections, sometimes by more than one person. All these problems create layers of uncertainty that present the researcher with significant difficulties. Some sense can be discerned, but faithfully reproducing parts of these transcripts would simply have produced unreadable results. We therefore decided to provide edited versions of these transcripts, which we refer to as 'plausible reconstructions'. Clearly, they cannot be taken as entirely faithful renditions. At the same time, though, we do believe they capture the gist of those conversations.

Sometimes, breaks occur in the transcripts when tapes are changed. One transcript of a conversation in the Victor Verster cottage mentions a tape being changed 'on the Revox machine' – a high-quality reel-to-reel tape recorder in use at the time. Presumably, other tape recorders were running as well, but the eavesdroppers seldom succeeded in constructing seamless records of the conversations. Of course, they could not ask their subjects to stop talking while the tapes were being changed.

At least one conversation with a group of visitors in the cottage at Victor Verster Prison was taped not only by the Department of Prisons but also by the National Intelligence Service (NIS). One file in the Coetsee archive contains two transcripts – a complete one by the Department of Prisons, and the other, selected pages from an NIS transcript which the prison officials identify and acknowledge.

This indicates that Mandela's conversations – at least those in the cottage – were not only recorded by the prisons service, but also by NIS. Indeed, Niël Barnard, director-general of NIS at the time, confirms this in his book *Secret Revolution: Memoirs of a Spy Boss* (2015), and also claims that Mandela was well aware of it. (Barnard formed part of a secret government working group that held a series of discussions with Mandela from 1988 onwards about his political beliefs.) Yet Barnard's account contains some anomalies. After briefly citing several conversations between Mandela and some of his visitors, he goes on to say:

'How did we know what Mandela and his comrades told each other in the cottage at Victor Verster? Well, no intelligence service worth its salt will not record such vital historic conversations – especially if it formed part of those conversations. And no true freedom fighter – after all, Mandela was the founder of Umkhonto we Sizwe – would be so naïve as to think his conversations with a spy boss would not be recorded. Mandela was not born yesterday.'[1]

The clandestine recordings were an open secret, Barnard continues, and he and Mandela never discussed the matter directly. Some of the warders at Victor Verster were aware of this and probably told Mandela about it, but he never mentioned it or raised any objections. This was probably because Mandela was aware that he was not the elected leader of the ANC and did not have a mandate to conduct discussions with government representatives. As a result, Barnard argues, the taped conversations might have been an insurance policy that would enable him at a later stage to show which undertakings he had made, and which not.

Barnard claims that, ironically, the surveillance strengthened their mutual trust. During a few conversations at the cottage, Mandela took his arm and said: 'Let's go outside and talk under the tree.' But the tree was also bugged. 'When we got there, I looked up at the branches and said: "Let's rather talk elsewhere in the garden." He smiled, and we walked away together.'

While inconsistent in some respects, this passage seems to confirm that NIS recorded two kinds of conversations – those between

Mandela and the government working group (including Barnard), and conversations between him and other visitors. However, it also suggests that this was done by NIS alone. Barnard must have known that at least some of the conversations were also being taped by Coetsee's surveillance system within the prisons service. Why he does not acknowledge this is unclear.

////

On 18 July 2012 the Rivonia trialist Denis Goldberg, who spent 22 years in Pretoria Central Prison, and other members of the Ex-Political Prisoners' Association commemorated Mandela Day by planting trees outside the cottage at Victor Verster Prison. Goldberg and the other former prisoners were taken on a tour of the cottage by Warrant Officer Jack Swart, Mandela's personal chef during that time. During the tour, Swart pointed out a hole in a tree where a microphone had been placed to record Mandela's 'every conversation'. He also showed the visitors a small room just off the kitchen which, he said, was the only room in the house which was not bugged.[2]

Talking to a reporter, Goldberg expressed concern about several aspects of South Africa's post-apartheid order. However, he added that anyone who said South Africa should have righted itself in the 18 years since the first democratic elections in 1994 was mistaken. 'They didn't read history. History takes time. Sadly, 18 years is nothing.'[3]

1
Let the games begin . . .

> 'All that is required of Mandela now . . . is that he should
> unconditionally reject violence as a political instrument.
> This is, after all, a norm which is respected in
> all civilized countries of the world . . .'

ON THURSDAY, 31 January 1985, State President P.W. Botha announced in parliament that the South African government was prepared to consider Nelson Mandela's release from prison, provided he was prepared to renounce the use of violence for political ends.

While this was less well known, the government had made numerous offers to release Mandela in previous years.[1] However, all of these hinged on him accepting release to the 'Republic' of Transkei, which would have amounted to a tacit recognition of the apartheid homelands system, and isolated him from his own movement as well as resurgent political resistance in 'white' South Africa.

At that stage, the Transkei was governed by K.D. (Kaiser) Matanzima, Mandela's nephew, who had decided to collaborate with the homelands system. He offered Mandela a comfortable home, but also undertook to ensure that Mandela would 'abide by the law'. In this setting, Mandela would have been marginalised to the point of becoming a forgotten man, which – for a time – is clearly what the authorities (and probably Matanzima) wished to achieve. For these reasons, Mandela consistently rejected these offers, or simply did not respond.

Botha's statement in parliament attracted widespread attention, both because it underscored that, amid mounting international pressure and rising internal unrest, Mandela had become a far greater political problem, and also because it meant the government had given up on trying to persuade him to accept release to the Transkei.

By then, Mandela had been incarcerated for more than 20 years. This included a period he describes, in *Long Walk to Freedom*, as 'The Dark Years' during which he and fellow 'security prisoners' endured brutal conditions on Robben Island, and a subsequent period he describes as 'Beginning to Hope' in which conditions on the Island improved and he and others began to enjoy greater contact with the outside world. This period ended in 1982 when he and four other prominent 'security prisoners' – Walter Sisulu, Ahmed Kathrada, Raymond Mhlaba and Andrew Mlangeni – were abruptly moved from Robben Island to Pollsmoor Prison, a maximum security prison on the Cape Peninsula.

In sharp contrast with their conditions on the Island, they were installed in a penthouse on top of the main prison building, comprising a large room with four properly made beds, and separate ablution facilities. (Previously, they had slept on mats on their cell floors.) It was connected to a large outside terrace where they were allowed out during the day. No reason for the move was provided, However, Mandela and his colleagues believed the authorities were attempting to 'cut off the head of the ANC on the island by removing its leadership'.[2]

Nevertheless, the food was much better; they were permitted a fairly wide range of newspapers and magazines, and were also given a radio (which, to their regret, only received local stations and not the BBC World Service). Mandela started a vegetable garden on the terrace, in oil drums cut in half that were supplied by the prisons service. In May 1984, he received the first 'contact' visit from his wife, Winnie, his daughter Zenani (known as Zeni), and a granddaughter during which he could hug them for the first time in 21 years.

Given their improved connections with the outside world,

Mandela and his colleagues were aware that the anti-apartheid struggle was intensifying, that new grassroots political movements – including the United Democratic Front (UDF) – were being formed inside the country, and that the ANC was experiencing a 'new birth of popularity'. Also, countries across the globe were beginning to impose economic sanctions on South Africa.

////

In this context, there were other indications that the process surrounding Mandela had begun to accelerate. On Monday, 21 January, just ten days before Botha's statement in parliament, a prominent British and European politician, Lord Nicholas Bethell, was allowed to interview Mandela in Pollsmoor Prison. Bethell had a standing interest in human rights issues, and had been petitioning the South African government for permission to visit Mandela for a long time. However, after many months of routine refusals, it had become expedient to allow Bethell to interview Mandela.

A member of the Conservative Party, Bethell was a staunch anti-communist who had campaigned against human rights abuses in the Soviet Union. He was the first foreigner to be allowed to visit Mandela in prison, and the first person allowed to publish an interview with him. Put differently, this was the first time that Mandela's views would be placed on public record in 22 years.[3]

Bethell's account of the interview was published at length in the British *Mail on Sunday* six days later, on 27 January 1985. It went on to receive global media coverage – notably because it contained what were thought to be the first public comments by Mandela on prospects for negotiations with the NP government, including the conditions under which the ANC would suspend its 'armed struggle'.

The Coetsee archive contains both typed and handwritten transcripts of their conversation. Revealingly, Bethell told Mandela that he had seen Kobie Coetsee earlier that morning, and would see

35

him again later the same day. This points to the conclusion that Coetsee (and presumably P.W. Botha) had allowed Bethell to interview Mandela and publish the results in order to achieve several interrelated objectives. The first was to gauge Mandela's current stance on the renunciation of violence; the second, to discredit the ANC by displaying its commitment to 'terrorism' to the international community; the third, to convey to Mandela that Western governments, including the British government led by Margaret Thatcher, still disapproved of the ANC's adoption of the 'armed struggle'; and the fourth, to add to pressure on Mandela to renounce violence in the process.

////

Nine days later, on Wednesday, 30 January, the Minister of Law and Order, Louis le Grange, referred in parliament to speculation that the government was considering releasing Mandela as 'an old ANC story'. However, Botha made his offer of release the very next day. His motivation was as follows:

Lord Bethell and the *Mail on Sunday*, which had published his findings on visits to two South African prisons as well as Mandela, had asked the South African government to release Mandela on humanitarian grounds. Two eminent black leaders, President Kaiser Matanzima of Transkei and Chief Minister Mangosuthu Buthelezi of KwaZulu, had also called on him to do so.

In fact, Matanzima had for years appealed to the South African government to have Mandela and a number of other Transkei citizens who were serving prison sentences in South Africa released to the Transkei. Matanzima had indicated that Mandela and some of the other prisoners belonged to his people, that Mandela was related to him, and that he would provide them and their families with suitable houses in order to enable them to resume a normal family life. He also indicated that, should they be released, these people 'would not act contrary to the provisions of any law'.

The government was willing to give sympathetic consideration to Matanzima's requests, but it seemed that Mandela and his associates preferred to stay in prison rather than be released in their country of origin. Botha then went on to say:

'The government is not insensitive to the fact that Mr Mandela and others have spent a very long time in prison – I am personally not insensitive about this – even though they were duly convicted in open court. The government is also willing to consider Mr Mandela's release in the Republic of South Africa on condition that he gives a commitment that he will not make himself guilty of planning, instigating or committing acts of violence for the furtherance of political objectives, but will conduct himself in such a way that he will not again have to be arrested . . .

'As I have indicated, the Government is willing to consider Mr Mandela's release, but I am sure that Parliament will understand that we cannot do so if Mr Mandela himself says that the moment he leaves prison he will continue with his commitment to violence.

'It is therefore not the South African Government which now stands in the way of Mr Mandela's freedom. It is he himself. The choice is his. All that is required of him now is that he should unconditionally reject violence as a political instrument. This is, after all, a norm which is respected in all civilized countries in the world . . .'[4]

Helen Suzman asked Botha whether this same offer would also extend to some of the other prisoners who were in jail and had been there for years. He replied: 'Yes, if they unconditionally accept the provisions I laid down.' He would not take any further questions.

The government lost no time in getting Botha's offer to Mandela. One of his surviving prison notebooks contains the following cryptic entry: '31 JANUARY 1986: Commanding officer supplies me at 12.15 am with copy of President Botha's speech. At 3.13 I have 40 minutes consultations with 4 comrades from roof.'

////

Three weeks later, Mandela publicly rejected Botha's offer in a statement read out by his daughter Zindzi at a rally of the United Democratic Front (UDF), held in the Jabulani Stadium in Soweto to celebrate Archbishop Desmond Tutu's reception of the Nobel Peace Prize. Known as 'My Father Says', the statement has achieved historical prominence, and appears on the website of the Nelson Mandela Foundation as well as those of numerous other archives. Extracts appear below:

> My father and his comrades at Pollsmoor Prison send their greetings to you, the freedom-loving people of this our tragic land, in the full confidence that you will carry on the struggle for freedom . . . [They] are grateful to the United Democratic Front who without hesitation made this venue available to them so that they could speak to you today . . .
>
> My father says: I am a member of the African National Congress. I have always been a member of the African National Congress and I will remain a member of the African National Congress until the day I die. Oliver Tambo is much more than a brother to me. He is my greatest friend and comrade for nearly fifty years. . . . There is no difference between his views and mine.
>
> I am surprised at the conditions that the government wants to impose on me. I am not a violent man. My colleagues and I wrote in 1952 to Malan asking for a round table conference to find a solution to the problems of our country, but that was ignored. When Strijdom was in power, we made the same offer. Again it was ignored. When Verwoerd was in power we asked for a national convention for all the people in South Africa to decide on their future. This, too, was in vain.
>
> It was only then, when all other forms of resistance were no longer open to us, that we turned to armed struggle. Let Botha show that he is different to [his predecessors] Malan, Strijdom and Verwoerd. Let him renounce violence. Let him say that he will dismantle apartheid. Let him unban the people's organisation, the African National Congress. Let him free all who have been imprisoned, banished or exiled for their opposition to apartheid. Let him guarantee free political activity so that people may decide who will govern them.

I cherish my own freedom dearly, but I care even more for your freedom. Too many have died since I went to prison. Too many have suffered for the love of freedom. I owe it to their widows, to their orphans, to their mothers and to their fathers who have grieved and wept for them. Not only I have suffered during these long, lonely, wasted years. I am not less life-loving than you are. But I cannot sell my birthright, nor am I prepared to sell the birthright of the people to be free. I am in prison as the representative of the people and of your organisation, the African National Congress, which was banned.

What freedom am I being offered while the organisation of the people remains banned? What freedom am I being offered when I may be arrested on a pass offence? What freedom am I being offered to live my life as a family with my dear wife who remains in banishment in Brandfort? What freedom am I being offered when I must ask for permission to live in an urban area? What freedom am I being offered when I need a stamp in my pass book to seek work? What freedom am I being offered when my very South African citizenship is not respected?

Only free men can negotiate. Prisoners cannot enter into contracts . . . I cannot and will not give any undertaking at a time when I and you, the people, are not free. Your freedom and mine cannot be separated. I will return.

////

The statement made a considerable impact. As Mandela points out in *Long Walk to Freedom*, it was his first public statement in South Africa in 21 years, and worked to rekindle popular interest in the ANC.

Mandela also explains how the statement was generated. After listening to Botha's speech on the radio, he made a request to the prison commander for an urgent visit by Winnie and his lawyer, Ismail Ayob, so that he could dictate his response. Permission was delayed, and he eventually saw them on Friday, 8 February, just two days before the rally. A young warder tried to prevent them from having a 'political conversation', but Mandela stared him down by demanding that he contact the State President. He then handed Winnie and Ismail his prepared statement, which was read out at the rally.[5] What is less well known is that Mandela and his four colleagues in Pollsmoor also responded to the offer in a letter to P.W. Botha.

2
The missing letter to P.W. Botha

'The simple fact is that you are South Africa's head of government, you enjoy the support of the majority of the white population, and you can help change the course of South African history . . .'

THE ORIGINAL LETTER to P.W. Botha, in Mandela's ornate handwriting, resides in the Coetsee archive. Besides Mandela, it was signed by Ahmed Kathrada, Walter Sisulu, Andrew Mlangeni and Raymond Mhlaba. At this point, however, *Long Walk to Freedom* presents the reader with a curious puzzle. Mandela refers to a letter in a single sentence: 'Winnie and Ismail were not given permission to visit for a week, and in the meantime I wrote a letter to the foreign minister, Pik Botha, rejecting the conditions for my release, while also preparing a public response.'[1]

While Mandela might conceivably have written to R.F. (Pik) Botha, this is unlikely, and no such letter has ever turned up. What seems to have happened is that, when Mandela spoke about the letter to P.W. Botha, he was misunderstood by his ghost-writer, Richard Stengel. If this is the case, it is odd that, despite the editorial resources lavished on *Long Walk to Freedom*, this error was never detected and rectified. Secondly, Mandela omits to mention that the letter was ostensibly a joint effort, written by himself as well as his four colleagues in Pollsmoor Prison. In contrast to 'My Father Says', he also does not quote from it.

However, indications are that, at that time at least, he did regard the letter as significant. When Helen Suzman and a fellow member of parliament, Tiaan van der Merwe, visited him at Pollsmoor Prison more than a year later, he told them that, after Botha had made his offer of conditional release, he also replied to him in writing. (This also speaks to the agonisingly long time frames and restrictions Mandela then had to endure in the course of communicating with the outside world.)

Permission to give a copy to Winnie Mandela was refused. According to the covert transcript of the conversation, he then told his visitors: 'That letter would have exposed the government. They suppressed it. We said we were prepared to negotiate. He [Botha] says the opposite.' He added that this was what Botha had told the Commonwealth Eminent Persons Group (EPG), which had visited South Africa in the interim.

////

If Mandela did regard the letter as important, it was with good reason. It differs substantially from the statement read out at the Soweto rally. Among other things, it contains a virulent attack on P.W. Botha. It condemns his offer as ' . . . no more than a shrewd and calculated attempt to mislead the world into the belief that you have magnanimously offered us release from prison which we ourselves have rejected. Coming in the face of such unprecedented and widespread demands for our release, your remarks can only be seen as the height of cynical politicking . . .

'. . . No self-respecting human being will demean and humiliate himself by making a commitment of the nature you demand. You ought not to perpetuate our imprisonment by the simple expedient of setting conditions which, to your own knowledge, we will never under any circumstances accept. . . .

'. . . It would seem that you have no intention whatsoever of using democratic and peaceful forms of dealing with black grievances, [and] the real purpose of attaching conditions to your offer is to ensure that the NP should enjoy the monopoly of committing violence against defenceless people . . .

'. . . You say you are personally prepared to go a long way to release the tensions in inter-group relations in this country, but that you are not prepared to lead the whites to abdication. By making this statement you have again categorically reaffirmed that you remain obsessed with the preservation of domination by the white minority. You should not be surprised, therefore, if . . . the vast masses of the oppressed people continue to regard you as a mere broker of the interests of the white tribe, and consequently unfit to handle national affairs . . .

'. . . You state that you cannot talk with people who do not want to cooperate, that you hold talks with every possible leader who is prepared to renounce violence. Coming from the leader of the NP this statement is a shocking revelation as it shows more than anything else, that there is not a single figure in that party today who is advanced enough to understand the basic problems of our country who has profited from the bitter experiences of the 37 years of NP rule, and who is prepared to take a bold lead towards the building of a truly democratic South Africa . . .'

Botha is also taken to task for his adverse response to allegations at the UN that Mandela's health had deteriorated and that he was being detained under inhumane conditions: 'There is no need for you to be sanctimonious in this regard. The United Nations is an important and responsible organ of world peace . . . Its affairs are handled by the finest brains on earth, by men whose integrity is flawless. If they make such allegations, they do so in the honest belief that they were true . . .'

However, the letter also spells out the ANC's formal demands at the time, namely that the government should itself renounce violence; dismantle apartheid; unban the ANC; free all those who had been imprisoned, banished or exiled for their opposition to apartheid; and guarantee free political activity. These are presented as steps to be taken by Botha and his government if a 'looming confrontation' is to be averted, and amount to Mandela's (and possibly the ANC's) conditions for a peaceful settlement of the South African conflict. These same demands – formulated in a less formal way – are also embedded in Mandela's statement read out at the Soweto rally.

Most significantly, though – as suggested by Mandela in his conversation with Suzman and Van der Merwe – the letter also contains a definite feeler in the direction of engagement. In a marked shift in tone, it states:

'Despite your commitment to the maintenance of white supremacy, your attempt to create new apartheid structures, and your hostility to a non-racial system of government in this country . . . the simple fact is that you are South Africa's head of government, you enjoy the support of the majority of the white population and you can help change the course of South African history. A beginning can be made if you accept and agree to implement the five-point programme on pages 4–5 of this document. If you accept the programme our people would readily cooperate with you to sort out whatever problems arise as far as the implementation thereof is concerned.

'In this regard, we have taken note of the fact that you no longer insist on some of us being released to the Transkei. We have also noted the restrained tone which you adopted when you made the offer in Parliament. We hope you will show the same flexibility and examine these proposals objectively. That flexibility and objectivity may help to create a better climate for a fruitful national debate.'

This passage is carefully worded; for instance, use of the word 'negotiate' is avoided. However, in line with Mandela's remark to his Progressive Federal Party visitors, it signals an unmistakable invitation to Botha to engage with the ANC. It is equally startling today to realise that the NP government eventually met all or almost all of those conditions.

////

Whether the letter ever reached Botha is unknown, and if it did, so is his reaction. Maybe Coetsee decided it was too provocative, and never gave it to him. The only annotation on the letter itself is 'Bêre 913' ('Place in the 913 file'). If Botha ever read the letter, he never commented on it in public.

In February 2010, the Nelson Mandela Foundation staged a commemoration of Mandela's rejection of Botha's offer of conditional release. To mark the occasion, the Foundation interviewed Zindzi Mandela, who had read out the 'My Father Says' statement. She recalled: 'I wasn't worried about us on stage, but I was nervous because Mummy [Winnie Mandela, who was banned to Brandfort at the time] was in the crowd with a scarf on her head, cheap sunglasses, no make-up, and looked like an ordinary aunty from the township, because she insisted on being there.'

The Foundation also interviewed Ahmed Kathrada, who described how Mandela's response to Botha's offer was crafted. The item on the Foundation website quotes him as saying: 'Madiba had been called to the office and [was] informed of this offer of Botha and then he was given, I think, a copy of Hansard . . . a page or two of Hansard where Botha had made this offer. We then discussed it, and it didn't take long for us to unanimously reject the offer. We discussed it among the five of us and, of course, rejected it. And Madiba then, of course, drafted a reply, which we all agreed to. We all helped with the reply and then, of course, he drafted the speech that Zindzi read at a rally in Jabulani.' If this account is correct, it is instructive to note that Mandela was not the only Rivonia trialist who, in the mid-1980s, started to make overtures to the Botha regime.[2]

In the meantime, numerous other 'security prisoners' quietly accepted Botha's offer. They included the Rivonia trialist Denis Goldberg, who had been held in Pretoria Central for 22 years. Goldberg was released on 28 February 1985 and put on a plane to Israel where he was reunited with his family. He later worked for the ANC in London, and returned to South Africa in 2002. He was made to sign a document. He said later that he had grown tired of prison, and he knew in any case that negotiations had effectively begun.

3

Tardy ministers and the State Security Council

'The SSC resolved that certain ministers, after collaboration with one another and with relevant role players . . . would devise a strategy for releasing, from a position of power, security prisoners from both the right and the left, before Christmas . . .'

BOTHA'S OFFER of release and Mandela's response seem reasonably straightforward – a simple binary of action and reaction. However, the Coetsee archive reveals that this was far from the truth. Indeed, key documents in the archive contain some startling revelations that substantially rewrite previous histories of this period.

The first is a top-secret memorandum written and signed by Kobie Coetsee, and addressed to the chairman of the State Security Council (unnamed, but known to have been P.W. Botha). Dated 13 December 1984, it was written in preparation for an SSC meeting the next day. A translation of the complete memorandum follows:

THE CHAIRMAN OF THE STATE SECURITY COUNCIL
MEETING OF THE STATE SECURITY COUNCIL: 14 DECEMBER 1984:
SECURITY PRISONERS
On 3 December, the State Security Council took the following decision (item 3 of the Minutes):
  (a) 'That the relevant ministers, in collaboration with one another and with institutions such as President Matanzima and Chief Minister Buthelezi, will work out a strategy for releasing, from a position of strength, certain security prisoners from the right and left before Christmas;' and

(b) 'That the Minister of Justice would submit the strategy to the State Security Council on 14 December 1984.'

The relevant Ministers are Ministers Botha, De Klerk, Le Grange, Viljoen and myself. I have consulted the Ministers both verbally and telephonically, and asked them via their staff to submit any inputs to me by Wednesday 12 December. No written inputs have been received. Minister Botha indicated that he wanted to hold more consultations, that he would prepare inputs, and that those inputs would be sent to me by 13 December, failing which they would be submitted to the meeting. [While this was not stated, it is reasonably clear that 'Minister Botha' was a reference to the Minister of Foreign Affairs, Pik Botha, an *ex officio* member of the SSC, and not its chairman, P.W. Botha.]

Officials of the Departments of Justice, the Interior and Foreign Affairs as well as the Directorate Security Legislation have deliberated about the available statutory powers for removing relevant people born in the Transkei from the RSA to the Transkei. The identified possibilities are discussed in Appendix C. To summarise, the conclusion is that no legal authorisation for such a forced removal exists that does not hold serious risks of revision in the Supreme Court, and of possibly being set aside. Such litigation could also bring with its serious political disadvantages, especially as it would involve issues such as citizenship, guaranteed rights, and the removal of persons . . .

Appendix B contains deliberations about each of these prisoners . . . with relevant political and security considerations . . . as well as recommendations about release. Immediate release (that is to say, before Christmas) is only recommended in the case of G[ovan] Mbeki. In respect of Mandela, the recommendation is also positive, with a time scale to be determined either via negotiations with the Transkei and suitable legislation, or the model for Mbeki, based on experience with his release. As far as this person and others are concerned, the question is whether this could be done so that release could hold the maximum advantage and the minimum disadvantage in respect of political and security – so that we will not be worse off after release than we are now.

In formulating these recommendations, I have taken the following into consideration: legal authorisation for removing relevant people to the Transkei . . .; the contents of the 'Green Book' (Total Planning – Book 1 / Policy); the National Intelligence Assessment, which has just become available; the ANC Strategy as adopted by the State Security Council and the draft UDF strategy. Communication and action can only be planned after decisions have been taken.

STAMPED: H.J. COETSEE, Minister of Justice, 1984-12-13

The appendices then follow. Appendix A analyses the eligibility of prisoners in terms of the length of their sentences, their age, and the time spent in prison. Those in category I – prisoners serving life sentences who were older than 65 and had served 20 years of their sentences – include only 'G. Mbeki, N. Mandela and W. Sisulu'. Appendix B analyses the pros and cons of their potential release in terms of seven categories, namely policy considerations; grounds for release; means of release; political aspects; security aspects; strategy (effectively, the recommendations); and time frame.

In the case of Mandela, no fewer than six 'possibilities' are mapped out across all seven categories. Possibility One comprises handing 'subject' to the Transkei for detention, either at the full discretion of the Transkei, or on conditions and guarantees approved by the RSA. After citing a host of political and security disadvantages, this option is rejected as 'not feasible – at least not in the short term'.

Possibility Two comprises unconditional release followed by immediate deportation to the Transkei, with the legal implication that Mandela's 'host' could deal with him at will. This option, the document says, would only be feasible if the legal uncertainties could be eliminated.

Possibility Three comprises unconditional release followed by immediate deportation, but preceded by negotiations with the subject aimed at (a) securing his agreement to be released in the

Transkei; and (b) an undertaking that he will not make it necessary for him to be rearrested. This is recommended as the 'second option'.

Possibility Four comprises unconditional release in the RSA after 'successful negotiations with the subject', aimed at securing his agreement to do nothing that would make it necessary for him to be rearrested. 'However, it is doubtful that subject will sign such document.' As a result, this option is 'not regarded as feasible'.

Possibility Five comprises unconditional release on the grounds of age; the fact that 'subject' has served 20 years of his sentence; as well as requests by black leaders, 'not because they regard him as their leader, but because they regard this as advisable'. This is recommended as the 'first option, in tandem with experience in respect of Mbeki's release. Simultaneously with Mbeki's release, it could be announced that Mandela was also under consideration, but proof should be provided that this would not lead to unrest – or that such a step could only be taken in a climate of public order.'

Possibility Six comprises conditional release (parole), aimed at restricting 'subject'. It could include employment, as well as reporting to the South African Police. Negative factors would include continued agitation for his unconditional release, and the deliberate flouting of parole conditions. This would create opportunities for conflict with the authorities. 'It will not be possible to restrict the subject, and he could rather be detained in prison for this purpose.' For these reasons, this option is also 'not recommended'.

////

The implications are inescapable. At an unknown point, but probably in the course of 1984, the SSC took a decision in principle to release political prisoners 'from both the left and the right' before Christmas 1984, with the unstated but reasonably obvious implication that 'prisoners from the left' would include long-term 'security prisoners' such as the Rivonia trialists, including Mandela, Mbeki and Sisulu. At this stage, the SSC still seemed intent on releasing them to the Transkei.

Pursuant to this, Coetsee then recommended that Govan Mbeki be released before Christmas 1984; that the government should announce that it was also considering Mandela's release; and that he should then be released, at an unspecified time but presumably soon afterwards, provided Mbeki's release did not have adverse consequences. Most importantly, Mandela would no longer be released to the Transkei, but to the Republic of South Africa. No formal undertakings or ultimatums were mentioned. Significantly, all the options for release to the Transkei (and, by extension, any other 'independent homeland') were rejected as 'inadvisable' or 'not feasible', and Coetsee conjured up a host of legal obstacles in this regard.

This begins to speak to Coetsee's assertion to co-author Jan-Ad Stemmet two days before his death that his archive would 'rewrite the story of Mandela's release'. Specifically, it speaks to Coetsee's assertion in the course of one of his interviews with the Irish researcher Padraig O'Malley some 25 years later that Mandela's release flowed from a structural (and non-racially formulated) change in policy regarding the release of 'security prisoners', introduced by himself in a deliberately obscure speech in the Senate, which had enabled the release of Breyten Breytenbach in December 1982 – in the full knowledge or with the clear intent that this would eventually result in Mandela's release as well.

Given the document's elaborate officialese, and the fact that the 'recommended' option of unconditional release in the RSA is buried as Possibility five, it also speaks to Coetsee's admission to O'Malley that he sometimes deliberately used obfuscation to advance his political agenda.

The second salient document in the Coetsee archive is a top-secret memorandum written on 23 January 1985 by the director-general of Justice, S.S. (Fanie) van der Merwe. This was two days after the Bethell interview, and seven days before Botha's statement in parliament. Addressed to Coetsee, the memorandum was clearly written after Van der Merwe had studied the Bethell transcript. It casts light on the December meeting of the SSC, as well as the consequences of Bethell's visit. The entire memorandum minus some paragraph numbering is reproduced below.

NO. 913 PRISONER NELSON MANDELA: POLLSMOOR PRISON: MANAGEMENT [*HANTERING*]
MINISTER
On 14 December 1984, the State Security Council, among other things, took the following decision with respect to abovementioned prisoner:

> 'that he [presumably P.W. Botha] will have no objection if Mandela be informed that numerous people and institutions have asked for him to be released, and that release upon the request of the president and prime minister of Transkei will only be considered if he [Mandela] should undertake to abide by the Law'.

Subsequent to this, Lord Bethell (Britain) spoke to Mandela in the course of an orientation visit on 21 January 1985 to SA Prisons during which he also had the opportunity to conduct discussions with a number of prisoners. In the course of the discussion, which took place in the presence of the Head of Pollsmoor Prison (Major Van Sittert), Mandela expressed himself as follows about the use of violence by the ANC, with which he associated himself:

1. The policy of the RSA government had left the ANC with no other choice;
2. Attempts at 'constructive engagement' by the ANC since 1912 had failed;
3. Violence was primarily aimed at so-called hard targets, such as military installations, and not at persons;
4. If soft targets (individuals in charge of or in defence of such hard

51

targets, or even civilians) were to fall victim in the process, this was regrettable;

5. That the ANC was still prepared to negotiate with the RSA government, but only unconditionally, and not under condition that violent actions should first cease.

Aforesaid attitude once again confirms what we already know and/or suspect, namely that to date there is scant indication that Mandela will renounce violence, even if this should result in his release. His attitude is that he has already spent 22 years in prison for this cause, and that he will not capitulate at this stage for personal benefit.

The question therefore arises whether, taking account of the advantages and disadvantages spelled out below, it would still be advisable to confront him with an opportunity to give a firm commitment in this regard:

(a) Advantages:
(i) Gives the Government an opportunity to motivate Mandela's non-release on the grounds that he advocates violence. [The Government] will be able to substantiate this in writing.

(b) Disadvantages:
(i) He [Mandela] could grab the opportunity to give such an undertaking, but could qualify it in such a way that it could rob the undertaking of any value, or embarrass the government.
(ii) A declaration in favour of violence would increase his stature as a determined leader, and limit the government's future options should it become advantageous to release him – this would also make it difficult for Mandela to change his stance at a later stage.
(iii) It would detract from the government's strongman image to be seen at all to approach Mandela with such a proposal – it could be interpreted as a peace offering to the ANC.

PROPOSAL

That, in the light of the foregoing considerations, no effect is given to the [SSC] decision cited [above], but that, added to the results of a discussion on 23 January between Professor Samuel Dash (USA) [a law professor at Georgetown University in Washington DC] and Mandela, for purposes of the record, an arrangement should be made that the Commanding Officer of Pollsmoor Prison, Brigadier F.C. Munro, during a routine discussion which he has to conduct with Mandela in any case, should explore the same terrain. This would have the character of an incidental and informal person to person discussion, and not one of government to prisoner.

This will allow the government to state that Mandela's prognosis is such that he cannot be released at this stage, given that he still advocates violence, and therefore remains part of the armed struggle. At the same time, this will not imply a firm commitment from his side. Therefore, his stature should not benefit from this, while it would give the government an adequate opportunity, from a position of power, and should this become necessary and strategically advisable, to release him unconditionally in terms of a prognosis that may then read differently – a management strategy [*hanteringswyse*] that allows for far greater freedom of movement.

////

These documents allow us to unravel this hidden sequence of events for the first time. Specifically, how do Coetsee's recommendation to the SSC, the council's eventual decision, Van der Merwe's recommendation to the SSC, and P.W. Botha's later offer to Mandela and others follow on and differ from one another?

Firstly, the initial decision of the SSC seems to reflect a reasonably unequivocal determination to release 'security prisoners from the right and left', including Mbeki, Mandela and Sisulu. This corresponds with Coetsee's assertion in later years that the release of Mandela emanated from a policy change relating to the release of long-term 'security prisoners' introduced by himself in 1982.

Next, Coetsee proposes the release first of Govan Mbeki as a litmus test and then – provided this does not result in political unrest – the effectively unconditional release of Mandela. No personal commitment or undertaking by Mandela is mentioned.

Next, at its meeting on 14 December, the SSC (in effect P.W. Botha) decides 'he will have no objection' if Mandela is informed that various people and institutions have asked for him to be released, but that this will only be considered if he undertakes to 'abide by the law'. While these people are said to include Matanzima and other homeland leaders, the offer no longer seems to imply that Mandela would be released to the Transkei. However, this introduces the notion of a personal commitment by Mandela, which was not present in Coetsee's recommendation.

Next, expectations that Mandela would tell Bethell he was prepared to renounce political violence – or that Bethell would persuade him to do so – have a predictable but disappointing outcome. Accordingly, Van der Merwe recommends to the next meeting of the SSC that the previous resolution would need to be abandoned for the time being, but proposes – remarkably – that the situation should be kept as fluid as possible and options kept open, thereby avoiding both sides painting themselves into a corner.

Indeed, Van der Merwe's memorandum seems to be a desperate attempt to prevent Botha from presenting Mandela with any kind of ultimatum. By then, senior prison staff were on intimate and even cordial terms with Mandela, perhaps to the point of feeling protective about him, and Van der Merwe knew precisely what the outcome of the SSC decision (effectively Botha's) would be. Whether this intervention was either initiated or encouraged by Coetsee is unknown. It is also unknown whether the SSC met between the date of the letter and Botha's eventual statement in parliament. But the die had been cast.

Next, Botha announces in parliament that he is prepared to release Mandela and other 'security prisoners', provided they formally renounce violence. On the one hand, the move signifies that Botha and the government have finally abandoned their long-held objective of releasing Mandela to the Transkei. On the other, Botha's announcement does exactly what Van der Merwe tried to avoid, namely to harden positions on both sides. Once again, it appears that, albeit seven months before his infamous speech in Durban, Botha moved to the bank of the Rubicon, and then stepped back from it.

The response from Mandela and his four 'comrades from the roof' is predictable. It would take two more years before Coetsee would start talking to Mandela; four more before Govan Mbeki would be released from Robben Island; and five more before Mandela walked out of Victor Verster Prison.

While it would be specious to suggest that their earlier release would have hastened the resolution of the South African political conflict, the intervening years saw two states of emergency and the deaths of many thousands of people, both in South Africa and in the broader southern African region, which bore much of the brunt of the South African conflict.

////

Later in 1985, Mandela writes, he was taken to the Volks Hospital in Cape Town 'under heavy guard' for a prostate operation. Besides Winnie, he had a surprising and unexpected visitor in the form of Kobie Coetsee, who dropped by the hospital unannounced 'as if he were visiting an old friend'. On the way back to Pollsmoor Prison, he was told that he would be separated from his colleagues, and was placed in a new cell unit comprising three rooms and a separate toilet. Again, no explanation was provided.[1]

While he was not happy about being separated from his colleagues, he realised that his solitude gave him a new opportunity, namely to begin discussions with the South African government. 'I had concluded that the time had come when the struggle could best be pushed forward through negotiations . . . My solitude would give me an opportunity to take the first steps in that direction, without the kind of scrutiny that might destroy such efforts.'

This would be extremely sensitive, and a decision to talk to the government was so important that it should only have been made by ANC headquarters in Lusaka. But he felt the process needed to begin, and he had neither the time nor the means to communicate fully with Oliver Tambo. 'Someone from outside needed to take the first step, and my new isolation gave me both the freedom to do so and the assurance, at least for a while, of the confidentiality of my efforts . . .'

In a candid passage, Mandela writes: 'I chose to tell no one what I was about to do. Not my colleagues upstairs, nor those in Lusaka. The ANC is a collective, but the government had made collectivity in this case impossible. I did not have the security or the time to discuss these issues with my organisation. I knew that my colleagues upstairs would condemn my proposal, and that would kill my initiative even before it was born. There are times when a leader must move out ahead of the flock, go off in a new direction, confident that he is leading his people the right way . . .'

Within a few weeks, he wrote to Coetsee to propose talks about talks, but received no response. However, another opportunity to be heard came in early 1986.

4

Brothers in arms

> 'When I leave here I will be going to Lusaka.
> Are there any messages to our brothers? . . . Of course,
> this will be confidential . . .'

IN OCTOBER 1985, at a summit in Nassau, British Commonwealth leaders decided to send a delegation of 'eminent persons' to South Africa to report back on whether sanctions were an appropriate means of bringing about the end of apartheid. In early 1986, a seven-member Eminent Persons Group (EPG), led by General Olusegun Obasanjo, former military leader of Nigeria, and Malcolm Fraser, the former Australian prime minister, arrived in South Africa on their fact-finding mission. The group also included Lord Barber, a former British cabinet minister, and John Malecela, a former Tanzanian foreign minister.[1]

In February 1986, Obasanjo was allowed to visit Mandela to discuss the delegation's brief. All Mandela says about this meeting is that Obasanjo was 'eager to facilitate a meeting between myself and the full group'. With the government's permission, the meeting with the full group was scheduled for May. The prison authorities had a fitted suit made for the occasion, so that he could meet the delegation on an equal footing. (Mandela records that a smiling Brigadier Munro, Officer Commanding, Pollsmoor Prison, told him he looked 'more like a prime minister than a prisoner'.)

At the meeting between Mandela and the EPG, they were joined by two 'significant observers': Kobie Coetsee and Lieutenant-General W.H. (Willie) Willemse, the Commissioner of Prisons. Despite the fact that he pressed them to remain, as he had nothing to hide, they left shortly after the session started. 'Before they took their leave,' Mandela writes, 'I told them the time had come for negotiations, not fighting, and that the government and the ANC should sit down and talk.'

At the outset, he set ground rules for the discussions. He told the EPG that the head of his movement was Oliver Tambo, and that they had to go and see him in Lusaka. They could tell Tambo what Mandela's views were, but they were his personal views alone. 'They don't even represent the views of my colleagues, here in prison. That said, I favoured the ANC beginning discussions with the government.'

Various members of the group expressed concerns about his political ideology and a South Africa under ANC leadership. He told them he was a nationalist, not a communist, that nationalists came in every hue and colour, and that he was firmly committed to a non-racial society. He believed in the Freedom Charter, which embodied principles of democracy and human rights, and that it was not a blueprint for socialism. 'I spoke of my concern that the white minority should feel a sense of security in any new South Africa. I told them I thought many of our problems were a result of lack of communication between the government and the ANC, and that some of these could be resolved through actual talks.'

The group questioned him extensively on the use of violence. 'While I was not yet willing to renounce violence, I argued in the strongest possible terms that violence could never be the ultimate solution to the situation in South Africa, and that men and women by their very nature required some kind of negotiated understanding. While I once again reiterated that these were my views and not those of the ANC, I suggested that if the government withdrew the army and police from the townships, the ANC might agree to a suspension of the armed struggle as a prelude to talks. I told them that my release alone would not stem the violence in the country or stimulate negotiations.' The EPG was scheduled to see him again. 'I was optimistic, as they had been to both Lusaka and Pretoria, and I hoped that the seed of negotiations had been sown.'

Recounting an infamous chain of events, Mandela writes: 'But the day before we were to meet, the South African government took a step that sabotaged whatever goodwill had been engendered by the visit. On the day the EPG was scheduled to meet cabinet ministers, the South African Defence Force, under the orders of President Botha, launched air raid and commando attacks on ANC bases in Botswana, Zambia and Zimbabwe. This utterly poisoned the talks, and the EPG immediately left South Africa . . .'

////

Both meetings, with Obasanjo and with the full group, were recorded, and transcripts – stamped SECRET – appear in the Coetsee archive. Both make for interesting reading. Among other things, they show that Mandela's account is accurate in some respects, and substantially inaccurate in others.

The first transcript records that the meeting with Obasanjo took place at 1.05 pm on 21 February. Obasanjo calls him 'my brother'. After a while, Mandela starts to call Obasanjo 'my brother' as well. Among other things, Obasanjo makes Mandela an interesting offer, which he politely refuses. An edited version of the transcript follows.

> Obasanjo: It's nice to see you. I was on the plane, and there was Winnie. How are you?
> Mandela: I am fine . . . very well. Nigeria is typical of Africa. There are songs about you. You are our hero. Nigeria is the biggest state in Africa. I was there in 1962 during the Monrovia conference [a short-lived association of African states] in Lagos and I met a million personalities, and I always feel very close to Nigeria. Everything I read about it, there is a feeling of belonging, and I felt very honoured when the university gave me that prize [honorary doctorate of law degree

from Ahmadu Bello University]. Rest assured that Nigeria will be one of my very first priorities . . .

O: I am happy that you are informed.

M: I have got a radio and I get newspapers.

O: I'm surprised.

M: I am following your movements, and I have got a file on the seven of you, and please do convey my regards to General Babangida [president of Nigeria].

O: I will.

M: And indicate to him just what Nigeria means to me.

O: I will post your comments.

M: One of the reasons I am in high spirits is the knowledge that I have got powerful friends and your coming here and the way you have handled the situation. I like that very much.

O: Thank you . . .

M: Your steps, what you have done, have created a favourable impression not only to us but to the whole party (ANC) as well, and they can now see that these are men who are heads of state and will know what diplomacy is. You have done it very well. That's why they allow you to come, because of the way in which you have done it. I have of course committed that I will not tell anybody that you have been here.

O: I told them to do so.

M: I will honour that.

O: The ministers keeps on saying that Nelson is a man of honour. I know that he (Nelson) is a man of his word, and will do so.

M: I am happy to hear that.

O [perhaps talking about Kobie Coetsee]: My impression of him too is that he is a man of fibre. He has got problems, but he is a man of honour.

Let me use the short period that we have. I don't know whether the group as a whole will be allowed to see you. But that request will be formally made. I have told the minister. I will associate myself with that request. I will of course be reporting to them.

Some of our brothers assist us wherever designated, and when they talked to me I explained that we can't do more than our mandate prescribes. We don't want to raise expectations. But we do believe that we just might have . . . I don't know if you feel that way. How do you think we can approach this task before us, for whatever it's worth . . . I found the word 'dialogue' has become abused.

M: Yes.

O: And of course the Commonwealth do let us talk of negotiations. And the minister and government also talk of negotiations. We have talked to people and of course we will continue to talk to people, and it's a good thing they allowed the whole group to come here. We have maintained a low profile.

When I leave here I will be going to Lusaka. Are there any messages to our brothers? I will be glad to . . . of course, this will be confidential . . .

M: This is a wonderful and great moment for me, and a great honour. I do want you to have clean hands, and there are messages I would have liked to have given to you. Because you have given an undertaking to them that you will keep this quiet, and I have done so too, they would not like us to use it for purposes which are not consistent with the undertaking . . .

This delegation, my brother, is a very important delegation. I have no doubt that even Lusaka will endorse it. You can tell them that I give this delegation my full blessing, and when the time comes when it is permissible for us to reveal things, you can say that you discussed the matter with me. You were strengthened because you heard that I endorsed the idea.

O: This is a great moment for me, and I must say that talking to ministers and government, one is amazed at their own understanding . . . They are seeing things happening [perhaps ripening], and I think what a group like ours wants to do is to try and see how we can move on government and people to whom the government has not been talking for god knows how long, to really find a process of genuine negotiations where there will be understanding on either side, and where there will be respect on either side.

M: To evade discussions with the ANC and to insist on this question of the conditions that I must renounce violence – that we cannot do, that we will never do.

O: What has caused this?

M: For fifty years we continued with the policy of no violence, with peaceful struggles, in which we went out of our way to discourage violence, and the ruling party went all out to smash even the little privileges we still had to the extent that today we have none. In that situation we had no alternative but to take this decision.

But we are interested in normalising the situation. One of my several desires is that I should contribute towards the building of my country, and if I am given that opportunity I will do so. But I will never do so on the basis that I should renounce violence. The atmosphere must first be created. They are also making a mistake by still holding up the ANC as a . . .

O: A communist . . .

M: Yes. Through all these years we have had a lot of eminent persons who are not only not communists but anti-communists. The tradition of this organisation (ANC) is just like the principle of it . . .

O: They take in everybody . . .

M: Yes, anybody. No matter what his use is as long as he is determined to fight against racial discrimination. That's the basis.

O: And that's all.

M: That's all . . . they know that, it's in the records. I led a movement in the mid-forties. No, let me say, I was part of a movement by the younger people who expelled communists from the organisation. People like Prof. Z.K. Matthews said the tradition of this organisation is that any African who is over the age of 18 and who is against racial discrimination is entitled to become a member.

O: When you say African does it mean black, coloured, white and . . .

M: Well, at that time we had only blacks in mind. It was only later that others could join.

M: Now apart from this the government itself has been working with communists. You see, it's a question of what your interests are. And they are cooperating in numerous respects in the interests of SA (with communists).

O: Yes.

M: And quite apart from that I have quoted to them that during the last war Britain, France and America were in alliance with the Soviet Union.

O: Yes.

M: It became necessary and even today they are working together with the Soviet Union not only in the United Nations, but in every way. So why should anybody not want us to have dealings with people who are uniting against a common evil? What they must understand is the fact that the man who is regarded as a Marxist, a communist, is not there in the capacity as a member of the Communist Party, but he is there purely as a black, white etc. who feels there is need for change in this country.

O: Yes.

M: And that is all. We also resent some of the organisations to which they belong. They themselves have got a number of societies to which they belong. They have got an organisation called the Broederbond.

O: Broederbond?

M: Yes, the Broederbond. It means the Union of Brothers. They post members of that society in key positions. People like the State President and the Ministers.

O: Broederbond . . . [laughs] How do you spell that? . . .

M: B-R-O-E-D-E-R-B-O-N-D. They have got that body, but still they are not prepared to work with us. Oliver Tambo is a Christian, a religious man.

O: Yes, he is so nice.

M: Completely humble.

O: Is he a communist?

M: No, no, he is not a communist.

O: I agree with that.

M: Then why should the communists put him up, a man who is not only a non-communist but also a Christian, and put him in that position (leader of the ANC)? He is a very religious man.

O: Thank you, Nelson, I believe that and I hope and pray that something will happen to smooth things out without unnecessary bloodshed in this country. This is a beautiful country with fantastic infrastructure. This must be there for everybody to make use of. A country that must be saved for all its citizens. And I mean all the citizens of the country.

Although you have not been out of jail for 24 years, there are problems which you must be aware of. The country is polarised – there are differences not only between whites and blacks but between blacks and blacks. What do you say about this? That's a very important question, my brother.

M: That's a very important question. When I was asked about that by a journalist, I said the differences between blacks – that is, Africans, coloureds and Asians – are not matters for the press. If there are differences, I will discuss them directly with the black leaders themselves. My policy is to try and keep good relations with all African leaders, even those who are working inside these institutions (homelands). When I go out . . . if I will ever go out . . .

O: You will go out . . .

M: I will speak to each and every one. I know exactly what to say to everybody. My task is to provide a liberation movement first before attending to any other problems. I don't think that is insurmountable . . . Even with all the difficulties that I have, I have tried to keep in touch with K.D. [Matanzima]. I sent him a letter which was published because of its significance. When I was in hospital, he sent me a message of goodwill. We are friends.

[Major Van Sittert enters and points to the time.]

M: You must thank the university for me and then of course General Babangida, and tell him what I have told you. And of course all the other members of the EPG. I think they are doing an excellent job . . .

////

The Coetsee archive contains a handwritten note by Mandela on lined and perforated government-issue A4 paper. Dated 21 February 1986, and addressed to the Officer Commanding, Pollsmoor Maximum Prison, it reads:

'I am ready and willing to receive General Obasanjo, and undertake not to give publicity to the meeting. In particular, I undertake not to make it known to other people. Signed: N.R. Mandela.'

5

The birth of an idea

'If you can intercede for me, I would like to speak to my colleagues on Robben Island, as well as those in South Africa outside prison . . .'

THE EPG visited Mandela on Friday, 16 May 1986, accompanied by Kobie Coetzee.[1] While Coetsee did leave the meeting after a while, it started with a significant exchange between him and Mandela. It turns out that Jan Heunis, a state law adviser and the son of Chris Heunis, then Minister of Constitutional Development and Planning, sat in on the entire meeting. The group was due to meet a Constitutional Committee, chaired by Heunis senior, four days later, on Monday, 19 May. A detailed transcript of the meeting with Mandela appears in the Coetsee archive. Stamped 'SECRET', it also states that it is the fourth of only seven copies.

Obasanjo – who seems to chair the meeting – thanks Coetsee for their opportunity to meet Mandela, and expresses regret that he has to leave. He then gives Mandela a chance to speak. Mandela also expresses his regret that Coetsee won't stay for the meeting. As a cabinet minister, he says, it's important for him to bear in mind the significance of contact between the ANC and the government. He has met Coetsee previously, although briefly, and feels strongly that more meetings will be valuable.

At the meeting, he would speak freely, and Coetsee would have an opportunity to listen to some of the issues that worried Mandela and his colleagues. Some of the government's problems would then disappear. 'There are of course very serious issues which divide us, and they cannot be resolved by us merely sitting together for two or three hours.' But the act of talking is highly significant, and would reveal a lack of mutual confidence that is leading to a waste of human and other resources.

If the minister chooses not to be present, he hopes he will see him again soon. 'I have very much desired organised discussions with members of the cabinet in order to allay the fears which they seem to have and to assure them of my co-operation, not only as an individual, but as a member of an organisation.' But he goes on to say: 'I am a loyal member of the ANC, and my views can only carry weight if they are expressed as part of the ANC . . .'

One of his difficulties is that he is not in contact with members of his organisation, in prison or outside. He is not complaining about the fact that he is staying alone, and his living conditions are extremely good. However, he and his four colleagues are isolated from the rest of the prison population, and for discussions such as these, it is necessary to keep on exchanging views. 'Because what you are interested in is that whatever rapport is established must also be a rapport with members of my organisation who play an important role in influencing decisions.'

He also assures Coetsee that his colleagues are men of goodwill. 'They do not want to be reduced to a position whereby they pull down what has been built up. They are essentially constructive people who want to play a role in normalising the situation in this country . . .

'The advantage of having a discussion with members of the government is precisely because this will create an atmosphere of normality in which we can develop the mutual confidence for tackling very sensitive issues, with no mutual suspicion, which we could prove to the entire South African population with a common vote . . . This is why I attach such importance to this group.'

Seeming to cut Mandela short, Coetsee says: 'I appreciate the rapport that has been established between us, and I am also pleased that it is possible to arrange an event of this nature . . . You will know exactly what I am saying to you, and I think you also appreciate my position as a member of the government . . .

I believe the purpose of the meeting could be to canvass certain issues, and I believe those issues could be better canvassed without my being present . . . Again, I think you understand exactly what I am saying . . . [So] I think the moment for our departure has arrived, and I will take you up on your invitation to see you more on a personal level.' Coetsee then leaves.

Obasanjo says the group wants to fill Mandela in on what has happened since his last visit. It has met with government ministers, members of parliament, businessmen, ordinary citizens, UDF leaders and trade unionists, as well as an ANC delegation outside the country. Flowing from this, it has assessed the situation and concluded that, 'within certain parameters', the situation in South Africa could be resolved through negotiation.

'As a result, we have come up with up with an idea of our own – a possible negotiating concept – which we thought could advance the process for peace and harmony in this country.' He hands Mandela a document (presumably setting out the negotiating concept), and asks him to read it. He says the group passed the proposal on to the government two months previously. The latter eventually responded by saying it would not give an 'absolute yes or absolute no'.

Among other things, the document explores some fears the government would have if this concept was adopted – particularly about violence, and the reaction of the international community if acts of violence did not abate, and the government acted to quell the violence. 'We said that, within the limits of what we could foresee, embarking on negotiations would in itself de-escalate violence.

'If this process is to be embarked upon, we are here . . . to apprise you of the progress we have made . . . We are also here for you to give us your views, your idea of the South African problem, and the possibilities of how to get there.'

Lord Barber also says it would be helpful to get 'some sort of reaction' from Mandela. However, it would be understandable if he 'does not go far', because he has only read the document very quickly, and has not yet consulted his colleagues.

Barber then summarises the negotiating concept as follows: 'The guts of the matter is first the release of prisoners like yourself as well as detainees. Secondly, the unbanning of the ANC and the PAC [Pan Africanist Congress], and thirdly, the opportunity to have free discussions and meetings and the abolition of detention without trial. On the other side, we would ask the ANC and others to do two things, namely to enter into negotiations with an open agenda, and that the black community should be represented by people of their own choosing. They would also have to agree to suspend violence.'

Surprisingly, he goes on to say it would be 'grossly unfair to ask the ANC to suspend violence forever . . . Negotiations might break down, and then all bets would be off. The position would then be as it was before. It is very important not to ask them to suspend violence forever, because this will be unreasonable. The ANC would not agree to that.'

It is clear, Barber continues, that members of government 'should be talked to'. They are obsessed with what would happen if these conditions were imposed. 'It is reasonable to tell you that government officials have also talked about the suspension of violence – not renunciation. Of course, this is not to be made public.'

Mandela then asks: 'What officials?' Fraser replies that they are 'government officials, as well as ministers . . .'

Fraser then joins in: 'As far as the government is concerned, the most important thing now is to diminish these fears. We have explored [this], and if the concept is accepted, a suspension of violence would be the acceptable thing. Take Port Elizabeth, for instance. There was rioting and violence, and they had to send troops in. We have explored these fears on the government side, and they have to lay them to rest. If there is any guidance on this, it would be good.'

Mandela: 'As far as I am concerned, I have no problem with this document. I have not studied this closely, but there have been hints in the press . . . so I am conversant with its contents. The problem is that what you are actually interested in is not my view, but my [ability] to express the view of the organisation to which I belong. To give a clear view of this, you have to consult with your colleagues, the organisation.

'I can convince my colleagues to use these ideas as a starting point. My colleagues outside and inside the country are very amenable to persuasion. They have a greater responsibility than members of the government. People in prison seek realistic solutions much more than people outside. [So] it will not be difficult to assert this document as a starting point. The advantage is that it leaves the government a lot of room to manoeuvre, and we can in the course of discussion twist their arm and it would be easy to do so.'

Fraser: 'Our idea is only that it is a starting point.'

Mandela: 'My problem is that I have no contact with my colleagues inside or outside prison in South Africa. I see my colleagues here whenever I want, but some of our leaders are on Robben Island, and it would be necessary to consult with them. The wider the backing, the better. It is important that I consult with my people on Robben Island. Not all of them, which would be ideal, but with the leaders. The government can also allow colleagues outside prison to come and see me here. It would be very fruitful, if I could do that.'

Fraser asks: 'What about people from outside the country?'

Mandela: 'No. They won't allow me to go to Lusaka. [But] if they can say that we spoke to colleagues here and outside prison, that will be important, and our people in Lusaka will never interfere.'

Fraser asks again: 'Can we help here?'

Mandela: 'If you can intercede for me, I would like to speak to my colleagues on Robben Island, as well as those in South Africa outside prison. You would have to convince the government. It will not help to discuss it with the Officer Commanding here. I would only see the recognised leaders, but those outside also have leaders. We can then decide that this plan has a chance.

'Let's try it out. We can then advise our people in Lusaka... They are responsible people, but they can be directed by us from here. The matter rests with you. Tell them [the government] that it is important that my views should express the views of my colleagues. I am putting the task to you...'

Fraser: 'There will be no problem at all. We will talk to them. Of course, we will also talk to the ANC in Lusaka.'

Mandela asks whether they are aware of divisions within government on the proposals, which could be expected in 'any organisation made up of human beings'.... 'I know you have met the Minister of Foreign Affairs. Anybody else?'

Fraser: 'We are meeting the Constitutional Committee on Monday. That is very important – even critical.'

Barber says they have seen no one else, and that people are waiting for a speech by the State President. Fraser adds that the group previously met 'eight or nine'. They don't think they will meet the State President. 'We are moving step by step.'

Mandela asks whether they are coming back from Lusaka. Fraser confirms that they are, and that they will be back on Sunday or Monday.

Mandela: 'This allays my concern. I was under the impression that you were only meeting with Pik Botha, and that you were on the verge of leaving.'

Fraser: 'No, no.'

Obasanjo: 'That would not be correct.'

Mandela says the intervention might be seen as a delaying tactic in lieu of sanctions. 'Surely you won't allow that? I have to tell my colleagues that I raised this issue, and that this was your reaction.'

Fraser says the group is working to a tight schedule. Their six months are up by end June, and they must have a report by then. 'If we see that things are progressing well, but time is too short, we will say this to the [Commonwealth] prime ministers, and they will accept that. Unlike Namibia, we will not put you and the ANC in a situation that drags on and on. The prime ministers are meeting in August, and this will be discussed.' He adds that the South African government is aware of this as well.

Mandela asks what will happen if the prime ministers feel that sanctions should be applied, and Britain disagrees. Fraser says this will only happen if the mission fails. The Commonwealth without Britain is 'unimaginable'. In the United States, many institutions are not investing in companies doing trade with South Africa. All this would gather pace if the discussions fail.

'If they do, there will be no other attempt in a very long time, and this will trigger all sorts of repercussions. Those who believe in violence rather than negotiations will be strengthened, and America won't be able to stand back. This makes it important to exhaust all avenues, and get the negotiations started.'

Next, Mandela himself raises the issue of communism: 'The State President made a statement after you left. He said those members of the ANC who were nationalists could come back if they renounced violence. Political scientists then went to their files to see who was a communist and who was not. That will cause a lot of problems, because we don't want the government to decide how we are composed. This is our affair.'

Barber: 'We agree. The ANC must decide. [But] the government also says that blacks must choose their own leaders. What has been said in the past can be left aside. The government realises that if our mission fails, there is nothing left. We have succeeded so far. We have behaved impeccably. We are trusted.'

Mandela: '. . . But you are aware that the State President made the statement after you were here.'

Obasanjo: 'That is part and parcel of politics, Nelson . . .'

Fraser: 'Let us be practical. If we said only non-communist people could come back, it could blow the whole operation.'

Heunis explains that Botha made the remark in parliament in the House of Representatives.[2]

Mandela persists: 'If a member of the NP says a person is a communist, we have to be careful. This is no reason to attack their integrity, because it's part of their background, and they are trained to think like that. To them, anybody who has been educated in the socialist countries is a communist. Three ANC leaders – Tambo, [Alfred] Nzo and [Thomas] Nkobi[3] – are well-known nationalists. What has happened the last 24 years, I don't know.'

John Malecela points out that the government says it will no longer prescribe who should represent blacks, so this is now an 'open agenda'.

Mandela: 'I am happy about that . . . [but] there is no other organisation behind the ANC. If they are dominated by the communists, and you talk to Tambo and Nzo, you are not talking to the real policy-makers, because this would be the Communist Party. There is no such thing. You are dealing with the ANC.'

Barber asks Mandela for his views about Chief Buthelezi. 'People say he has let down the side.' Responding, Mandela says Buthelezi is a 'freedom fighter in his own right'. He differs from the ANC, but he is a force that should not be ignored. He goes on to say that the liberation movement should not be divided, and that it is the task of the ANC to unite it.

'One of my first tasks would be to convince my colleagues that we should close ranks and not allow a man like him to be regarded with reservations. Let us bring him under our wing. I regard him as important, and have said so openly. I have a formidable case to convince my colleagues. He will have to see Oliver Tambo. There were problems but they are friends. To answer, I say that I regard Buthelezi as an important figure.'

Obasanjo asks whether anyone wants anything to be clarified. In an apparent summary of the proceedings, Heunis then remarks that Mandela regards the EPG document as a starting point, and will try to convince his colleagues. He then asks him: 'If the government accepts it, will you accept it?'

Mandela: 'I will accept it whether the government does or not.' [Some laughter.] He asks Heunis to accept his remark 'in the spirit in which it was made'.

Heunis: 'Thank you very much, sir.'

Mandela adds: 'I accept this as a starting point. My only reservations are that I would like my views to be that of the movement.'

Fraser says the government is concerned about violence. Among other places, it had to use troops in Port Elizabeth. 'Is it reasonable to tell the government to talk to Mandela, Tambo and others of importance to try and calm the situation so that the military is not used? Is that reasonable in the context of the negotiations going on?'

Mandela: 'The way I see it is, if there are responses from both sides, from the government and the ANC, there can be no difficulty at all, because at the same time when the ANC suspends violence, the government must also pull out the army and police from the townships.'

Fraser: 'The government is concerned about how much violence the ANC controls.'

Mandela: 'The people involved in this are well known. There are cases where criminal elements take advantage, but generally speaking it is a result of political issues. Take the last funeral in the Eastern Cape. Mkhuseli Jack [a UDF activist in Port Elizabeth] went to the police and asked them to pull out. He said they could not control it all. The police agreed, and according to the papers it all went peacefully. In Alexandra, you have leaders and they arranged a funeral.

'To solve this, there will have to be a great deal of consultation. The mere release of Nelson Mandela is not going to solve this. I and my colleagues as a team will have to go to the people and persuade them that this is harmful. Forget the government, so many people are dying, it is necessary to call this off, for in this way we will get the support of our people and of whites in the country. We will be able to isolate the government by doing that . . . [Laughter] . . . If we and the other organisations work together, we can control this.'

Obasanjo: 'This is what we are trying to achieve . . .'

Barber: 'I get the feeling that they (government) are not confident... If all hell breaks loose in a township... are they going to be criticised? They feel this is a tremendous gamble they are taking...'

Obasanjo says something about Mandela being freed, Tambo returning, and people marching to Pretoria. [Laughter]

Mandela: 'I can see why the government is reluctant about this, but contact [between us] will have the effect of removing those fears, because we are interested even from a selfish point of view to put an end to violence. I do want to go out and lead a normal life with my family, and to join my children. I am not prepared to do so under humiliating conditions. I want to leave prison as I came, with the same image.

'But I will not abuse that. I want this uprising to come to an end. I want conditions to be normal. I understand their fears. They do not know the leaders of the black population.'

[People talk about the available time.]

Mandela: 'If there are no further questions...?'

Obasanjo: 'In view of our impending discussions in Lusaka. Anything on that?'

Mandela: 'You can indicate what my views are. It will be sufficient to point out that these are my views, without me consulting my colleagues here, but I have no doubt they would agree. I saw them last Friday.'

Obasanjo: 'Can you give us your view of South Africa?'

Mandela: 'It is difficult for a man in prison. The men in control of the organisation are in Lusaka...' Mandela goes on to say that the ANC's policy is spelled out in the Freedom Charter, the 'most devastating attack I know of on discrimination in all its ramifications, economic, political, social... And it calls for a new order, not on the basis of any change in the system of production. We visualise the existing system of production, except in certain sectors of the economy... We have seen countries nationalising and then later de-nationalising, so your advice will be valuable...

'We believe that this programme will receive the support not only of blacks but of whites as well, because a substantial number of whites have the same problem we have. I do not know what the position is now. Perhaps Mr Heunis will tell us. But during the Treason Trial which ended in March 1961, we investigated and found that almost half of the province of the Free State was owned by one enterprise. So the masses of the people, whites too, have not got the land to divide.

'I therefore say, let land be divided amongst those who can work it. This will receive the support of whites as well. There is the complaint by farmers of the big inroads made by big corporations. This is a problem affecting all the sections of the population.'

Fraser: 'Do you have a view on controlling the young generation?'

Mandela: 'We have an organisation of youth, COSAS [Congress of South African Students, aligned to the UDF], which is banned. But to get an idea of how this organisation can control the youth, you have to look at a report that was published by Professor [Tjaart] Van der Walt of the University of Potchefstroom [in 1985 on black education in the Vaal Triangle]. He conducted this investigation of the disturbance which took place at Sharpeville [in 1984]. He had a number of commendable things to say about COSAS. He found them responsible. More intelligent than their white counterparts, and very brilliant youngsters. That organisation has a massive following in this country.

'The youth tend to be left today because of the development which is taking place in neighbouring states. Mozambique, Marxist, Zimbabwe, Marxist, Angola, Marxist – I don't know what the position of SWAPO is, but there is a belief that there is a strong Marxist presence there. This has affected the youth, and it's a problem that will stay. It may well be that the Freedom Charter is not progressive enough for them, but that is our policy at the present moment.

'Well, I am very happy to have met you., I hope it is not the last time. I am encouraged to know you are not leaving for good . . .'

Mandela then asks Obasanjo to arrange for Frieda Matthews to come and visit him. He explains that she is the widow of Z.K. Matthews, former president of the ANC in the Cape, and lives in Gaborone in Botswana. Obasanjo should approach Foreign Minister Pik Botha on this issue. (The transcript notes that the matter has been taken up with Security Services [Colonel Gillingham], and will be dealt with administratively.)

////

This is a highly informative conversation. Besides casting light on the activities of the EPG, as well as Mandela's interaction with it, it also elucidates his beliefs and strategies at that time. Specifically, it reveals that Mandela had only met Coetsee once before – presumably at Volks Hospital – and that Mandela used the meeting with the group as much to talk to Coetsee as to the EPG.

It also shows that Mandela was already thinking about talking to political leaders in prison as well as outside – at this stage, to persuade them to regard the EPG proposals as a point of departure towards a negotiated settlement – and was so enthusiastic about it that he asked the EPG to persuade the South African government to allow such a discussion. Although the EPG initiative would soon collapse, the idea endured, to be implemented in a few years' time.

Remarkably, beyond its formal brief, the transcript also reveals that the EPG thought it could broker constitutional negotiations in South Africa, with the apparent support of Minister Chris Heunis and officials – including his son – in the Department of Constitutional Development and Planning.

Three days later, the group were in their meeting with Heunis when an official entered the room to inform the minister that raids had been launched on ANC bases in Botswana, Zambia and Zimbabwe. It was clear Heunis did not know this was going to happen. Research has revealed that the raids were ordered by P.W. Botha himself without the knowledge of the chief of the Defence Force,

General Magnus Malan, who was in hospital at the time. Botha did so in his capacity as commander-in-chief of the SADF. The EPG flew out of the country almost immediately. On 12 June 1986, the government imposed a nationwide state of emergency.

6

A meeting with Kobie Coetsee

'I wish to see you on a matter of national importance...'

IN JUNE 1986, the month after the EPG had left South Africa, Mandela wrote to General Willie Willemse, Commissioner of Prisons, saying that he wished to see him on a matter of national importance. He handed the letter to Brigadier Munro, Officer Commanding, Pollsmoor Prison. That weekend, Munro told him to prepare for a meeting with Willemse, who was coming down from Pretoria. They eventually met in Willemse's house in the grounds of Pollsmoor Prison.

In *Long Walk to Freedom*, Mandela writes: 'Willemse is a direct fellow, and we got down to business immediately. I told him I wanted to see Kobie Coetsee... He asked me why. I hesitated for a moment, reluctant to discuss political matters with a prison official. But I responded with frankness: "I want to see the minister in order to raise the question of talks between the government and the ANC."'

Willemse phoned Coetsee, who, he said, 'just happened to be in Cape Town'. Minutes later, they left the General's house in a small convoy, bound for Coetsee's official residence. (Mandela notes that the 'ease and rapidity' with which this meeting was set up made him suspect that it 'might have been planned in advance'.) In any event, Coetsee greeted him warmly, and they settled down on comfortable chairs in his lounge.

Mandela then writes that he spent three hours in conversation with Coetsee, during which he was struck by his sophistication and willingness to listen. Coetsee asked knowledgeable and relevant questions, which reflected a familiarity with the issues that divided the government and the ANC. 'He asked me under what circumstances we would suspend the armed struggle; whether or not I spoke for the ANC as a whole; and whether I envisioned any constitutional guarantees for minorities in a new South Africa. His questions went to the heart of the issues dividing the government and the ANC.'

Mandela sensed Coetsee wanted some resolution: '"What is the next step?" he asked. I told him I wanted to see the state president and the foreign minister, Pik Botha.'[1] Coetsee wrote this down on a notepad, and said he would send Mandela's request through the proper channels. They shook hands, and he was driven back to Pollsmoor.

'I was greatly encouraged,' Mandela writes. 'I sensed the government was anxious to overcome the impasse in the country, that they were now convinced they had to depart from their old positions. In ghostly outline, I saw the beginnings of a compromise...' But again, 'after this promising start', nothing happened. Weeks and then months passed 'without a word from Coetsee'. In some frustration, Mandela wrote him another letter.[2]

////

What Mandela did not know is that Coetsee informed P.W. Botha about the discussion before it took place, wrote a memorandum about it on the same day, and discussed it with Botha the next. (While Mandela recalls that the meeting took place in June, it actually occurred on Sunday, 20 July, and the discussion with Botha on Monday, 21 July.) The memorandum and a summary of Coetsee's discussion with Botha appear in the archive. Written in Afrikaans, they are stamped 'TOP SECRET' – and not without reason. A handwritten note states that it is the second of only three typed copies. Translations of the complete documents follow.

BACKGROUND

913 asks to meet with the Commissioner of Prisons (Komvang), and indicates that he has had some ideas that may interest the Minister. Komvang and Minister arrange that the former should conduct an exploratory conversation with 913, and that, should he conclude that this is a political matter which the Minister should take note of, he would contact the Minister. The conversation takes place on Sunday 20 July 1986, and Minister decides to meet with 913. Minister informs State President. Conversation takes place. Komvang and CO Pollsmoor withdraw after opening conversation.

Minister and 913 agree that the conversation is confidential. Besides disclosures to the State President, nothing will be disclosed unless both parties agree. With 913's knowledge, the Minister makes notes of the conversation.

SUMMARY OF CONVERSATION

The Minister states that there are forces misusing the Mandela image to their advantage and not the advantage of 913, and that any initiative will have to take account of realities in the RSA [Republic of South Africa], the standpoint of the State President about violence, and the fact that 913 is associated with communism, which is rejected by the RSA.

913 explains that, after lengthy deliberation, he has concluded that an initiative is required, that the obstacles can be addressed with new formulations that will still conform to the State President's requirements in respect of violence. At this point, Komvang and the CO withdraw.

913 continues and says his 'suggestion' will meet the State President's conditions and also that the conditions laid down by the organisation (the ANC). When I start to respond, 913 says hastily: 'My sole idea is to put forward an idea to the State President of how he can establish whether his conditions are being met by me . . . by everyone.'

He says he is not trying to negotiate his release. He wants to indicate to the State President that he can play a role without leaving prison. He says the State President is obliged to listen to anyone who wants to make a contribution to normalising the situation in the RSA. He is not prepared to deviate from his duty of uniting Blacks and Whites in South Africa. He says this in response to my statement that there are many people who do not want to see peace in South Africa.

In response, I say to him that it is unthinkable for the State President to conduct a conversation with him that could [transcript illegible] negotiations or result in an agreement while he is still in prison.

913 sees the direction the conversation is taking, and tries to steer it in another direction. I repeatedly have to bring him back to this, and indicate that it is obvious that he needs to get out of prison should he have a role to play. I emphasise that the whole question of violence and the standpoint of the State President has to be dealt with in this light before he can leave prison. He repeatedly says that the idea he wants to convey to the State President will address precisely this problem.

I respond by saying that should this need to result in a conversation between him and the State President, I would need to make a plan to place him outside the conventional prison – the words I used were 'as a matter of transition'.

913 responds by saying that such a thing would need to happen without his collaboration because 'I must see the State President with my reputation intact', in a reference to credibility 'with the people that matter'.

(My comment: 913 is clearly not averse to learning more about the 'situation of transition', BUT when I indicate at a certain point that this could result in release from prison so that he could participate as an individual, could take part in politics in a peaceful manner, he is caught unawares, becomes agitated, and declares: 'To release me in an atmosphere of hostilities . . . would be disastrous.')

Besides the issue of the Idea he wants to convey to the State President, he also wants to discuss the following: 'If I work with him towards a mutual understanding, I am sure it will be possible to normalise matters in our country without outside interference.' He later puts this as follows: 'I would be prepared to prepare the ground, to play a role in normalising the situation, and create an atmosphere to resolve differences.' (In the course of the preceding discussion with Komvang, he said: 'I have thus far been an opponent, but would now like to make a positive contribution.')

913 is initially hesitant to discuss the Idea with me, because according to him it is about the issue of violence and formulation, about conditions and solutions that could be resolved by means of formulation but only between him and the State President.

Eventually, it emerges that the Idea comprises the following (after I return repeatedly to the issue of violence): 'We (the State President and I) must try to find a situation whereby we suspend violence. This is immediately followed by discussion – without any call to renounce violence. If the two of us (the State President and I) take a decision to suspend violence, and the conference immediately follows, then people will believe us and will listen.' (He responds in this way after I tell him that the unruly elements may not respond to his call.)

In preparation for his initiative, 913 proposes to speak to his colleagues at Pollsmoor, as well as selected prisoners on Robben Island as well as 'certain people' inside South Africa. (Comment: compare the EPG proposals, but it is noticeable that he does not propose a prior conversation with the ANC.)

When I tell 913 that a 'suspension of violence' will not be acceptable to the State President, but a 'cessation' would, he says that he had taken cognisance of this earlier, and made a note of it. He says he fully understands the Government's standpoint in respect of the cessation of violence, as this would be the standpoint of any Government (even a communist one) before it would talk to anyone. It is in this spirit that he wants to convey his Idea to the State President.

About the issue of Communism:
I tell him that there are many people who believe he is not a communist, despite the document found at Rivonia.

He responds in a strange way: 'As matters stand, I am not prepared to deny that because then I will [have] conceded to be examined about my political beliefs.' His response:
1. Chief Justice Rumpff found that the Freedom Charter did not underwrite/was not supportive of Communism.
2. Look at the top management of the ANC – Tambo or Nzo. Not one

was a communist, and they had also not studied in Russia. (Note: that Thabo Mbeki's name was a 'prominent omission'.)

3. In 1946/7, he passed a resolution to excise communism from the ANC, but did not take this further because of the British example, where the Communist Party is a legal party. (Professor Z.K. Matthews had advised him that the role of the ANC should be to 'unite all people opposed to race discrimination'.)

Time frame: I indicate to 913 that I will convey his request to the State President, and that we may conceivably talk again. 913 welcomes this and says: 'We must not be in a great hurry over matters so important and delicate; we should think very clearly.'

He proposes that if anything should happen it should only happen by the end of August when Howe has concluded his visit and 'the dust has settled'. [Following the collapse of the EPG initiative, a European Community mission led by the British Foreign Secretary, Sir Geoffrey Howe, was due to visit South Africa to assess the situation in the country.]

I ask him whether [his wife] Winnie's standpoint about the issue of whether he should speak to Howe is also his, upon which he responds as follows: 'There are leaders (colleagues of mine) that responded sensibly by saying that they would meet him without compromising themselves. Others, like Tutu, said they would not see him. If he (913) could have advised them, they would have responded differently, with more wisdom. However, as matters stand he cannot do otherwise but to fall in behind them – for the sake of solidarity. (On this point, 913 is uncomfortable and uncertain.)

Observation: 913 does not display the same confidence as previously.

Deduction: 913 is trying to regain lost ground after the failed EPG initiative;

and/or sees that he is running out of options, that his role is being determined for him from outside; and that he therefore has to try to reach agreement with the RSA Government while retaining maximum possible black support;

and/or 913 wants to start negotiating with the State President at any price in order to prove his leadership;

and/or 913 fears being released without showing any results, as he would then have no bargaining power vis-à-vis the ANC and UDF.

For this reason, 913 does not welcome the idea of unconditional release, and prefers to reach an agreement with the State President from the protection of prison (and the 'mystique' which he and the outside world believe he has developed).

Recommendation: To be discussed.

SUMMARY OF DISCUSSION WITH STATE PRESIDENT: MONDAY, 21 JULY 1986

1. Primarily interested in the reaction which he [913] will show towards Howe, should the latter ask to see 913. The State President seemingly accepts a proposal as follows:

   That he has reason to believe that 913 does not see any advantage for himself in foreign interference in his case; and that therefore the State President is not disposed to giving him permission [to meet with Howe].

   NB: I stated unambiguously that this would be a better formulation than saying that 913 is not prepared to speak to Howe.

2. The State President states that we will allow no further foreign visitors to 913.

3. We recommend that the SA Prisons Service launch a further investigation with the objectives of depopularising and depoliticising 913, [and] to develop options that could include:

   (a) Unconditional release at a stage where, in the government's view, he would have the least possible negative impact on the security situation; or

   (b) Release on parole (which we do not recommend because this would give 913 an opportunity to embark on a new initiative involving conflict); or

   (c) Another model of detention.

4. When considering the aforementioned, the restriction should be borne in mind that a conversation with 913 by the State President (and Government) is not possible as long as he is a prisoner.

////

These are among the most significant and most seminal records in the entire Coetsee archive. They show that, while at that stage Mandela would have been well aware of his rising global status, he was receiving far more attention behind the scenes than he could possibly have imagined. They illustrate the murky and often claustrophobic space in which government strategy towards Mandela was being determined – notably the convoluted framework nurtured by Coetsee, punctuated by the extreme and often chaotically destructive interventions by P.W. Botha. They also introduce seminal themes in the process surrounding Mandela's release that would persist over the next four years.

While Mandela wrote candidly and frankly in *Long Walk to Freedom* about his decision to start talking to the NP government, it remains informative to learn how openly he offered to collaborate with the State President and others in order to 'normalise' the South African situation, and the lengths he was prepared to go in doing so. This is particularly true about his main proposal, or 'idea', namely that the government and the ANC should mutually agree to suspend violence, to be followed immediately by a 'conference', a proposal which cut across the fundamental tenets of ANC policy at the time. As the previous chapter shows, this concept might well have been partly based on the EPG's proposed 'negotiating concept'.

The conversation also foreshadows Mandela's proposed campaign to talk to political prisoners as well as other political leaders inside the country. Again, this idea first emerged in Mandela's conversation with the EPG, and Coetsee's notes reveal how these themes were carried forward.

The summary of Coetsee's discussion with P.W. Botha appears to be an uneasy – or crafty – mix between the latter's thoughts and decisions and Coetsee's own agenda. While Botha was apparently prepared to tell Sir Geoffrey Howe that Mandela did not want to speak to him, without any further explanation, Coetsee seems to have persuaded him to adopt a softer formulation (which, while kinder to Mandela, was also not entirely accurate). Despite rapidly mounting international pressure for access to Mandela, Botha was still prepared to summarily order all foreign visits to be terminated. This directive seems to have held sway for a considerable period.

At the same time, while it remains unclear precisely who made the recommendations in point three, and to whom they were being made, they foreshadow 'unconditional release', albeit at a moment when this would most serve to undermine Mandela, a full four years before this actually happened.

They also propose 'another model of detention' – a seemingly bland phrase whose meaning is made clear in the memorandum itself. Coetsee still argues (or, at least, pretends to argue) that the State President will not talk to Mandela under any circumstances while he is still in prison, and that he needs to renounce violence in order to get out. However, he then goes on to mention a startling solution of his own, namely that, in order to enable a conversation with the State President, Mandela might need to be placed 'outside the conventional prison', in a 'transitional' environment. This is an unmistakable reference to Coetsee's plans to place Mandela in open detention – two and a half years before it happened, when Mandela was moved into a warder's cottage at Victor Verster Prison. And transition to what? It could only be his eventual release.

Moreover, the fact that this proposal is so openly stated in a memorandum expressly written for P.W. Botha, as well as its precise wording, suggests that Coetsee and Botha discussed it previously. This suggests, in turn, that Botha must have – at least tacitly – approved of the idea. Indeed, it reminds one that when Mandela was moved to Victor Verster in December 1988, Botha was still State President, and that this must have happened with his knowledge and at least a degree of approval. Moreover, the closing paragraph in the 'summary' amounts, unmistakably, to a strategic argument in favour of releasing Mandela.

The last intriguing feature is Mandela's agitated response to the proposal of a 'situation of transition', clearly involving his eventual release. This leads Coetsee to suggest that Mandela might 'fear being released without showing any results', as he would then have no bargaining power vis-à-vis the ANC and UDF. This is followed by the startling assertion that Mandela 'does not welcome the idea of unconditional release', preferring to come to an agreement with the State President from the protection of prison (and the 'mystique' that went with it).

This begins to cast some light on one of the most puzzling themes in the process surrounding Mandela's release, which surfaced repeatedly in the feverish closing negotiations: his attempt to use his prison status as a kind of inverse bargaining chip by declining to agree to his release – taken literally, a refusal to leave prison – without a 'package' he could present to the ANC in exile in Lusaka.

////

Although he did not get a direct response from Coetsee, Mandela writes in *Long Walk to Freedom*, there were other signs that the government was preparing him for a different kind of existence. On the day before Christmas 1986, Lieutenant-Colonel Gawie Marx, deputy commander of Pollsmoor Prison, took him on a drive through Cape Town – the first of many similar excursions during which he and younger warders sometimes also stopped for tea. 'Much as I enjoyed these little adventures,' he writes, 'I well knew that the authorities had a motive other than keeping me diverted.' He sensed that they wanted to acclimatise him to life in contemporary South Africa, and perhaps get him so used to 'small freedoms' that he might be willing to compromise in order to get out of prison.[3]

In 1987 he resumed contact with Coetsee, and they had several private meetings at his residence. Later that year, the government made its first concrete proposal, namely the appointment of a working group to conduct private discussions with Mandela. Headed by Coetsee, the committee would also comprise General Willemse,

Fanie van der Merwe, and Dr Niël Barnard, head of the NIS. According to Coetsee, this would be done with the 'full knowledge of the State President'.

Mandela was disturbed by the presence of the spy chief, Barnard, but eventually agreed. He wanted to address three crucial matters: consult his colleagues on the 'third floor'; communicate with Tambo in Lusaka; and draft a memorandum to P.W. Botha, setting out his views and those of the ANC. This would create talking points for future discussions.

He requested a meeting with his colleagues, which – to his surprise – was summarily refused. He could only assume that it reflected a 'great deal of nervousness' about the prospect of secret talks between himself and the government. Later, he was allowed to see them one by one. He told them he had discussed with Coetsee the idea of starting talks with the government, and that the government seemed interested. Sisulu was 'lukewarm', saying he wouldn't stop Mandela, but hoped he knew what he was doing. Mhlaba and Mlangeni responded positively, and Kathrada more or less responded like Sisulu.

Soon afterwards he received a note from Tambo, who had heard reports that Mandela was having secret discussions with the government and expressed his concern. In a letter, Mandela replied that he was talking to the government about one thing only, namely a meeting with the National Executive Committee of the ANC. The time had come for such talks, and he would not compromise the organisation in any way. He also began to draft his memorandum to P.W. Botha.

The meetings with the secret working group began in May 1988 and continued at irregular intervals. The discussions centred on four themes, namely the armed struggle, the ANC's alliance with the South African Communist Party (SACP), the idea of nationalisation, and majority rule. Committee members insisted that the ANC should renounce violence and give up the armed struggle before the government would agree to negotiations, and before he could meet President Botha.

7

Mandela's 'political testament'

'I make this move without consultation with the ANC . . .'

IN THE WINTER of 1988, Mandela writes, he was finally told that President P.W. Botha was planning to see him before the end of August. The country was still in turmoil. The government had reimposed states of emergency in 1987 and 1988. International pressure was mounting, more international companies were disinvesting from South Africa, and the American Congress had passed a sweeping sanctions bill.[1]

In 1987, the ANC held a 75th birthday conference in Tanzania where Tambo declared that the armed struggle would be intensified until the South African government was prepared to negotiate the abolition of apartheid. Two years before, at the Kabwe conference, the ANC had pledged that no discussions with the government could be held until all ANC leaders were released from prison.

Despite Mandela's optimism about the secret talks, it was a difficult time. He had recently had a visit from Winnie and learnt that No. 8115 Orlando West, the house in which they had first lived after their marriage and which he regarded as home, had been burned down. Invaluable family records, photographs and keepsakes had been lost.

If Botha had indeed seen Mandela in August 1988 – presumably on the basis of progress made during the talks with the secret working group – this would have been a significant event. Botha was still the head of government as well as the NP, and the meeting would presumably have had some concrete purpose. However, on two levels, fate intervened. Firstly, Mandela fell ill, which delayed the process significantly, Secondly, in January 1989, Botha suffered a stroke, which had a major impact on his mental state and eventually led to him being removed from power.

Mandela writes that he was suffering from a cough which he could not shake, and often felt too weak to exercise. One day, during a meeting in the prison's visiting area with his attorney, Ismail Ayob, he felt ill and vomited. Eventually he was taken to Tygerberg Hospital, where he was diagnosed with tuberculosis. He spent the next six weeks at Tygerberg, recuperating and receiving treatment. In December, he was moved to the Constantiaberg Clinic, a private hospital near Pollsmoor 'that had never had a black patient before'.[2]

While still at the clinic, Kobie Coetsee told him that he wanted to put him in a situation that was 'halfway between confinement and freedom'. On 10 December 1988, he was taken to Victor Verster Prison outside the town of Paarl, some 60 kilometres from Cape Town, where he was ensconced in a cottage formerly occupied by a prison official in a remote area in the prison grounds. It had three bedrooms and a small swimming pool, and was shaded by tall trees. The concrete walls around the cottage were topped with razor wire, and the entrances were guarded. (Also, while Mandela does not say so, the cottage and garden were heavily bugged.). The Prisons Service provided him with a chef, Warrant Officer Jack Swart, who produced meals for Mandela and a growing stream of visitors.

On the afternoon of his arrival, as noted previously, he was visited by Coetsee, who brought a case of wine as a house-warming gift. He told Mandela the cottage would be his last home before becoming a free man. The reason behind this move was that he should have a place where he could hold discussions 'in privacy and comfort'.

Meetings with the secret committee continued, but stalled on the same issues: the armed struggle, the ANC's association with the SACP, and majority rule. Mandela was still pressing Coetsee for a meeting with Botha. By this time, he was allowed to communicate with his comrades at Pollsmoor and on Robben Island. (Mandela writes that this included the ANC in Lusaka, but this seems implausible. There are no documents in the Coetsee archive to support this assertion. Any communications with Lusaka would have been closely monitored, and records would almost certainly have been kept by Coetsee. Indeed, this is exactly what happened when Mandela was eventually allowed to phone key figures in Lusaka in January 1990.)

In January 1989, he was visited by his four comrades from Pollsmoor, and they began to discuss a memorandum he planned to send to Botha. 'It reiterated most of the points I had made during the secret committee meetings, but I wanted to make sure the state president heard them directly from me.'

Whether this actually happened is unclear. Mandela states that he sent the memorandum to Botha in March. In his book *Secret Revolution: Memoirs of a Spy Boss*, Dr Niël Barnard writes that Mandela sent the document to the President via Kobie Coetsee without his (Barnard's) knowledge, and only handed it to the secret committee in July. Both these claims are contradicted by the transcript of a conversation between Mandela and Barnard in April, in which they clearly refer to the memorandum.

Be that as it may, Barnard devotes a whole chapter to the memorandum, which he describes as 'Mandela's political testament'. He notes that the committee accepted the document as a 'non-paper' (a discussion document without official status), and responded in a counter-memorandum. After criticising it on various grounds, Barnard writes that, in his view, it was a 'blessing' that the memorandum never received official status, and adds that both sides let the document die a silent death. He does imply, though, that Botha read the document because, after noting that Mandela had sent it to the President via Coetsee a few months earlier, he adds: 'This made the warm reception which Mandela received in Tuynhuys all the more remarkable.'[3]

The memorandum was made public in January 1990. After a brief controversy, outlined in chapter 20, its political relevance rapidly dissipated. However, it retains historical value because, among other things, it contains a frank statement of Mandela's intention to facilitate a negotiated settlement between the government and the ANC, and an acknowledgement that he was doing so without the movement's knowledge or consent. It also contains a two-stage proposal for a negotiated settlement that did not conform to the latest ANC policies, and which the ANC later repudiated. A summary appears below.[4]

////

Mandela starts by saying he considers it necessary 'in the national interest' for the ANC and the government to meet urgently to negotiate an effective political settlement. He is making this move without consultation with the ANC. He is acting on his own initiative, in the hope that the organisation will in due course endorse his actions. His task is to bring the country's two major political bodies to the negotiating table.

He is not asking to be freed, but hopes the government will give him an opportunity to sound out the views of his colleagues inside and outside the country. His initiative will only have any significance if it is formally endorsed by the ANC.

In a pointer to the intended purpose of the memorandum – a meeting with Botha – he writes: 'I come here with an open mind, and the impression I will carry away from this meeting will be determined almost exclusively by the manner in which you respond to my proposal. It is in this spirit that I have undertaken this mission, and I sincerely hope that nothing will be done or said here which will force me to revise my views on this aspect.'

He then deals with three main issues, which, he says, seem to constitute an obstacle to a meeting between the ANC and the government, namely that the ANC should renounce violence, sever its ties with the SACP, and abandon its demand for majority rule.

The ANC has no vested interest in violence. It abhors any action which may cause loss of life, destruction of property and human misery. It has worked long and patiently for a peaceful and non-racial state. However, it regards the armed struggle as a legitimate form of self-defence against a morally repugnant system of government which will not even allow peaceful forms of protest.

From the early days, the organisation diligently sought peaceful solutions and talked patiently to successive South African governments, including the current one. Its demands were not only ignored but met with force. Violent struggle was the only possible response to this challenge.

The real problem facing the government is not that the ANC refuses to renounce violence, but the fact that it is not yet ready for negotiation and for sharing political power with blacks. It is still committed to white domination, and is only prepared to tolerate blacks who are willing to serve in apartheid structures. White South Africa should accept that the ANC will not suspend or abandon the armed struggle until the government has shown its willingness to surrender its monopoly of political power, and to negotiate directly and in good faith with acknowledged black leaders.

He equally rejects the charge that the ANC is dominated by the SACP. Cooperation between the ANC and SACP is limited to the struggle against racial oppression and for a just society, and the former has never adopted or cooperated with communism itself. Members of the SACP have always been free to join the ANC, but then become fully bound by the policy of the organisation as set out in the Freedom Charter. As members of the ANC engaged in the anti-apartheid struggle, their Marxist ideology is not directly relevant. Throughout the years, the SACP has accepted the leading role of the ANC, a position which is respected by SACP members who join the ANC.

The government had also accused the ANC of being agents of the Soviet Union. On the contrary, the ANC is non-aligned, and welcomes support from the East and the West, from socialist and capitalist countries. The only difference, as it has explained previously, is that socialist countries supply it with weapons, which the West refuses to do. 'We have no intention whatsoever of changing our stand on this question.' As regards his own position, as previously stated, he did not belong to any organisation besides the ANC.

Majority rule is a pillar of democratic rule in many countries of the world, and is also fully accepted in white politics. 'Only now that the reality has dawned that apartheid had failed, and that blacks will one day have an effective voice in government, are we told by whites here and their Western friends that majority rule is a disaster to be avoided at all costs.

'Majority rule is acceptable to whites as long as it is considered within the context of white politics. If black political aspirations are to be accommodated, then some other formula must be found, provided that that formula does not raise blacks to a position of equality with whites. White South Africa has to accept that there will never be peace and stability in this country until this principle is fully applied.'

In a concluding section, Mandela declares: 'The key to the whole situation is a negotiated settlement, and a meeting between the government and the ANC will be the first major step towards lasting peace in the country, better relations with its neighbours, admission to the Organisation of African Unity, re-admission to the United Nations, other world bodies and international markets, and improved international relations generally.'

Turning to his proposed model for negotiations, Mandela writes that, at such a meeting, two central themes will have to be addressed: firstly, the demand for majority rule in a unitary state, and, secondly, the concern of white South Africa over this demand, as well as the insistence of whites on structural guarantees that majority rule will not result in domination of the white minority. The most crucial task that will face the government and the ANC will be to reconcile these two positions. This will only be achieved if both parties are willing to compromise.

Negotiations may need to be undertaken in at least two stages. In the first, the ANC and the government will work out the preconditions for a proper climate for negotiations. The second stage will be the actual negotiations themselves. Any other approach could lead to 'irresolvable stalemate'.

Lastly, Mandela writes: 'The move I have taken provides you with the opportunity to overcome the current deadlock, and to normalise the country's political situation. I hope you will seize it without delay.' In the event, Botha did not do so, for reasons that were unforeseen at the time.

8

Botha crosses the Rubicon, and then tries to swim back

*'The Afrikaner is ready to talk,
and to make a positive contribution . . .'*

FOLLOWING his stroke in January 1989, Botha had resigned as head of the NP, but retained his position as State President. As Mandela observes, this created an unparalleled situation in the country's history: in the South African parliamentary system, the leader of the majority party became the head of state. President Botha was now the head of state but not of his party.[1]

Political violence and international pressure continued to intensify. In view of government restrictions on their operations, the UDF and the Congress of South African Trade Unions (COSATU) arranged to cooperate in a loose alliance known as the Mass Democratic Movement (MDM), which began organising a countrywide campaign of civil disobedience to challenge apartheid institutions. On the international front, Tambo held talks with the governments of Great Britain and the Soviet Union, and in January 1987 met the US secretary of state, George Shultz, in Washington. Sanctions against South Africa remained in force and even increased.

On Tuesday, 4 July 1989, Mandela writes, he was visited by General Willemse, who told him he would be taken to see Botha the next day. A tailor quickly made him a new suit. Early the next morning, Major Marais, the commander of Victor Verster Prison, inspected his appearance and adjusted the knot in his tie. He was then driven to Pollsmoor Prison, where General Willemse's wife served breakfast, and then to Tuynhuys, the official presidential office in the centre of Cape Town, next to the Houses of Parliament. In the lobby in front of Botha's office, they were met by Kobie Coetsee, Niël Barnard, and various prison officials.

During prior discussions about a possible meeting, Coetsee and Barnard had advised him to avoid controversial issues. Recalling an incident also widely recounted by Barnard, Mandela writes: 'While we were waiting, Dr Barnard looked down and noticed that my shoelaces were not properly tied. He quickly knelt down to tie them for me. I realised just how nervous they were, and that did not make me any calmer. The door then opened and I walked in expecting the worst.'

From the opposite side of his 'grand office', Botha walked towards him, smiling broadly and holding out his hand. 'In fact, from that very first moment, he completely disarmed me. He was . . . courteous, deferential and friendly.' Photographs were taken. Tea was served, and the conversation with Botha began. 'From the first, it was not as though we were engaged in tense political arguments but a lively and interesting tutorial. We did not discuss substantive issues so much as history and South African culture.'

The meeting lasted for less than half an hour, and was 'friendly and breezy' until the end. It was then, Mandela writes, that he raised a serious issue. 'I asked Mr Botha to release unconditionally all political prisoners, including myself.' The was the only tense moment in the meeting, and Botha said he could not do that.

'Then there was a brief discussion as to what we should say if news of the meeting leaked out. We quickly drafted a bland statement saying that we had met for tea in an effort to promote peace in the country. Once this was agreed upon, Mr Botha rose and shook my hand, saying what a pleasure it had been. Indeed, it had been. I thanked him, and left the way I had come.'

While the meeting was not a breakthrough in terms of negotiations, Mandela writes, it was one in another sense. 'Mr Botha had long talked about the need to cross the Rubicon, but he never did it himself until that morning at Tuynhuys. Now, I felt, there was no turning back.'

The next Monday, Botha handed around photographs of his meeting with Mandela to shocked members of the State Security Council.[2] Coetsee eventually released a brief statement confirming that a 'courtesy visit' had taken place, that no policy matters had been discussed and no negotiations had taken place, but that Botha and Mandela had confirmed their support for 'peaceful development in South Africa'.[3]

////

Mandela's rendition of the conversation is selective and inaccurate. He and Botha did in fact touch on several 'controversial' issues, including his preconditions for negotiations. Among other things, he told Botha the government should take certain steps to normalise the situation. In exchange, the ANC could renounce violence and also take other steps 'without either the government or the ANC losing face'.

In turn, Botha told Mandela that a decision had been made to release Walter Sisulu. The onus would rest on Sisulu not to misuse his release and 'start a new propaganda campaign'. Also, though in heavily didactic terms, Botha expressed seemingly genuine concern about and interest in development in Africa, and spoke about the role of Afrikaners in a future dispensation in South and southern Africa in markedly conciliatory terms, envisaging a shared future following an end to white domination. The Afrikaner, he said, was 'ready to talk, and make a positive contribution'.

All this emerges from a more detailed record of the conversation in the Coetsee archive. Stamped 'SECRET', the document is headed 'Conversation: Tuynhuys, 5 July 1989'. It was written in Afrikaans by Barnard, based on his notes taken during the meeting. A translation of the entire document (with some paragraph numbering omitted) appears below.

CONVERSATION: TUYNHUYS, 5 JULY 1989

SP [State President] welcomes M[andela]. General conversation about their mutual health and circumstances, including Kaiser Matanzima, childhood years, the Anglo-Boer War, and the role of Pres. Steyn. Thereafter a general conversation about African leaders such as Houphouët-Boigny, Chissano, Mobutu, Savimbi, situation in Angola, Mozambique and SWA [South West Africa]. The SP makes the statement that Angola is key to the resolution of the southern African question, and that a peaceful solution in Angola would benefit Zambia and Zaire [now the Democratic Republic of Congo] as well. They agree on the importance of the opening of the Benguela railway line, and that Pres. Kaunda [of Zambia] might agree with this as well.

M expresses the wish that the relationship between the SP and Kaunda should improve. Discuss political contradictions, and M mentions that he has told the Minister that he would like to see a victory for the National Party in the coming elections, despite the fact that he is opposed to everything the National Party stands for. This may also cause him problems.

SP remarks that problems are there to be solved. Life is full of problems. M confirms this and remarks that problems can become large but that there is always hope for a solution. SP says the situation in Africa could improve significantly. He has gained this insight after visiting African countries and speaking to their leaders. President Banda [of Malawi] is a very good old friend and they have spent hours together. President Banda agreed that Africa could open the doors to better circumstances for many people. What Africa needs is peaceful development, education, training, job creation, and the exploitation of its riches to the benefit of all.

SP remarks that, in his conversations with Kaunda, he emphasised the need for Africa to come to an agreement with the Afrikaner, and that this would benefit the entire southern Africa. He says there is too much interference from outside in South Africa's domestic affairs. A solution for this has to be found. M says he has a good understanding of this and that he has come to know the Afrikaner better while in prison. He has had the further privilege while in prison of exchanging viewpoints with Minister

Coetsee. He emphasises that current developments are conducive to negotiations. According to M such a climate could only be created if the Government attends to the demands of the ANC, like the legalisation of the ANC and the lifting of the state of emergency. However, he does not want to misuse this occasion to conduct such a serious conversation. The Government must take certain steps to normalise the situation. In exchange, the ANC could renounce violence and also take other steps without either the Government or the ANC losing face.

SP says this is merely an informal discussion and an opportunity to exchange ideas. SP says he has done a great deal to advance the peace process in SWA. In the RSA, violence will only lead to more violence and destruction. Since assuming his position (1978) he has gone out of his way to combat violence. His ideal was rather to strive towards the comprehensive upliftment and development of the people of the RSA.

SP's standpoint is that violence must be ended and that opportunity for discussions [*geleentheid tot gesprekvoering*] can contribute to this ideal being realised. Instead of violence, people must rather resolve their problems around the negotiating table. SP believes M is in a position to make a contribution to a peaceful solution. However, M must not forget the contribution the Afrikaner can make in this regard. The Afrikaner loves this soil, and has no other home. The Afrikaner is ready to talk, and make a positive contribution. With SP's visit to Africa he saw how underdeveloped Africa was, and he believes the RSA can make a major contribution to resolving Africa's problems.

M gives the assurance that the ANC leadership does not differ from that of the Government, and that there are no parties inside or outside parliament that have a better record in terms of a commitment to peace than the ANC. SP warns that the ANC must not make the mistake of listening to everyone who claims to speak on behalf of South Africa and its people. The ANC must re-evaluate its position. SP praises M for not wishing to talk to everyone who applied to visit him purely for their own publicity.

M discusses the position of [Walter] Sisulu and expresses the hope that Sisulu will be released because this would make his own task a lot easier.

Should Sisulu be released and misuse his release, the SP would have every reason to doubt M's word, but the opposite is also true.

SP states that a decision has already been taken to release Sisulu, that it could be expected from him not to start a new propaganda campaign, and that M's honour would be at stake. M says he has already spoken with Sisulu and that he should be released as soon as possible – even before the return of his wife [from overseas where she led a UDF delegation]. SP invites M to stay in touch. They thank each other and wish each other good health.

Minister Coetsee discusses how the conversation will eventually be made known to the media so that M and the SP will be protected. It will be stated that this was just an informal visit and conversation. M agrees, everyone departs.

[Signed] N. Barnard, 17/2/90.

////

Barnard sent these minutes to Botha at his retirement home, Die Anker, at Wilderness on the Cape South Coast on 19 February 1990. A covering letter, pointing out that the contents of the minutes were subject to the Protection of Information Act, suggests that a controversy had arisen around the substance of the meeting. This was indeed the case, and much of it is in the public domain. Barnard's version, as recorded in his book *Secret Revolution*, is as follows.[4] Botha and his private secretary, Ters Ehlers, made a hidden tape recording of the meeting with Mandela. A few days later, Ehlers handed the tape to Barnard, which was, according to civil service rules, the 'correct procedure'. Barnard writes that he felt uncomfortable about the tape, as Mandela's permission had not been asked beforehand. He was also worried that the contents could be misused for political purposes, a fear which 'later proved to be justified'. After consulting with his deputy, Mike Louw, and listening to the tape, he decided to have it incinerated.

Although Botha had retired to Wilderness, Barnard writes, he retained a lively interest in politics. He did not receive F.W. de Klerk's historic speech in parliament on 2 February 1990 with 'great enthusiasm', and later that year announced his intention to resign from the NP. On 15 February, four days after Mandela's release, the Afrikaans-language daily *Die Volksblad* published a front-page photograph of Mandela, Barnard and Botha taken during the Tuynhuys meeting. Commentators widely declared that this encounter had opened the door for Mandela's release and, by implication, the unbanning of the liberation movements and other steps announced on 2 February. According to Barnard, Botha decided that he 'did not wish to be remembered in this way'. He then recalled the tape recording made by him and Ehlers, and believed he could use it to show that he had actually taken a hard line with Mandela, notably that he had told him he would not be released unless he renounced violence and distanced himself from the SACP.

At that point, he contacted Barnard, demanding that the tape be returned. After exchanges with the NIS stretching over several months, Botha asked F.W. de Klerk to intervene, and the latter asked Barnard to visit the former President in Wilderness to try to lay the matter to rest. He eventually met Botha at Die Anker on Tuesday, 12 November 1991.

Botha's first wife, Elize, sat in on the conversation, which was also taped. An irrational and agitated Botha would not accept that the tape recording no longer existed. He was also dissatisfied with the written minutes on the grounds that they did not reflect how firmly he had acted towards Mandela. Later in the week, Botha gave transcripts of his recording of this meeting with Barnard to two Sunday newspapers, which had a 'field day'.[5] In response, the NIS issued a 'rare' statement to clarify the matter, stating that, despite its far-reaching historical and political significance, the Tuynhuys recording had 'no decisive security-related value', and that the NIS had felt that 'any further retention or utilisation of the tape could only lead to embarrassment and would have no future use'. It also noted that the tape had been in Botha's possession for a considerable period, but no transcript was made.[6]

Botha then laid a charge against Barnard with the ombudsman, Judge Piet van der Walt, who found that Barnard had made an 'error of judgement' in destroying the tape without consulting Botha, that the recording possibly had historical value, and that it was 'undesirable' for such a decision to have been left to the discretion of the head of the NIS.

Barnard then writes that he respected the judge's findings, and accepted full responsibility for his decision. 'At the same time, I am still thankful that I had the opportunity to use authoritarian authority to take a decision in the national interest.' He adds that these events were the 'biggest humiliation' he had experienced in his life. However, when *'tannie* [aunt] Elize' died unexpectedly of a heart attack a few years later, he attended the funeral service, where he was reconciled with her 'difficult husband'.

Fresh light is cast on the dispute by another document in the Coetsee archive – a personal and top-secret memorandum written by Barnard and sent to President F.W. de Klerk on Saturday, 16 November, together with a copy of the minutes of the meeting with Mandela sent to Botha in February 1990.

In his memoirs, Barnard writes that the conversation between Botha and Mandela was taped without his prior knowledge. In his memorandum to De Klerk, however, he writes that, during the conversation with Botha, he 'acknowledged that the tape was made, and that I was aware of this. However, I did not give the instruction for the tape to be made. NIS was also not responsible for the recording, and moreover the tape was in the possession of former President Botha's office personnel from 5 July 1989 until it was handed to me after his retirement on 15 August'. Perhaps the remark in his memoirs was a simple oversight.

A second issue concerns Barnard's rendition of the conversation itself. In his memoirs, he speaks about the written minutes, but provides another, markedly different, account of the conversation in the main text, including numerous direct quotes. No source for this account is cited. In his memorandum to De Klerk, he writes that, during their conversation, Botha claimed he was certain that the tape and a transcription still existed. 'I consistently denied this strongly.' Perhaps Barnard has a truly exceptional memory.

9

'A conjuncture of circumstances'

The advent of the Harare Declaration

IN THE MEANTIME, a policy document appeared on the scene that would have a major impact on events going forward. Known as the Harare Declaration, it contained a new framework – developed by the ANC and endorsed by the Organisation of African Unity (OAU) as well as the United Nations – for a negotiated settlement of the South African conflict.

It was adopted by an OAU ad hoc committee on southern Africa that convened in Harare on 21 August 1989 – just seven days after P.W. Botha's resignation, and six days after F.W. de Klerk became acting President. It went on to be adopted by a full OAU summit, and then – with slight alterations – by the Commonwealth of Nations as well as the UN.

Famously, in a preamble, it stated: 'We believe that a conjuncture of circumstances exists which, if there is a demonstrable readiness on the part of the Pretoria regime to engage in negotiations genuinely and seriously, could end apartheid through negotiations. Such an eventuality would be an expression of the long-standing preference of the people of South Africa to arrive at a political settlement . . .'[1]

////

The Harare Declaration was the product of a long and complex process.[2] From the 1960s onwards, ANC policy documents had spoken of a 'seizure of power' in South Africa – in other words, its formal aim was to overthrow the NP government.³ However, from the mid-1980s, given major shifts in regional and global power politics, the ANC realised it might be forced to negotiate with Pretoria. Indeed, in 1983, in anticipation of the Nkomati Accord between South Africa and Mozambique, the ANC 'started to explore . . . scenarios for negotiation, lest they be caught flat-footed'.⁴

From then on, pressure on the ANC mounted. In 1987, Tambo set up an ANC task team to draft guidelines for a 'free South Africa'. Headed by Zola Skweyiya, and including Kader Asmal, Penuell Maduna, Brigitte Mabandla, Albie Sachs and Jack Simons, among others, the team came up with constitutional guidelines for a democratic South Africa, including a Bill of Rights.

In the same year, on 9 October, the ANC's National Executive Committee (NEC) issued a 'Statement on the Question of Negotiations', which foreshadowed the Harare Declaration. It still provides useful insights into the ANC's underlying reasoning and orientation.⁵

The statement argued that the Botha regime had 'neither the desire nor the intention to engage in meaningful negotiations'. However, it went on to say that the ANC had never been opposed to genuine negotiations, provided they were aimed at transforming the country into a united and non-racial democracy. The question of whether to negotiate, and on what conditions, should be put to the ANC's entire leadership, including those who were imprisoned and should be released unconditionally.

Significantly, the statement went on to deal with the three demands made by the NP government in the P.W. Botha era, namely that the ANC should renounce violence and abandon the armed struggle; distance itself from the SACP; and abandon its demand for majority rule. On the armed struggle, it declared: 'We reject unequivocally the cynical demand of the Pretoria regime that we should unilaterally abandon or suspend the armed struggle. The source of violence in our country is the apartheid system. It is that violence which must end.' However, establishing the germ of a new approach, it stated that any cessation of hostilities would have to be negotiated and entail agreed action by both sides as part of creating a democratic South Africa.

On the SACP, it said: 'We reject all efforts to dictate to us who our allies should or should not be, and how our membership should be composed. Specifically, we will not bow down to pressures intended to drive a wedge between the ANC and the SACP, a tried and tested ally in the struggle for a democratic South Africa. Neither shall we submit to attempts to divide and weaken our movement by carrying out a witch hunt against various members on the basis of their ideological beliefs.'

However, extending the anti-apartheid struggle beyond the confines of the ANC and its allies, it said: 'The conflict in our country is between the forces of national liberation and democracy on the one hand, and those of racism and reaction on the other. Any negotiations would have to be conducted by these two forces as represented by their various organisational formations.'

On group and minority rights, it said the ANC accepted that a new constitution could include an entrenched bill of rights. However, it was opposed to any attempt to perpetuate apartheid by advancing the concept of group and minority rights.

In a key passage, presaging the approach adopted and elaborated in the Harare Declaration, it stated: 'We insist that before any negotiations take place, the apartheid regime would have to demonstrate its seriousness by implementing various measures to create a climate conducive to such negotiations.

'These would include the unconditional release of all political prisoners, detainees, all captured freedom fighters and prisoners of war as well as the cessation of all political trials. The state of emergency would have to be lifted, and the army and the police withdrawn from the townships and confined to their barracks. Similarly, all repressive legislation and all laws empowering the regime to limit freedom of assembly, speech, the press and so on would have to be repealed.'

Perhaps in response to rumours about Mandela, and disquiet within the organisation about talks between some ANC leaders in exile and a growing stream of visitors from South Africa to Lusaka, it declared: 'We take this opportunity once more to reaffirm that the ANC is opposed to any secret negotiations. We firmly believe that the people themselves must participate in shaping their destiny and would therefore have to be involved in any process of negotiations.'

Seemingly laying down a new interim line on the armed struggle, it said: 'There is, as yet, no prospect for genuine negotiations because the Botha regime continues to believe that it can maintain the apartheid system through force and terror. We therefore have no choice but to intensify the mass political and armed struggle for the overthrow of the illegal apartheid regime and the transfer of power to the people.' It also called on the international community to impose 'comprehensive and mandatory' sanctions against South Africa.

////

In 1988, following continued discussions within the ANC, Tambo appointed a team to develop a fresh ANC perspective on negotiations, 'aimed at ensuring that the ANC would gain the tactical and strategic initiative'. The team, headed by Neo Mnumzana and including Joel Netshitenzhe and Ngoako Ramatlhodi, produced a draft of the ANC's terms for negotiations, which the ANC then canvassed for adoption by the OAU and UN. The document was adopted by the ANC's NEC in 1989 and sent to the presidents of Tanzania, Angola, Zambia, Zimbabwe and Botswana. The governments of Cuba and the Soviet Union also commented on the document.[6]

A week before an OAU summit in Harare in August 1989, Tambo, along with Steve Tshwete, Ramatlhodi, Penuell Maduna, Thabo Mbeki and Pallo Jordan, flew around the Frontline States in a small jet provided by Kaunda to present the document to their heads of state. All the presidents suggested some improvements.

On 7 and 8 August 1989, the ANC's National Working Committee discussed a final draft. Shortly afterwards, exhausted by his efforts, Tambo suffered a stroke. When, on 21 August, the document was adopted by the OAU subcommittee on southern Africa, he was lying in a Lusaka military hospital, unable to talk and partially paralysed. The ANC secretary-general, Alfred Nzo, represented the organisation at the OAU meeting.

As noted previously, the document went on to be adopted by an OAU Heads of State summit in Addis Ababa, Ethiopia, and then, with slight alterations, by the Commonwealth of Nations and the United Nations.

////

The Harare Declaration was a sophisticated document that incorporated a programmatic approach to negotiations. Among other things, it was designed to circumvent the impasse around the armed struggle. It also repeatedly urged both sides to turn to the negotiating table.

In a preamble, it said the OAU recognised the reality that permanent peace and stability in Southern Africa could only be achieved when apartheid had been liquidated and South Africa transformed into a united, democratic and non-racial country. 'We therefore reiterate that all the necessary measures should be adopted now to bring a speedy end to the apartheid system, in the interest of all the people of southern Africa, our continent and the world at large.

'We believe that, as a result of the liberation struggle and international pressure against apartheid, as well as global efforts to liquidate regional conflicts, possibilities exist for further movement towards the resolution of the problems facing the people of South Africa . . .'

In an often-quoted passage, it said: 'We believe a conjuncture of circumstances exists which, if there is a demonstrable readiness on the part of the Pretoria regime to engage in negotiations genuinely and seriously, could create the possibility to end apartheid through negotiations . . . Such an eventuality would be an expression of the long-standing preference of the people of South Africa to arrive at a political settlement. We would therefore encourage the people of South Africa, as part of their overall struggle, to negotiate an end to the apartheid system and agree on all the measures that are necessary to transform their country into a nonracial democracy.'

In a section headed 'Climate for negotiations', it stated: 'We believe it is essential, before any negotiations take place, that the necessary climate for negotiations be created. The apartheid regime has the urgent responsibility to respond positively to this universally acclaimed demand and thus create this climate.'

In line with this, the present regime should release all political prisoner and detainees unconditionally and refrain from imposing any restrictions on them; lift all bans and restrictions on all proscribed and restricted organisations and people; remove all troops from the townships; end the state of emergency, and repeal all legislation designed to circumscribe political activity; and cease all political executions.

It added: 'These measures are necessary to produce the conditions in which free discussion can take place – an essential condition to ensure that the people themselves participate in the process of remaking their country. The measures listed above should therefore precede negotiations.'

Following the creation of this climate, negotiations should proceed along the following lines:
- Discussions should take place between the liberation movement and the South African regime to 'achieve the suspension of hostilities on both sides by agreeing to a mutually binding ceasefire'.

- Negotiations should then proceed to establish the basis for the adoption of a new constitution by agreeing, among other things, on the principles enunciated previously.
- Having agreed on these principles, the parties should then negotiate the necessary mechanism for drawing up the new constitution.
- The parties should then agree on the role to be played by the international community in ensuring a successful transition to a democratic order.
- Next, the parties should agree on the formation of an interim government to supervise the drafting and adoption of a new constitution; govern and administer the country; and effect the transition to a democratic order, including the holding of elections.
- 'After the adoption of the new constitution, all armed hostilities will be deemed to have formally terminated.'
- The international community would then lift the sanctions imposed on apartheid South Africa.

////

In November 1989, President F.W. de Klerk publicly rejected key aspects of the Harare Declaration. In an interview with the *Washington Post* – said to be his first with a newspaper since becoming State President in September – he ruled out the possibility of a transitional government governing South Africa while a new, non-racial constitution was being drawn up.[7]

The report quoted him as saying: 'We are not prepared to move into a situation where a lawfully elected government will be suspended and an interim government will come about.' But once a new constitution was negotiated under the supervision of the current government, the existing authority in Pretoria would have to accept this and give way to a new government.

According to the report, De Klerk also made it clear that whatever new political order evolved from negotiations, power in South Africa would be shared on the basis of racially defined groups and not according to the principle of majority rule.

He also said Mandela's release was under 'constant consideration'. While he declined to say when Mandela would be freed, he said there was place at the negotiating table for him 'and other leading figures in radical organisations', including the ANC, who were committed to peaceful negotiations. He tacitly acknowledged that some of his cabinet ministers had been in discussions with Mandela. Asked if he planned to meet with Mandela himself, he replied: 'I wouldn't announce it if I had any plans in advance.'

In practice, however, as the Coetsee archive reveals, he and his team began to work to meet at least some of the demands set out in the Harare Declaration. This amounted to a fundamental shift in the process surrounding Mandela's release. Until then, the ANC had been perpetually on the back foot, compelled to respond to conditions laid down by P.W. Botha, namely that he was not prepared to negotiate with the ANC unless it renounced the armed struggle, dissociate itself from the SACP, and abandoned the notion of majority rule.

Now, in a shift coinciding with F.W. de Klerk's presidency, the pendulum had swung the other way. From now on, amid mounting pressures, it was up to De Klerk and his government to respond to the terms laid down in the Harare Declaration.

10
'A large piece of bitterness . . .'

A conversation between Mandela, 'Zeni and Muzi',
September 1989

ON 1 September 1989, the Commissioner of Prisons, General Willie Willemse, sent Coetsee a summary of a monitored conversation between Mandela, 'Zeni and Muzi', together with a covering letter. Zeni (Zenani) was Zindzi Mandela's elder sister, and Muzi was her husband, Prince Thumbumuzi Dlamini of Swaziland (now eSwatini). They were living in the United States, where they had met while studying at Boston University, and were presumably visiting South Africa at the time.

Stamped 'Confidential', the covering letter reads as follows: 'Herewith a significant document which airs in some detail a large piece of bitterness, resentment and frustration which client [Mandela] has harboured towards his wife over many years, and he can do little about. It appears as if things are now moving to some sort of conclusion. She pays him no heed, for numerous reasons among which certain physical needs must apparently not be discounted.

'It is clear that he wants to get the daughter [Zindzi] away from what he regards as this corrupting influence . . . thus the urgent need for a passport for her so that she can join the family [Zeni and Muzi] in the USA. A situation whose advantages must be exploited. Dr B [presumably Dr Niël Barnard] has also been informed.'

A photocopy of the record of the conversation is appended to the letter. The record is handwritten on a standard form for the 'monitoring of discussions' (*gespreksmonitering*), with three pre-printed columns, namely 'synopsis', 'elucidation' and 'responsibility'. The 'synopsis' – as well as intermittent comments in the 'elucidation' column – reads as follows (translated from Afrikaans). Some names have been withheld, and some sentences deleted.

VISIT: ZENI & MUZI TO 913

1. 913 says he wants to talk to the team [Zeni and Muzi] about the visit by Brenda Fassie that had been denied, as well as letters that were kept back. ('*These aspects can be raised in the next round of discussions.*')
2. 913 says he has a good reason to see Muzi and Zeni on their own. 913 says she (W) had made many mistakes and that he is under pressure from his colleagues. ('*Her infidelity would be the theme.*')
3. 913 says Winnie must work on [Wilton] Mkwayi's case together with [the Rev.] Frank Chikane. ('*I wonder whether 913 can still afford any matters to be managed by Winnie. She does not follow instructions.*')
4. 913 says Winnie must also apply to see [Elias] Motsoaledi.
5. Zeni talks about W's problems, and that Ayob [Mandela's lawyer] is the cause thereof.
6. 913 says they are not alone. This is a government house and they are listening to us in the sitting room. ('*So he is aware that his discussions are being monitored.*' *In the only entry in the 'responsibility' column, Willemse then wrote: 'So where did the rest of the conversation take place? Still in the sitting room or dining room?*')
7. 913 says Winnie has no respect for the community, the ANC, the family, or himself, and also not for herself. He talks about Winnie who went around with married men. This is why 913 says she has no respect. A wife who today goes with a married man and tomorrow with someone else is a wife of loose morals. Winnie is such a person. 913 says he then went underground. 913 says he was in London with Mary Benson, and she had told him that Winnie had attended a concert with a married man. 913 says she also had relationships with other men. He had told her that he was going to Durban and was arrested in the course of his return. 913 says that it was clear to him

that the police knew that he was in Durban. 913 says Winnie had spoken about where he was. She (W) had told this to someone with whom she had an intimate relationship. This person wanted her and 913 was betrayed. Winnie was arrested and she had said where 913's comrades were – there is no doubt about this. 913 says Fikile Bam was also arrested as a result of Winnie's relationships with informants. 913 says other men had taken over his home. She had also had a relationship with a certain M __ . [name withheld.] A certain M __ [name withheld] (PAC) who had been released from Robben Island also went to stay with her. (*'This point is mainly about Winnie's infidelity and lack of responsibility.'*)

8. 913 says Winnie's most recent friend is A __ M __ [name withheld] (RMC [Release Mandela Campaign]). 913 says A __ had had the wall around the house built, and Ayob had paid him R6 000 towards this.
9. 913 says he had done his best to save the marriage. They must talk to her (Winnie). 913 says an 'embarrassing situation' is approaching. 913 says he will not allow her [Winnie] to attend the graduation ceremony if this matter/question has not been thrashed out. This is why 913 wanted to see her over the weekend.
10. 913 says the government is treating him well, but is trying in a very subtle way to drive a wedge between them.
11. 913 says the visitors should tell R[aymond] Tucker to come and see 913 about the new house. (*'Tucker is 913's advocate who handles these matters.'*)
12. Muzi says 913 should talk to the government that Zindzi should get a passport to go to them (Muzi and Zeni). 913 says Zindzi should be taken away from Winnie, because he cannot stand it any longer.
13. [sentence deleted.]
14. 913 says Winnie is living like a rich woman, but is bankrupt. The ambassadors have been warned not to give her any more money.
15. 913 says he also wants to see [Archbishop Desmond] Tutu and his wife, and [the Rev. Allan] Boesak and his wife.
16. [sentence deleted.]

11

The management of Nelson Mandela

'Due to various strategic considerations . . . the question is no longer whether he [Mandela] should be released, but rather when, in what way, and under what circumstances . . .'

A SECRET DOCUMENT dated 3 October 1989 appears in the Coetsee archive. It comprises a three-page memorandum titled 'The Management of Nelson Mandela' [*Die hantering van Nelson Mandela*], plus a two-page 'follow-up note' entitled 'Options about which a decision in principle needs to be taken'.

The authors are not identified. However, the memorandum refers to a team working under the authority of the Minister of Justice. The document comprises no more than five pages of double-spaced typing. However, it is one of the most significant items in the Coetsee archive. Written in a dispassionate, quasi-analytical style, it seeks to provide a fresh strategic framework for dealing with Mandela. In the process, it becomes the first document in the archive – and the first known government document – to explicitly recommend Mandela's unconditional release.

It starts by noting that the current international climate in favour of the peaceful resolution of conflicts, the accompanying emphasis on negotiation and dialogue, the demand for reconciliation in the RSA and for Mandela's release, thus allowing him – in the view of the international community – to play a role in resolving the South African problem, has once again brought his release to the fore, 'also with respect to his role in the government's own efforts towards democratisation'.

His release has been considered and reconsidered on various occasions over the previous ten years, and the nature of his detention has changed. He was moved from Robben Island to Pollsmoor, where he found himself in a relatively comfortable situation, and then to Victor Verster Prison. In this period, his release was linked to various conditions, among others that he should renounce violence. The memorandum then states: 'Due to various strategic considerations as well as expectations created around him, the question is no longer whether he should be released, but rather when, in what way, and under what circumstances.'

When considering his release, it says, the following factors should be considered:

- The government has the strategic initiative in respect of Mandela, especially due to the international expectations surrounding his possible role in the peaceful resolution of the South African question. This means that, in the current climate, actions in terms of his release could not be seen as reactive. His release could also be regarded as confirmation of the seriousness of the government's intentions in respect of the envisaged democratisation process in the RSA.
- Mandela's stature in the international community, within the ANC and internally is still on a high level – a factor that enhances his strategic value.
- Notwithstanding the demands by Western leaders for his immediate release, they also appear to be realistic about this, and only expect it to happen in a few months' time.
- Following his conversation with Mr P.W. Botha, Mandela expressed himself in favour of a peaceful resolution of the South African problem.
- Almost all significant internal leaders believe that no constructive dialogue or negotiations can take place without Mandela's release.
- Mandela's release will hold certain international advantages for the RSA, at least in the short and medium term.
- While his release may not cause a split in ANC ranks, it

could force the organisation to make certain adaptations and make certain choices in respect of leadership and strategy.
- It must be accepted that Mandela cannot be ideologically 'reoriented'. However, this means that he will retain his credibility among his followers. It can also be accepted that he currently finds himself among those in the ANC in favour of negotiations.

'In light of the foregoing,' the document states, 'and especially the fact that Mandela sees himself as a "bridge builder" between the government and the ANC, it is envisaged that this should indeed be his role within the broad framework of the government's path towards the future [*toekomspad*].'

Within this broad framework, Mandela should be utilised to involve those favouring negotiations in the ANC and the internal extra-parliamentary groupings in a negotiation and settlement process. He could already play a decisive role, especially in a pre-negotiation phase, in his current situation of detention.

However, this would require that he not be released in a political vacuum, that an understanding between him and the government should be reached (without compromising his credibility), and that he should enjoy increasing freedoms (such as providing him with access to opinion formers). 'The last-named factor should enable him to play, in a controlled way, a bigger political role that will have a moderating influence on himself, the ANC, and internal groupings.'

The follow-up note sets out two options. Option 1 would entail 'neutralising or scaling down' Mandela's role and standpoint by releasing him unconditionally as soon as possible without any 'deal'; employing propaganda action against him; delivering him to the normal workings of national and international political processes; or 'via the Winnie factor'.

'To the extent to which efforts to neutralise him may not succeed,' the note states, 'this option has the potential to drive him in an uncompromised manner into the ANC camp, which will strengthen its ranks when his inherent ability to coordinate opposing factions is taken into consideration.'

Option 2 would entail Mandela 'becoming part of a resolution'. In terms of this solution, 'release is a reality that cannot be postponed beyond 1990'. The intervening time should be utilised for an interactive process aimed at tying him as far as possible to a peaceful, democratic and negotiated solution.

In this period, he should be exposed by means of correspondence and discussions to a broad spectrum of political actors, initially focused internally but gradually extending to southern Africa, Africa and even beyond, within a broad and accountable plan of action.

In terms of this principle, the document notes, a mandate must be given for initiating his exposure to regional leaders within his sphere of influence, paired with other figures as might be suggested by 'the Team' and with the approval of the Minister of Justice. (This single sentence had far-reaching consequences, as we shall see.) 'This modus operandi,' the document concludes, 'will place him in an interactive role with the community, and will allow his impact to be evaluated while control over his movements is retained.'

It is clear that the document seeks to provide a reasoned, strategic rationale for Mandela's release, as punted by Coetsee and presumably Viljoen. Indeed, the quasi-academic language suggests that the latter might have been involved in drafting it. It spells out a far-reaching and ambitious framework for utilising Mandela to advance a negotiated settlement and moderate the political climate – even while still in prison. In the process, it demonstrates a significant convergence between the government's own strategic concerns and calculations on the one hand and Mandela's proposals for acting as 'mediator' on the other, constituting a framework that endured at least until February 1990. In doing so, the document becomes nothing less than a fresh and overarching blueprint for Mandela's release. From then on, the process accelerated rapidly – and the next step was not long in coming.

12

The release of the 'eight'

*'The plan that you have put together –
like the A-team – has almost become our own plan . . .
Almost down to the minutest detail . . .'*

ON 10 OCTOBER 1989, only three and a half weeks after his inauguration as President, De Klerk announced the release of the remaining eight long-term 'security prisoners' besides Mandela – the Rivonia trialists Walter Sisulu, Ahmed Kathrada, Andrew Mlangeni, Raymond Mhlaba and Elias Motsoaledi, plus the 'little Rivonia trialist' Wilton Mkwayi, the veteran Cape ANC leader Oscar Mpetha, and the PAC leader Jafta (Jeff) Masemola.

This clearly seemed to herald the release of Mandela himself. As *The Guardian* put it the next morning: 'If President F.W. de Klerk is prepared to let the former secretary-general of the African National Congress out of jail, Mr Mandela should not be far behind.' It went on to note, quite accurately: 'Whether that happens depends on the reception given in the black townships to Mr Sisulu and the other seven political prisoners to be freed. Fresh unrest will provide ammunition to the hard-line security chiefs who have seen their power diminish in the few months since Mr P.W. Botha was forced out of power.'[1]

In *The Last Trek,* De Klerk presents the release as part of a relatively seamless ongoing process – a continuation of the 'systematic release of high-profile prisoners' that had begun the previous year with the release of Govan Mbeki, aimed at setting 'orderly precedents for the inevitable release of Nelson Mandela himself'. In making the announcement, he recalls that he said the releases were intended to promote peaceful solutions to the problems of the country. He adds that Mandela was 'fully apprised' of the government's action. Discussions were held with him and he confirmed yet again that his own release was 'not then on the agenda'.[2]

In *Long Walk to Freedom*, Mandela also deals with the release and the process behind it in deceptively simple fashion. 'Even as De Klerk became president,' he writes, 'I continued to meet the secret negotiating committee. We were joined by Gerrit Viljoen, the Minister of Constitutional Development, a brilliant man with a doctorate in Classics, whose role was to bring our discussions into a constitutional framework. I pressed the government to display evidence of its good intentions, urging the state to show its bona fides by releasing my fellow political prisoners at Pollsmoor and Robben Island.'

Summarising a hugely complex process in a single sentence, he then writes: 'While I told the committee that my colleagues had to be released unconditionally, I said the government could expect disciplined behaviour from them after their release.' This was demonstrated by the conduct of Govan Mbeki, who had been released unconditionally at the end of 1987.

On 10 October, President De Klerk announced the release of Sisulu and seven of his former Robben Island comrades. 'That morning, I had been visited by Walter, Kathy, Ray and Andrew, who were still at Pollsmoor, and I was able to say goodbye. It was an emotional moment, but I knew I would not be too far behind.'[3]

What Mandela omits to say is that, earlier the same morning, he was also visited by Kobie Coetsee and Gerrit Viljoen in what appeared to be a gruelling last-minute horse-trading session about how many people would be released – and under what conditions – which must have lasted several hours. General Willemse sat in on the conversation. Records of the session appear in the Coetsee archive. The basic transcript is inaccurate and incomplete, confirming that it was compiled from a hidden recording.

There are two versions of the conversation – one with handwritten additions and corrections, and a second incorporating the first set of corrections with more content written in. Both sets of corrections appear to have been made by officials who listened to the tapes, with limited success. All this makes the transcript very difficult to decipher – a task made even harder by Coetsee's convoluted conversational style. Extracts from a plausible reconstruction follows.

////

The conversation starts with a courteous and elaborate interchange between Mandela and Dr Viljoen about the latter's career as an academic and university administrator and his transition to politics, first as administrator of South West Africa and then as cabinet minister. (This in fact suggests that it might have been their first meeting.)

Mandela then asks about the former State President, P.W. Botha. While the transcript is poor at this point, he seems to thank Coetsee and Viljoen for their assistance in preparing him for his meeting with Botha some three months previously. "It helped a great deal, and I am very much indebted to you . . .' After some further pleasantries, a possibly irritated Coetsee changes the tenor of the discussion, and monopolises it thereafter.

////

Coetsee: 'Well, Mr Mandela, to introduce the business of the day. We've been talking for a long time now about a release of individuals, and then you introduced the thought of a larger impact on the South African situation. Also, from your point of view, the impact on your people and the positive effect that this may have. I had the benefit of the notes which General Willemse took at your last meeting when you expressed the view that people might react positively if a larger group, at least four of the Rivonia trialists, were released.

'We took cognisance of your thoughts, prepared the ground, and promoted this idea or concept with the government and the State President. And I am now in the position to say that it is possible to realise this idea of yours, given circumstances which you yourself visualised that will have to prevail on the ground to make this a meaningful and successful exercise . . .

'The plan you have put together – like the A-team – has almost become our own plan. Almost down to the minutest detail, meaning that your idea to interview certain leaders from certain sectors, we have arranged to give effect to that. We have also arranged through General Willemse for you to see your colleagues.

'Now, if we understand your view correctly, it boils down to this, that you intend to extract a commitment from your colleagues that they will strive towards a peaceful and orderly integration into society without upheaval, and a commitment from the other gentlemen you will see that they will assist them and won't make it difficult for them. As I say, we have made your objectives our own, and it seems feasible, it seems attainable, and if we may perhaps share some of our difficulties with you, we may bring about adjustments in your ideas and your views . . .'

Coetsee goes on to say that, 'for financial reasons only', the government is under intense economic and financial pressure, but some organisations do not understand these problems, and are doing nothing to alleviate them. This includes COSATU, which, he says, has arranged a demonstration on an 'extraordinary scale . . . almost out of proportion to what can be regarded as reasonable.

'Therefore, releasing colleagues of a certain stature and influence is a very difficult exercise, and yet we think it is possible with your assistance. The profile of these gentlemen, if released later this week or next week, will have to be a profile that will not promote an atmosphere of demonstrations . . .'

Given this, he says, Mandela needs to get a commitment from his colleagues and the leaders of the various sectors he is about to see to bring about 'peaceful integration' and not to use their release to raise political tensions. 'If anything goes wrong, the two of us [presumably Coetsee and Viljoen] will have to find other jobs . . .'

Mandela assures Coetsee that the group would fully understand the importance of not doing anything that might worsen the political situation. 'I don't have the slightest doubt that they will honour this arrangement between us.' Moreover, they would convey his views on the matter to the ANC, which would never give instructions that would contradict his recommendations.

Coetsee asks how this would work in practice. Once released, the prisoners would communicate with their organisations. One could not tell beforehand whether their organisations would cooperate, but by then they would already have been released. This meant the exercise would have to be an act of faith, relying exclusively on Mandela's assurance. He would have preferred this, but Mandela could not always be everywhere. Therefore, there had to be some kind of commitment based on the trust and confidence indirectly established between the government, Mandela and the prisoners. 'Because indirectly it does exist . . .'

Mandela says he would also prefer to rely on an 'act of faith' between the government and himself. That afternoon, he is due to see Albertina Sisulu, co-president of the UDF; Chris Dlamini, president of COSATU; Cyril Ramaphosa, general secretary of the National Union of Mineworkers; Murphy Morobe, secretary of the UDF; and Cassim Saloojee, president of the Transvaal Indian Congress. 'If we say to them, we want you to make a commitment to some or other condition, we shouldn't have any problems. It would be sufficient for them to say to me that they accept this.'

Releasing the prisoners without formal conditions would create a good impression, because it would reflect a confident style which the State President has established, and which has persuaded some of the government's harshest critics to say that he should be given a chance. Any formal demands or conditions would not conform with this spirit.

'We should preserve this spirit, and I can assure you personally that we are not going to have any problems at all during the discussions. Mr Sisulu is very careful about what he says and wants to say... He would want to make a statement in accordance with our discussions, and he knows very well that I must be able to rely on his word.'

Coetsee asks whether Sisulu would effectively act as Mandela's spokesperson, or a spokesperson for the whole group. Mandela says it's difficult to say, because when the prisoners are released they will go to different areas and fit into various organisations. 'But I can assure you that they will promote the same spirit that I promoted inside the prison.'

Mandela then says: 'I would have liked to be in a position of saying to you that, after their release, I can be on the further list... But I am concerned not only about the people inside the country but also about my colleagues in Lusaka. I thought it would make you even happier if I got a positive statement from outside South Africa...'

Coetsee: 'That would be ideal, but time is of the essence, and we can't keep this to ourselves. After today, people will become aware that there is movement, people will put things together, and perhaps develop an answer which we might not like. So time is of the essence. If we have to clear this with Lusaka, it may take some time...'

Mandela: 'After I have had a chat, you can take any action you want, because I am quite convinced on the basis of previous discussions that I am not going to have any problems. It's just a repetition of what we have discussed before.'

Coetsee asks Mandela whether he envisages phoning Lusaka. Mandela confirms this. 'I don't think it's possible in any other way at the present moment.'

Coetsee: 'The last time you actually invited me to accompany you to Lusaka...'

Mandela: 'Well, I don't want to embarrass either you or the State

President by making such a request . . .' He goes on to say he has a 'good feeling' as far as his colleagues in Lusaka are concerned. 'I have a general idea of how they are going to react . . .'

Seemingly pressing for an announcement before Mandela's intended telephone call, Coetsee says: 'But could we regard that as a bonus? To tie things up in a nice little parcel? If we could have the commitment you have visualised from your colleagues and from the group you will see this afternoon, the way will be paved for the State President to announce. If there is a 100 per cent commitment, it will be possible for him to announce this decision to release them in the near future . . .

'The State President will be seeing [Archbishop Desmond] Tutu, [Rev. Allan] Boesak and your friend the Reverend [Frank] Chikane tomorrow. So it is not to forestall them, but to give this historical event its proper perspective . . . that we are of the opinion that the State President should make the announcement before then.'

Mandela agrees that it would be good strategy for the State President to make the announcement before having any discussions. The first opportunity would be that evening.

Coetsee reiterates that he is talking about a 100 per cent commitment. 'You will understand that, if from the left or the right, forces succeed in wrecking this exercise, then of course people will look around for culprits. We would need to advise the government that there is such a commitment. That this can reasonably be expected, namely that there will be a peaceful integration without upheaval . . . they will not allow themselves to be abused . . . that there won't be public demonstrations or participation in anything that will exceed the boundaries of an orderly welcome. Am I right in saying that this can be expected?'

Mandela agrees, but says the State President should not disclose that they had made such a commitment. Coetsee agrees, saying: 'This is just between us . . .'

Coetsee goes on to say: 'You have kept us posted of what you have accomplished with your colleagues and the other groups, and

I have advised the State President accordingly. So if you should be so kind as to inform General Willemse after the discussions – or at least late this afternoon – that you are satisfied, then I will know what to convey.'

Mandela: 'I doubt whether I will think back again, because this is the right thing to do.'

They go on to discuss the possible responses of individual prisoners. Coetsee suggests that, as discussed previously, Kathrada might act in an 'individual' way that could embarrass Mandela.

Masemola is in Diepkloof Prison in Johannesburg, and it doesn't seem possible to bring him to Victor Verster to talk to Mandela before his release. Coetsee then asks whether Mandela would insist on seeing him.

Mandela says he would like this, and would ask that Masemola be brought down immediately after his release. Despite the fact that Masemola is a member of another organisation [the PAC], they were close on Robben Island. 'I have no doubt that . . . not only will he feel grateful, but will also honour this appeal.'

They begin to discuss what seems to be a prior appeal by Mandela to release two other long-term prisoners, namely Elphas Mdlalose and Matthews Meyiwa. Coetsee says there are ten prisoners in the same category who haven't served the bulk of their sentences, and the government is not geared to deal with them. 'We have given this very serious thought, and we will continue to do so. But it is very difficult.

'We thought that releasing Mr Masemola and Mr Mpetha would perhaps cushion the situation, because people will ask, why the Rivonia trialists only? What of the others? So, in order to spare you embarrassment on this issue, we thought of Mr Masemola and Oscar Mpetha, together with the Rivonia leaders.'

Mandela says he is 'very sorry' that the government should find it difficult to release Mdlalose and Meyiwa. He has proposed this as a 'special case' because, while Mlangeni is a South Sotho and all the others are Xhosas, Meyiwa and Mdlalose are Zulus, and the absence of people representing this group is a serious weakness in the whole package. Releasing them would also bolster his relationship with Chief Mangosuthu Buthelezi. These were people he respected, and the release of Harry Gwala the previous year had brought them closer together.

Coetsee: 'But hasn't that [the release of Gwala] already been a token . . .'

Mandela: 'No, in the sense that it was done last year, and this package should be regarded as just one package, including these two people, and I really had hoped that I would find no difficulties in convincing you of this . . .'

Mandela goes on to say that a gesture like this would be widely welcomed because 'it would indicate the type of things that are coming, and all the communities right across the country will look at this matter . . .'

Seemingly indicating that the government might relent, Coetsee says: 'We may perhaps come up with a surprise package . . . You have activated an idea . . . but you must understand that we have a system, and we have to be seen to be applying a policy. Exceptions will create so many problems that we won't be able to contain the situation.'

Mandela continues to argue for the two additional releases. He mentions the case of a former NP deputy minister – 'not as a criticism, but purely to show how reasonable my request was. He was charged with a very serious offence. He was given ten years, which in the eyes of many people was very lenient. Five years was suspended, and he was released after he had served a third of his sentence . . .'

Hardening up his argument, he continues: 'The government has now considered that their policy of apartheid is wrong, and they are making an attempt to [address this] . . . which we have considered . . . Now, we hoped the government would treat the case of these two chaps as a special case of leniency . . . because I want us to have this sort of peace in this country . . .'

Coetsee: 'Now what were their offences? Were there any lives at stake?'

Mandela: 'I would really appeal to you . . . I have not made such a request before . . . we have just crossed quite a lot of sensitive motives, and once I realised your difficulty I am not going to push you. But [it has sometimes been humiliating to see the government deferring to] all sorts of people who are not regarded as seniors in our community at all . . . I would like to have the ability to bring the two major political parties in the country together . . . and I didn't push you. If on this occasion I do so, I think you must realise that there is some reason why . . . I would insist that you see what power [you may have to release Meyiwa and Mdlalose].'

Coetsee: 'Would you ask as a necessity that you should see them as well?'

Mandela: 'Well, you know, this would be the normal thing to do. To make sure that they won't do anything that will induce you to say, look, you said [they would not act in a provocative manner] . . . but now they . . .'

Coetsee: 'Well, I understand your sentiments about the package . . . they are useful and important. But I have to discuss it wider and higher. I will still do so today, and in the course of the day I will come back to you.'

Mandela then offers to endorse a public statement issued by Coetsee: 'You see, the way you worked on the question of the meeting with the former State President, and the statement that was issued. There was good cooperation, and I could go public and say that the statement which the Minister of Justice has issued is an accurate reflection of what I want . . . and we are able to establish mutual confidence . . . Although I do not lose my image as a member of the ANC. It is clear that I am a member of the ANC who is going for negotiating with the National Party, and there is a mutual confidence between us. I can defend your decision publicly . . . And I think that this decision must be improved between [extended to] these two people.'

Coetsee: 'Yes, you are the great negotiator now, I understand perfectly what you say. I will come back to you. Let us come back to the problem that I foresee. Everyone will ask, what about Mr Mandela?'

Mandela: 'Well, I don't know. What do you suggest?'

Coetsee: 'Well, I suggest that you consider a repetition of the sentiment that you expressed previously, that your release is not just now on the agenda. But that will carry a message loud and clear, more than ever before, and there will be many questions. Are you negotiating? What is the next stage, what is the next phase? And we will have to find answers, also to your satisfaction. So I don't know whether you . . . but it seems to me that this would indicate a message or sign to the same effect: your release is not on the agenda.'

Mandela says he would be prepared to do this, because it would reflect the truth. 'If you prepare a statement to that effect, let me see it and I am sure I would sign it.'

Finally, says Coetsee, they should consider the contents of a statement by the State President. The major features of such a statement would just be the names, and a signal that Mandela was 'completely in the know'. 'We will have to find very careful words for this element of the statement. It should not compromise you too much, but at the same time to show that you are there.'

Another important element was to acknowledge some people in Africa and elsewhere who had been calling for his release. Mandela says he doesn't object to this, as these were facts that should not be repressed. 'If [you mention that] people have demanded our release, this won't compromise me – they will merely be speaking the truth.'

Coetsee: 'Well, I think this more or less covers the area that we have to cover . . .'

////

The release of the eight political prisoners was announced on SABC TV the same evening. The statement said the decision to do so was made partly in response to requests by homeland leaders. It also said discussions had been held with Mandela, who had been 'fully apprised of the proposed action'. It also went on to say that Mandela had 'confirmed yet again that his own release was not on the agenda'.

Among those puzzled by this phrase was the British Prime Minister, Margaret Thatcher. De Klerk's statement – or a news report based on it – was read on the 8 pm news. Previously restricted British diplomatic cables published in 2019 reveal that De Klerk phoned Thatcher to tell her about his initiative at 6.20 pm. A confidential letter to selected recipients by Charles Powell, then Thatcher's private secretary, reads as follows:

No. 199 Letter from Mr Powell (No. 10) to Mr Peirce, 10 October 1989, Confidential (PREM 19/2861)

President de Klerk telephoned the Prime Minister at 18.20 this evening. The purpose of the call was to tell her that he would very shortly be issuing an important statement announcing the release of eight security prisoners. Against the background of his discussions with the Prime Minister and her recent message, he wanted to give her advance notice of this. The eight names on the list would include Sisulu and Mpetha. The list included virtually all those jailed at the same time as Mandela.

His statement would make clear that Mandela had been fully apprised of the proposed releases and had confirmed his understanding that his own release was not at present on the agenda.

The Prime Minister said that this was very good news and she was most grateful to President de Klerk for giving her advance notice. She wondered about the precise significance of the statement on Mandela. Did it imply that his time would come? President de Klerk said that it was intended to convey Mandela's own acknowledgement that his release was not possible at this point in time.

He continued it was very important for the South African government that their action should not be seen or interpreted as giving in to pressure from outside. His statement would try to give credit for the release to moderate black leaders like Chief Buthelezi and Chief Mabuza. The Prime Minister said that she fully understood this point.

The Prime Minister repeated her great pleasure at the news which President de Klerk had given her: it was a major step in the right direction. We naturally hoped it would be followed by the release of Mandela . . . [4]

////

While sometimes difficult to follow, the conversation on 10 October between Coetsee and Mandela reveals a great deal about the interaction between them, and the convergences and divergences between their various agendas. Specifically, it illuminates the hidden framework around the release of political prisoners. The gist is spelled out in Coetsee's opening remarks, namely that Mandela would try to persuade prisoners about to be released as well as leaders of opposition movements not to exploit their release to fuel further conflict but to help lower the political temperature in the country. These remarks indicate that this framework has been in place for some time.

In a previous conversation, Mandela and Barnard spoke only about the release of Walter Sisulu. Since then, this has expanded to include four more prisoners, and eventually a total of eight – possibly in the course of conversations with General Willemse.

The discussion also reveals that Mandela intends to extend his campaign to the ANC in exile, and that this has also been discussed previously. Astoundingly, it emerges that Mandela, in a previous conversation, invited Coetsee to accompany him to Lusaka. Presumably, he would then have returned to Victor Verster Prison. When Coetsee reminds Mandela of this offer, Mandela backpedals by suggesting that this might embarrass him (Coetsee) and De Klerk, which he would not like to happen. By then, however, Mandela has probably realised that those embarrassed by such a move would also include himself.

The discussion and subsequent statement also cast further light on Mandela's apparent reluctance to leave prison. When Coetsee asks him how the matter of his release should be addressed, Mandela responds: 'I don't know . . . What do you suggest?' This seems really strange until one realises it refers merely to the way in which the State President's statement should be worded. This suggests, in turn, that Mandela's attitude towards his release has previously been canvassed in discussions between him, Willemse and Coetsee. The actual wording, that his release was 'not on the agenda', harks back to a previous formulation.

Lastly, Mandela seems to feel that he, and not the government, is in control of the process surrounding his release, and that he can dictate when this will happen. This theme will be analysed in greater detail later. In the meantime, it made for some enigmatic formulations, in public statements and otherwise, which would continue to puzzle numerous people besides Thatcher – including people in Mandela's own movement – for some time.

In that period, an unnamed diplomat told the *Washington Times* that it was 'remarkable for a political prisoner to dictate the timing of his release, or for a government to accept his wishes. Clearly, it suits both sides for him to remain inside, if only that Pretoria needs to keep Mandela as their last card to play – and I suspect that Mr Mandela sees it as strategically important not to emerge at this time.'[5]

////

While, as noted previously, the conversation between Coetsee, Viljoen and Mandela implies that Coetsee was still bargaining with Mandela about which prisoners would be released, another document in the archive reveals that this might not have been the case at all. With an undated cover merely stating 'PLAN A', the document consists of six appendices outlining meticulous planning around the release of the eight security prisoners, plus Meyiwa and Mdlalose. If a main memorandum existed, it has got lost along the way.

The appendices comprise an action plan for the release of the ten prisoners; an examination of options for groups in which they should be released; measures to ensure that the release of prisoners from Pollsmoor, Robben Island and Johannesburg are handled in a 'strategic and functionally correct way'; and a draft media release. A time frame is given for various administrative and other steps leading up to the releases. The target date for the first step, described as 'considering the possible early release of the following security prisoners, in consultation with the security community', is given as 26 September, followed by several others leading up to 10 October.

This seems to reveal that this process began long before the meeting with Mandela on 10 October. If this is correct, it implies, in turn, that Coetsee was not really bargaining with Mandela, but merely informing him at the last minute that the releases would take place, creating the false impression that they were still negotiable in the process. While his motives are open to speculation, he clearly tries to extract further undertakings from Mandela about their future conduct. And why Meyiwa and Mdlalose were not released with the others is unknown.

13

'You are to blame . . .'

The Sisulu rally, and Mandela and Coetsee speak again

ON 29 October, Walter Sisulu and the other seven released prisoners appeared at a rally held at the recently opened Soccer City stadium in Soweto – the first in a series to be held around the country. It was organised by the National Reception Committee (NRC), a body formed to receive released political prisoners, chaired by Cyril Ramaphosa. The committee did not apply for permission to stage the event, but the Department of Justice – Coetsee's department – announced the previous Friday that the chief magistrate of Johannesburg had approved the rally in any case.[1]

Clearly a ground-breaking event, it attracted considerable media attention. Rather breathlessly, the *Los Angeles Times* reported the next day: 'Staging the largest anti-apartheid rally in South African history, 70 000 black and white activists rocked a giant soccer stadium with foot-stomping liberation songs, waved flags of the outlawed ANC and SACP, and roared a welcome for seven recently freed ANC leaders.

'Former ANC General Secretary Walter Sisulu, to approving shouts of "Amandla!" (Power!), called for an intensification of the sanctions campaign against Pretoria until the white minority-led government proves itself serious about negotiations . . .'

Speakers stood in front of a 50-foot-high banner that proclaimed 'ANC Lives. ANC Leads', flanked by the black, green and gold flag of the ANC and the red flag of the Communist Party. Thousands in the stands wore T-shirts with slogans supporting the banned organisations and vowing, 'The struggle continues'. During the ten-hour rally, which included hours of speeches 'laced with revolutionary rhetoric', they sang freedom songs and were led in chants of 'Unban the ANC!'

Such a rally, the report continued, which technically violated dozens of South African laws, would have been 'unthinkable' less than two months previously when F.W. de Klerk took office, promising to dismantle apartheid and launch negotiations with the black majority. Since then, De Klerk had begun to remove the police grip on peaceful protest 'one finger at a time', and had unconditionally released Sisulu and six other leading political activists. 'By approving Sunday's rally in advance and stationing unarmed police officers discreetly outside the stadium fences, the government continued to draw cautious international approval . . .'[2]

According to an account assembled by Thula Simpson, a historian at the University of Pretoria, the crowd did the *toyi-toyi*, a 'muscular march mimicking the movements of MK guerrillas in training'. When Sisulu and other ANC stalwarts emerged from beneath the grandstand, they were escorted by an honour guard of twenty young militants clad in khaki uniforms. The rally spokesman informed observers that these escorts were meant to symbolise MK. A message from Oliver Tambo was read out.[3]

The main address was delivered by Walter Sisulu. Clearly, the speech was very carefully worded. It turned out to be a collective effort. The *Washington Post* reported that MDM and COSATU leaders had spent the previous week in discussions with the freed prisoners, hammering out the line they would take. On Friday, the report claimed, one of them had flown to Zambia to consult the ANC leadership in exile. 'Imprisoned ANC leader Nelson Mandela provided inputs as well, with messages sent from his cell.' The complete address was rapidly published and is still widely available online.[4]

Throughout its history, Sisulu said, the ANC had been committed to the politics of peace and negotiations, but pleas to successive governments had fallen on deaf ears. 'This is why we formed

Umkhonto we Sizwe, the Spear of the Nation, to defend our people and fight for our freedom.'

He went on to say: 'Despite countless bitter experiences, we will not allow the past to stop us from constantly searching for the shortest possible path to freedom.' He then presented the recently announced Harare Declaration as the ANC's new framework for negotiations. 'If such a climate is created, the ANC is prepared, as the Harare Declaration says, to discuss the suspension of hostilities on both sides. [But] there can be no question of us unilaterally abandoning the armed struggle.

'We are looking forward to the election of a constituent assembly elected on the basis of universal adult franchise. If the government is serious about a lasting solution, they will agree to this logical step. In the meantime, our duty is to intensify the struggle until we are able to get the regime to discuss the issue of the normalisation of the situation in South Africa . . .'

Coetsee discussed the rally with Mandela a week later, on Sunday, 5 November. Again, General Willemse sat in on the meeting. Partly typed, with handwritten additions and corrections inserted, this transcript is also very difficult to decipher. Again, a summary of a plausible reconstruction appears below.

////

Mandela apologises for bringing Coetsee out on a Sunday. The three men then discuss their respective fitness, as well as Mandela's exercise routine. (Mandela explains that, in earlier years, he and others exercised at Orlando gym, and did road work twice a week. 'We weren't close to Johannesburg, and there was no transport, so we had to wake up at about two o'clock. But I got used to it.' Now, he still wakes up at three o'clock, and spends some time reading before shaving and exercising. Then he takes a bath, and returns to bed for an hour or so.) Coetsee asks Mandela whether he ever studied Latin, and tells him that a Latin textbook written by his father-in-law was prescribed for matrics in the Transkei.

Coetsee tells Mandela it is always a pleasure to see him and talk about current events, given that he is 'far more up to date than the average politician, or even people overseas'. They then get down to business, namely a post-mortem of the Sunday rally. Coetsee shares his 'concerns' with Mandela on several levels.

It emerges that Coetsee also saw Mandela the previous Wednesday evening, four days before the rally. There is no transcript of this meeting in the archive. It also emerges that, at this meeting, and possibly previously, Mandela agreed to ask the rally organisers – the National Reception Committee (NRC) – to present the gathering as a 'welcoming event' and not an ANC rally. It appears that Ramaphosa and another NRC member, Murphy Morobe, agreed, and even cancelled advertisements in some newspapers.

After the meeting, Coetsee now says to Mandela, he told the government he had 'no doubts' that the event would be orderly and a welcoming party alone. Moreover, *Sowetan* carried a front-page interview with the welcoming committee, saying that it would not be an ANC rally but a welcoming event. Then, however, *New Nation* carried a big advertisement which Ramaphosa and Morobe had previously placed that presented the event in a different light.

This, Coetsee tells Mandela, has provoked an adverse response from some government 'institutions', after he had told them not to worry. 'Those adverts . . . compromised my position, and naturally also yours. This is a problem in terms of my position as a reliable source, and challenges my authority . . .'

The rally, he says, has also been closely studied. The presence of the ANC and SACP flags, described as 'overwhelming' by some observers, suggested that, after Mandela's intervention and after Ramaphosa and his colleagues had taken a 'very decent position', instructions were issued 'from elsewhere' to give prominence to the Red Flag.

He has also studied Sisulu's speech. He was very careful not to acknowledge the SACP, except at the very end. 'But then,' Coetsee tells Mandela, 'there was the problem of the Red Flag, and he said some very interesting things about certain foreign powers. We have that on record.

'So it seems as though, after we had spoken, and after these other gentlemen took a decision which was reflected in the *Sowetan*, some other instructions were issued which gave the event a predominantly communist image. This of course is not so good ... I am conveying this to you because I know that you would be as concerned as I am about anything emerging that would affect this very difficult situation ...'

Coetsee then hands Mandela a recent speech by F.W. de Klerk in which he expressed a twofold concern about communism. The first was that communism was losing ground all over the world. The second was that there seemed to be a progression towards communism in South Africa. 'While, in his new South Africa, there will be room for everyone else, it will be very difficult to cope with economic philosophies that would not be socialism but something else ... another agenda ... that would be foreign to Africa ...' Part of De Klerk's concern is caused by the fact that he knows Mandela, but not the other released leaders. 'On the face of this, are they their own bosses?'

The government also did not like Sisulu's approach to sanctions. In fact, Coetsee remarks, he said 'nothing positive'. Others also had this attitude: 'For every Afrikaner who wants responsible solutions and is prepared to sit down and look afresh at the future, there is also an Afrikaner that criticises ... One could say, he didn't actually mean that, but we lost an opportunity. Whether he was influenced by Mrs Sisulu, whether she compromised herself when she went overseas and she had to live up to that – I don't know.

'I am looking for opportunities to bring about change, but to continue calling for sanctions puts this whole exercise back into the seventies. I want to ask you, should we talk to Mrs Sisulu? Would that have any purpose? Has she been compromised elsewhere?'

Winding up for now, Coetsee says: 'There is enough for me to be hopeful, and to say, well, we've achieved a lot. We are much closer. But sanctions are almost out of line . . . It will take years to destroy the government [in this way] . . . [Instead], we want to do business with the world, and the world wants to do business with us. So we are looking for pragmatism . . . a real commitment . . .'

Responding, Mandela thanks Coetsee for his input, and says he has no doubt that they will handle any problems that may arise. 'I have a very positive attitude towards what we believe about the future . . .'

It is 'absolutely important' for De Klerk to complete his current round of consultations with black leaders. He also hopes it won't take as long for him to see De Klerk as it did to see P.W. Botha. 'Meeting with him will not only enable me to [assist] him and you in so far as your colleagues are concerned, but also help me to persuade my own colleagues to adopt an attitude which I have fully explained to those who have now been released. Allowing me to be in contact with my colleagues is of crucial importance . . .'

Mandela then goes on the offensive: 'This is one of the mistakes which the government has made, of putting me at the centre of political debate in this country – which of course is what we expected – but at the same time cutting me off from the very people who are necessary if this momentum towards organisations should take place.

'This is one of the things on which I am going to [clash] with you, because there is no point in my undertaking this initiative if . . . [unclear] . . . But you and the government are the people who have isolated me from the very people whose attitudes [we want to influence] . . .'

The *Weekly Mail* wrote that the 'rally was ANC, but the day belonged to the Red Flag'; and that Sisulu called for the intensification of the struggle. 'How does this fit with "Mandela persuades his released comrades to discipline and control the ANC supporters"? "To calm the situation so that the government can proceed with the further normalisation of the security situation"? "To meet the preconditions . . ."?'

As regards the advertisements, the problem was that, although he spoke to the organisers, it was late in the day and close to the rally. They did say they would try to stop some adverts, but would not be able to stop all of them. 'If you had done this earlier, and if you had given me the opportunity to speak to our people . . .'

Seemingly forced on the defensive, Coetsee responds: 'No, you see, what I am trying to say to you is that you've succeeded – that Messrs Ramaphosa and Morobe wanted to cooperate. Every other newspaper cooperated, but *New Nation* deliberately did not, and then the Red Flag emerged over the whole country . . .'

Mandela goes on to say that he does not favour Coetsee seeking a meeting with Albertina Sisulu, given that he is advocating a meeting between the government and the ANC and not with individual members. This is the only solution, because the leadership would clarify the ANC's position no matter what the views of individual members might be. At present, senior members and the ANC don't want to meet with the government until certain preconditions are met.

This leads to a discussion of Mandela's proposed framework for negotiations in what appears to be an earlier draft of his eventual letter to F.W. de Klerk. Intriguingly, Mandela seems to acknowledge that the ANC has corrected his earlier viewpoint, but appears to indicate that he still favours his earlier, two-stage model for negotiations. He seems to ask Coetsee to help him persuade the ANC to adopt his own model.

Circling back, Mandela says: 'There can be no peace if . . . a person can't be given proper authority to be in contact with his colleagues.'

Coetsee: 'If I understand you correctly, then, you see your role as a facilitator between the government and the ANC?'

Mandela: 'Of course . . . before I even go to the summit to see my people there. I am making an issue of this for the simple reason that if I had seen Mrs Sisulu before she went abroad, you would probably not have had this problem . . .'

Coetsee: 'About sanctions?'

Mandela: 'About sanctions and about . . . [unclear] . . . You must have seen what she said when she came back here. She made a statement that Mandela had given me advice.'

He goes on to say that Sisulu himself has made some 'wonderful statements', especially one reported the previous week. This should give Coetsee an idea of what it meant for him to speak to his colleagues. 'He was speaking in his new role of acting on behalf of the organisation. You must understand the conditions under which he is working. Sometimes he has an opportunity to consult us, but in most cases he has to act alone.'

Coetsee: 'Mr Sisulu's remarks in his speech about the preconditions for talks has signalled to the government that he speaks on behalf of the ANC . . .'

Mandela: 'Well, I am not allowed to say so . . . whether he had all the instructions . . . in delivering his speech. But I can tell you that every sentence of this speech agreed with the policy of the ANC.' He goes back to explaining the advertisement in *New Nation*: 'They always have this huge page in every issue . . . It's quite possible that because they had already printed it, they found it difficult to reverse . . .'

On the question of sanctions and the remarks by Sisulu, Coetsee should appreciate that the 'people', not the ANC, had asked the world to apply sanctions. 'And you cannot expect members of the ANC not to defend sanctions when the world has actually responded to our request . . .'

Dealing with the issue of the SACP, Mandela seems to have a sudden emotional outburst. The transcript reads as follows: 'Now, as far as the Communist Party is concerned, again, if you had given me the opportunity to discuss this question with people from the various regions . . . you are to blame.'

Coetsee: 'I don't agree with you!!' [The two exclamation marks appear in the transcript.]

Mandela: 'You are making us lose valuable opportunities by not allowing me to see people from the various regions, and putting me directly to use. And you are doing this in spite of my commitments in the past. I made a commitment to the State President . . . saying that I am concerned about present conditions . . .

'I hope you won't leave without giving me permission to see my colleagues from the various regions, because this is the key. You are complaining, and all these things could have been avoided if you had allowed me to see these people . . .

'Why should there be such hesitation on this question? I have tried to cooperate, I have not hesitated, as you were saying. The statement you issued after my meeting with the State President is an actual statement. I did not hesitate. So why do you feel it is so risky for me to see my colleagues? . . . So that they themselves should not speak in a way in which I am trying not to speak to the country. The question of what they reflect must be rectified, but I can only rectify it if I am able to talk to people from all groups.'

Coetsee: 'Do we understand you correctly then that you would have persuaded them not to reflect the . . . [unclear].'

Mandela: [unclear]

Coetsee: 'General Willemse has studied a copy of the notes, and I doubt whether on his side all these things are legal, but some of the things I have to consult on. Because some of these people are still in detention, some have since been released, other restrictions have been removed. [But] I will make it my business to discuss this at the highest level . . .'

Mandela: 'I have raised this matter with the team on numerous occasions. I've raised it with you also, and you have given me your answers . . .'

Coetsee (still trying to mollify Mandela): 'We have accomplished so much, and the fact that some of it hasn't been done . . . you must really appreciate the position we have moved from . . .'

Mandela (still agitated): 'I appreciate that very much, but . . . I should remind you that . . . if we want people to promote peace, the most logical thing to do is to talk to people . . . That is why you are coming here ... There are no invitations to my colleagues who have been released. This shows the value of my discussions with them ... and with Mr Masemola as well ... I don't see any hesitation, because what stopped you.

'I think I saw you before September. Yes, I saw you before the big operation. It was on Monday the 18th. And I raised the question of the regions, and said it was urgent. The general here said, you are now allowed to see people from the northern region. Whereupon I said I must ask Mr Botha because he is the chairman, and you agreed. And he said he wanted to give some instructions. That was in August this year ... Then at that stage a message came through that ... a meeting was permitted between myself, Albertina Sisulu and Archie Gumede [both leaders of the UDF] ... Now, I want to talk to them in a matter of days ...'

Coetsee: 'I won't be able to say whether this will take place. As far as Mrs Sisulu is concerned, I think, General, you said to me she is leaving the country.'

Willemse confirms that she left the country at a certain stage, but then returned, and he only realised this after a decision was taken about the release of Sisulu and the other prisoners. 'Then, she was part of the visit that did take place with Mr Ramaphosa ...'

Coetsee: 'You see, that is why I say, Mr Mandela, that I would like to deal with this issue for once and for all in such a way that if I let you know this is going to happen, it will happen ...'

Mandela (seemingly calming down): 'I appreciate that very much, because I want you to remain as minister to take part in the development of the country ... Journalists both locally and abroad have commented on the good relationship between us, which has led to meaningful developments. Now, I can understand your position as far as people in other regions are concerned. But I also want to see people in prison. That doesn't really require any consultation.'

Coetsee: 'Just people on Robben Island? General, can that be arranged for tomorrow? The day after?'

Willemse: 'That is really a problem for us, you know ... [we need to find out if] people are available and if they haven't got medical appointments, or appointments with visiting family members. That is the one thing I cannot say out of hand at this particular moment.'

He goes on to say: 'I know you are also concerned about people from outside the system ... travelling from Johannesburg or far away ... But if it just depends on the chaps inside, there is no problem. The minister has indicated the principle, and I will arrange it. We can just sort out the management.'

Mandela reminds Willemse that he was able to bring Masemola down from Diepkloof Prison before his release, 'however this was arranged', and says this gave people a 'lot of respect'. He then adds: 'Many of these chaps are already off training – many have been to the Soviet Union. If the report came from Mr Gumede, which I think is the most senior man, then this move has to hold the future. You know they are committed to the young, the real revolutionaries ...'

Coetsee: 'I have seen papers on that. I have read everything ... and this does need correction ...'

Mandela says he wants to see five people from Diepkloof Prison. Coetsee asks Willemse whether he can handle this. Seemingly exasperated by his growing workload, Willemse says: 'This is also a matter of economics ... you know, running to and from [Cape Town] ... nowadays, a return ticket between Johannesburg and here costs R624. So you will again have to face the taxpayer in parliament about this type of thing. There are practical implications ...'

Coetsee then says: 'Mr Mandela, you are going to make so much money with your book. We have to talk about that. We would like to come and spend one evening with you, and we really have to try to press for time to talk about this book.'

Mandela: 'I would appreciate that ...' [Mandela apparently shows Coetsee and Willemse a document or manuscript.]

Coetsee: 'Can we just have a look at that? Perhaps I will remember, because of documents I have in my possession . . . I haven't seen this. Perhaps you can just ask Mr Marais to make a photocopy for us.'

Mandela: 'I also want to see people apart from the regions. Like Archbishop Tutu. I want him to come here, along with his wife. Because they are people who must also know what I am doing. I don't know if the General is going to settle this matter . . . he has already done this with Mdlalose . . .'

Coetsee: 'He has just recommended to me that the Reverend Frank Chikane [of the South African Council of Churches] should visit you.'

Mandela: 'I really want to see them, because the youth are the ones who are [in] trouble.'

Coetsee undertakes to let him know in a few days' time.

They briefly discuss a proposed visit by a chief, currently the chief executive of homeland President Lucas Mangope's office in Bophuthatswana, whom Mandela describes as 'very persistent', 'very noisy', and 'fond of national heroes'. He is on the list for January.

Coetsee then says he wants to ask Mandela for a strategy. 'We have a whole list of people who are trying to see you. Some want to come and play for you, some want to come and play for us, and so forth.' He talks about a prospective visitor who wants to hand a book to Mandela. The person is a theologian, with a 'very interesting style', who sent in a brilliant letter. 'You can read this, then you can see if you can trust me. He's got a very interesting history of this country in this century. I have always asked you whether you want to see these people. It gives a balanced image.'

Mandela: 'Why should I see him? I don't know who he is.'

Coetsee: 'I mentioned him just as well.'

Mandela: 'I would see anybody . . . [unclear].'

Coetsee: 'Even Eugène Terre'Blanche?'

Mandela: 'Now that is going too far . . . [but] the guys from this church, and so on, why should I see them? I am what I call a reconciliator; I want to know everybody. You know, if I made a public speech, if I had a discussion with Mr De Klerk, you should be surprised if I failed to get the right support . . .'

[Note in the transcript: 'Mr Mandela asked to see as many people representing political parties because he believes that the one way of getting across his point of view, he believes there is one way of taking as many people as possible. So he would even see the very far left, and also the very far right!!']

Mandela remarks that De Klerk has created 'quite a good impression . . . Because the Frontline States have now prevailed to see me, and Kaunda has said he wants a meeting with Botha [De Klerk?] . . .'

Coetsee returns to Mandela's book: 'I want to give you my perspective as a lawyer. People are going to try and catch me about you, your image and your history. And we are aware of the fact that you have been preparing [a manuscript]. I did not involve myself to the extent of wanting to go to war about it, but in principle I supported the idea, and so did the General, and now we believe that there are two sets of people writing about your life and who you really are.'

Mandela: 'We haven't got the time, minister, [but] let me put you at rest. I have stopped that . . .' He goes on to say that he will issue a statement stating that he will only collaborate with one agreed person. This would 'kill this idea' of a second biography. 'Now, about the people I want to come and visit me . . .'

Coetsee says he wants to make a suggestion that would save them time. Mandela should draw up a list of names, and give it to Major Marais, who would fax it to him. Otherwise, Mandela could write to any of the addresses they had used to correspond in the past.

Mandela: 'Now, the last thing I would like to raise is the question of the passports, which I raised before. My daughter Zindzi wants to complete her degree, and she might have to go to the

States for further study. And she has got the three children. I gave you the names.'

Coetsee. 'Very well. General, the passport is up to the team. And let's . . . [unclear] . . . people listed in the regions in the next half an hour.'

Willemse: 'Who we have is Zindzi and Fatima Meer. Those are the two passports. The only problem here was that it's just a matter of climate. . . . [unclear] . . . perhaps this will be resolved when you speak to these people [on the list] over the new few days . . .'

Mandela: 'No, I want to create a climate for us to do things positively . . . I am quite aware of your problems, but you should also be aware of ours. That's why it is necessary to speak to these people.'

Coetsee: 'I think the problem, sir, is not what we say the climate will be, the proof of the pudding is what's been observed . . .'

Mandela says he would also like his wife, Winnie, to have a passport. She had been invited to visit someone overseas in November, and he would really like her to go. 'My wife has had a very hard time, and for her to leave the country would mean a great deal.'

Coetsee: 'Yes, it's on my agenda.

'Now, today's *Sunday Star* carried a report about the people who were involved in the death of Stompie [Seipei]. It also says that the Attorney General has not yet indicated whether he is going to call Mrs Mandela as a witness. I am very sorry that that report was published. I don't know where they got it, but they did not get it from my system. Because I told General Willemse, when you mentioned the passport issue, long before the rally . . . that these were two very sensitive issues which I wanted to discuss with you . . .'

He goes on to talk about a meeting with the Attorney General aimed at 'assisting' the latter on this issue. 'He sensed that there was a special understanding between us, and he did sense that it was important. So he thought it advisable just to come and tell me that we've approached a very sensitive area. I am mentioning this just to tell you that I did not want it to appear in the newspaper. I didn't want anyone to realise that this is an issue. All I can tell you is that it has been leaked somewhere. We will leave it there . . .'

Lastly, Coetsee tells Mandela he also wants an Eastern Cape advocate, Ismail Mahomed, to come and talk to him. He had asked Mahomed to become a judge. Mahomed was ambivalent about this, on the grounds that he would not want people to think he was 'pandering to a system which he disapproves of and even disrespects', and said one person's opinion he would value would be Mandela's.

Mandela: 'Yes, I think it's better to tell him to come and see me, and it would be proper for me to express my opinion – what I thought for or against him doing so. I think it would be better if we discussed it. At the present moment there is a great sensitivity around these issues . . .'

////

This is a highly significant record that reveals a great deal about the dynamic between Mandela, Coetsee and other government representatives at that time. To highlight a few features, it emerges that Mandela's campaign to moderate the views of key figures in resistance politics and prepare the ground for negotiations was well under way. Among other things, we learn that Ramaphosa and Morobe took active steps to tone down the 'National Welcome Back Rally'.

It also reveals the extraordinary scope of Mandela's ambitions, namely to talk to a large number of leaders and other role players across a broad political spectrum. Lists had been made, appointments scheduled, and a new, expanded list to be submitted to Coetsee was in the offing. Willemse was made responsible for ferrying people to Victor Verster from all over the country. At that point, Mandela was already so busy that Coetsee and Willemse had to make an appointment to see him.

Besides this, it also reveals Mandela's extraordinary confidence that he could influence a broad range of people, and moderate their views and subsequent actions. This apparently includes moderating Albertina Sisulu's stance on sanctions, and persuading the MDM and the ANC to tone down their alliance with the SACP.

The transcript confirms that Sisulu's speech at the rally was very carefully crafted, with input from the ANC in Lusaka, and probably from Mandela himself. However, he asks for forbearance in respect of Sisulu's utterances given the pressures being exerted on him and the burden of speaking internally on behalf of Mandela and the ANC, which he has to bear alone: 'You must understand the conditions under which he is working. Sometimes he has an opportunity to consult us, but in most cases he has to act alone...'

The transcript also offers an insight into the dynamic between Mandela and Coetsee, who had by then been sparring with each other for several years. Presented with evidence that some of his promises have not materialised, Mandela adroitly turns defence into attack, accusing Coetsee and the government of placing him at the centre of politics in the country while not allowing him to talk to enough people.

The transcript reveals that Mandela still seemed to prefer his controversial two-stage model for negotiations to those in the Harare Declaration, and thought Coetsee could help him to popularise this model instead.

It also reveals some interaction between Coetsee and Mandela about a forthcoming book, probably, at that point, the biography *Higher than Hope* by Fatima Meer.[5] Coetsee displays a close interest in what Mandela is going to say about him and the period in question, as well as – perhaps with a tinge of envy – the book's commercial prospects.

In a closing flourish, Mandela effectively demands passports for several people – Winnie, Zindzi and her three children as well as

Fatima Meer – and, in a seeming confirmation of his famed human touch, agrees to see a black advocate who has qualms about accepting an invitation from Coetsee to step up to the bench. Whether this meeting ever happened is unknown, but Mahomed did accept a position on the bench in 1991. Later, in 1998, he would become the first black chief justice of South Africa.

14
'A grain of sand in an oyster . . .'

Mandela meets F.W. de Klerk, 13 December 1989

MANDELA eventually met F.W. de Klerk on 13 December. Once again, he was driven to Tuynhuys in the heart of Cape Town, next to the Houses of Parliament, and met De Klerk in the same room where he had had tea with P.W. Botha a few months before. De Klerk was accompanied by Kobie Coetsee, General Willemse, Dr Barnard, and Barnard's deputy, Mike Louw.

In the meantime, Mandela writes in *Long Walk to Freedom*, De Klerk had begun to dismantle the building blocks of apartheid. He opened beaches to people of all colours, and announced the repeal of the Separate Amenities Act. In November, he also announced that the National Security Management System – which Mandela describes as a 'secret structure set up under P.W. Botha to combat anti-apartheid forces' – would be dissolved.[1]

In early December, he was told a meeting with De Klerk was set for the 12th of that month. (It turned out to be the 13th.) By this time, he was able to consult his colleagues new and old, and had met at the cottage with leaders of the MDM, UDF and COSATU, as well as 'ANC people from various regions'.

As before, Mandela drafted a submission to De Klerk, which he calls a 'letter'. Whether or when this was handed to De Klerk is unknown. Mandela seemed to refer to an early draft in the course of his discussion with Coetsee and Willemse on 5 November, so it could have been handed to the working group. However, as will become clear, De Klerk was almost certainly familiar with its contents. An original version meticulously written out by Mandela in his old-school handwriting resides in the Coetsee archive.

In *Long Walk to Freedom*, Mandela says it was drafted 'with guidance from a number of colleagues'. This is evident from the letter itself, which is written in a very different style from his memorandum to P.W. Botha.[2] More significantly, it displays a marked shift towards the ANC's latest policies, notably the Harare Declaration. For this and other reasons, it is worth recollecting.

////

'I hope,' Mandela writes, 'that Ministers Kobie Coetsee and Gerrit Viljoen have informed you that I deeply appreciate your decision in terms of which eight fellow prisoners were freed on 15 October 1989, and for advising me of the fact in advance. The release was clearly a major development which rightly evoked praise here and abroad . . .'[3]

In his view, it has become urgent to take other measures to end the deadlock. This will be achieved if the government first creates a proper climate for negotiations, followed by a meeting with the ANC. Conflict will never be settled without an agreement with the ANC. He has spent more than three years urging the government to negotiate with the ANC, and he hopes he 'will not leave this place with empty hands'.

Seemingly responding to recent statements by De Klerk and other government spokespersons, he then addresses what he regards as the government's current precondition for negotiations, namely that the ANC should make an 'honest commitment to peace'.

Developing a line of argument in accord with the Harare Declaration and the ANC's 1988 policy statement, Mandela says the ANC will never make such a commitment at the instance of the government, or any other source. 'No serious political organisation will ever talk peace when an aggressive war is being waged against it.'

Moreover, the precondition that the ANC should commit itself to peace is inconsistent with a statement made by De Klerk shortly before the general election, in which he appealed to black leaders to negotiate with the government and refrain from setting preconditions. 'Although the government has called on blacks to set no preconditions, it considers itself free to do exactly that.'

He goes on to argue: 'The government ought to be aware that readiness to negotiate is in itself an honest commitment to peace. In this regard, the ANC is far ahead of the government. It has repeatedly declared its willingness to negotiate, provided a proper climate for such negotiations exists. The organisation has recently published a clear and detailed plan to this effect, which has already been approved by the Frontline States, the OAU, the Non-Aligned Movement, and by almost all the members of the Commonwealth of Nations.'

Reflecting the ANC's latest line on the armed struggle, he argues that 'on many occasions in the past' the ANC explicitly acknowledged its commitment to peaceful solutions, if channels for doing so were available, and vainly made 'impassioned overtures' to every South African government. This clearly shows that the ANC has an established record of a commitment to peace, and that its armed struggle is a purely defensive measure.

He then comments at length on a statement in De Klerk's inaugural address on 20 September that there is 'but one way to peace, to justice for all, that is the way of reconciliation, of seeking mutually acceptable solutions, of discussing what the new South Africa should look like, of constitutional negotiations with a view to a permanent understanding'.

Next, Mandela writes that, in previous discussions with the government team, he repeatedly urged that negotiations should take place in two stages. In the first, the government and the ANC would work out the preconditions for negotiations, and the second would consist of the actual negotiations themselves. In a revealing passage, he continues: 'Those were my personal views and not those of the ANC, which sees the problem quite differently. It seems to me that now that I am aware of the attitude of the ANC on the matter . . . we should work on the formula indicated by the organisation for the resolution of the present obstacles to negotiation.'

In his view, these are the policy of apartheid; the outdated concept of group rights; the government's plan to hold racially based elections to determine who should take part in negotiations; and its notion that a lasting solution can only be found after years of consultation and planning. 'We totally reject that view. There is nothing complicated in replacing minority rule with majority rule, [and] group domination with a non-racial social order.'

Mandela again appeals to De Klerk to release four fellow prisoners who are serving life sentences on Robben Island, namely Matthews Meyiwa and Elphas Mdlalose, plus Anthony Xaba and John Nene.

Moving towards a conclusion, he writes: 'I would like to believe that my exploratory efforts during the last three years have not been in vain, and that I have an important role still to play in helping to bring about a peaceful settlement.'

He closes with what at first seems like an insignificant and incongruous statement, but is actually anything but: 'In helping to promote dialogue between the ANC and the government, I hope to be able to avoid any act which may be interpreted as an attempt on my part to drive a wedge between you and the NP, or to portray you in a manner not consistent with your public image. I trust that you and other members of the government will fully reciprocate.'

////

In *The Last Trek*, De Klerk also writes about his meeting with Mandela – 'the man with whom I was destined to work for the following four years to make the transformation of South Africa a reality'.[4] Under the cover of darkness on the evening of 13 December, he recounts, Mandela was smuggled into the Tuynhuys basement garage and ushered into his office, where he was accompanied by Viljoen, Coetsee, Willemse, Barnard, and Louw.[5] After the usual greetings and pleasantries, the others withdrew and left Mandela and De Klerk to hold private talks.

So this, he thought to himself, was Nelson Mandela – the man who, during his 27 years of imprisonment, had become a global icon of the struggle against apartheid. 'Like a grain of sand trapped in an oyster', Mandela had been a continuous and growing source of irritation to previous governments. Over the years, layer after layer of myth – 'created by our own fears and the adulation of his supporters' – had accreted around him. Now, after 27 years, he and the political realities that he represented had emerged into the full glare of global and national attention.

Taller than De Klerk had expected, and slightly stooped by his 71 years, on first impression Mandela conveyed qualities of dignity, courtesy and self-confidence. He also had the ability to radiate unusual warmth and charm – 'when he so chose'. He was every inch a Thembu patriarch, and bore the mantle of authority with the 'ease of those who are not troubled by self-doubt'. 'His heritage, his volatile political career, and the hard lessons of self-control and fortitude he had learnt in prison had all prepared him for this moment of history.

'During most of the meeting, each of us cautiously sized up the other. . . .' Mandela raised the issue of the NP's commitment to group rights. He thought this was a mistake, and created the impression that the NP was trying to reintroduce apartheid by the back door. De Klerk reminded him that, in his memorandum to P.W. Botha, he had said that two broad issues would need to be addressed during negotiations: the ANC's demand for majority rule in a unitary state, and the insistence of whites on structural guarantees that majority rule would not result in domination of the white minority. The NP's support for group rights was simply a mechanism to provide such guarantees.

'I allowed him to do most of the talking,' De Klerk writes, 'and took his measure while he spoke. I think that we both reached more or less the same conclusions: that it would be possible for us to do business with each other.' They parted on a friendly note, with the assurance that they would meet again fairly soon. The next time, they would also discuss his release.

Mandela describes the conversation at greater length.[6] He confirms that he raised the issue of group rights, and that they discussed this for some time. 'I then brought up the question of my freedom, and said that if he expected me to go out to pasture upon my release, he was greatly mistaken. I reaffirmed that if I was released into the same conditions under which I had been arrested, I would go back to doing precisely those things for which I had been imprisoned . . .'

De Klerk listened carefully to what he had to say, and said he would take everything into consideration. 'I was able to write to our people in Lusaka that Mr De Klerk seemed to represent a true departure from the NP politicians of the past. Mr De Klerk, I said, echoing Mrs Thatcher's famous description of Mr Gorbachev, was a man we could do business with.' This is the same thing De Klerk said about Mandela in *The Last Trek* published four years later.

There is no record of this conversation in the Coetsee archive. However, it does contain the text of a media release about the meeting that was apparently never issued. Stamped 'TOP SECRET', it reads:

SP / MANDELA STATEMENT
I met Mr Mandela on the eve of his return to public life.
  Both of us strive towards a peaceful, prosperous and just South Africa. We differ about the road ahead – in some respects, dramatically so – but we agree that a road of confrontation and violence will not be [a road to the] salvation or prosperity of any South African. Therefore, I and Mr Mandela commit ourselves once again to a peaceful process for settling the South African question. To this end, a major responsibility rests on all individuals and parties to act in a reasonable and reconciliatory manner.

Mr Mandela and I also discussed the State of Emergency. He believes the lifting of the State of Emergency is essential to normalise the conduct of politics. I reaffirmed towards him that the Government is also striving towards lifting the State of Emergency as soon as possible. We agreed that the state of affairs should be reviewed from time to time, and that Mr Mandela will do everything in his power to try to ensure that the need for the continued maintenance of the State of Emergency will fall away as soon as possible.

The position of persons who are serving sentences as a result of crimes with political motives and of people who have committed such misdemeanours but have not yet been charged was also raised. We agreed that this was a matter that could only be addressed at a later stage in the negotiation process, but that exploratory conversations could already take place so that the positions of individuals could be clarified.

Mr Mandela expressed the wish that his release should take place in an orderly and dignified manner, and that everyone will act in such a way that emotions and radicalism will not triumph over the idea of a peaceful and orderly political process. The Government shares this point of view. The eyes of the world are therefore focused on all South Africans to prove that we are capable to negotiate our future in a restrained manner.

The statement would have been a sensation if it had been issued at the time. With the benefit of hindsight, it is not difficult to see why it did not see the light of day. (Among other considerations, it was probably written by Coetsee or his staff. It might have been turned down by De Klerk, or Mandela might simply have refused to support it.)

Firstly, it talks about Mandela's imminent release as a fait accompli. Secondly, it expresses a 'common commitment' to settling the South African conflict by peaceful means, which implies a renunciation of the armed struggle. Thirdly, it effectively states that Mandela agreed the state of emergency could not be lifted immediately, and that he would be partly responsible for creating the conditions needed for doing so. Fourthly, it suggests they agreed that the issue of amnesty should be deferred until later in a negotiating process. Fifthly, it expresses Mandela's support for a 'peaceful and orderly political process', resonating with a major theme in De Klerk's own thinking since his inaugural address earlier in the year.

Among other things, several of these 'agreements' amount to significant deviations by Mandela from the conditions set out in the Harare Declaration. But these are not the only revelations about the meeting in the Coetsee archive. Others will be dealt with in chapter 21.

In *Long Walk to Freedom*, Mandela jumps straight from his meeting with De Klerk to the latter's speech in parliament on 2 February 1990. But as the foregoing begins to indicate, a great deal happened in between.

////

On 18 December 1989, Mandela received a visit from the Rev. Frank Chikane, then secretary-general of the South African Council of Churches. A handwritten summary of their conversation appears in the archive, recorded on the standard printed form for monitoring conversations [*gespreksmonitering*].

The record is attached to a covering letter from General Willemse, addressed to the 'Director Efficacy' [*Direkteur Doeltreffendheid*]. He asks for a verbatim transcript of the conversation. Some aspects of the conversation are of interest to Minister Coetsee, and Brig. Gillingham of Security Services should see to it that he receives the record. The summary reads as follows:

> Chikane tells Mandela he has come to see him to clarify his viewpoint about the new house [in Orlando West, after the previous one had burned down]. 913 says he is going back to 8115 and the house must be enlarged. The plot next to the house should be retained. The new house should be completed and sold. The ANC and the UDF should issue a statement to this effect, and not the youth.

Frank and the ANC are worried about the young people around Winnie. 913 says that, if Frank prefers this, he will see the youth before he sees the UDF.

913 says he asked to see Mr De Klerk. He (913) says he is trying to phone [Alfred] Nzo [the ANC secretary-general based in Lusaka]. He wants to know what he should do. A major change is on its way. 913 says he told the SP that he wants to see the National Executive [Committee], either here (V.V.) [Victor Verster] or in Lusaka, or in a neutral country. They must not think they (the internal organisations) can do things inside the country without asking Lusaka. This is why he wants to talk to Nzo.

Mandela says during his meeting with the SP he raised some sensitive matters. He [the SP] reacted like a statesman. His problem was the whites.

913 says if he goes to Lusaka, he will see the whole group, and if they come here [to Victor Verster] he will see two or three.

Frank asks that, if [the people from] Lusaka come here, what guarantee will there be that they will be allowed to return. 913 says Minister Coetsee will keep his word, but he (913) will still ask for a written guarantee.

913 asks who is living next to 8115. Frank doesn't know. 913 says they will have to approach the people with caution. Pay him for his plot, and give him another, better house for free.

913 asks what the position is in respect of the RMC [Release Mandela Committee]. Frank says there are problems between the RMC and the UDF.

Clearly, this conversation points to some startling new developments. More information emerges from two records in the archive dated the very next day.

15

The men from COSATU

*'The SP says, his people are saying,
what have his initiatives brought him . . .?'*

ON 19 December, Mandela received a visit from a COSATU delegation comprising Cyril Ramaphosa, Chris Dlamini, Moses Mayekiso, John Gomomo and Sydney Mufamadi. A handwritten summary of their discussion appears in the archive. It is written in Afrikaans. A translation appears below.

1. 913 praises COSATU for its good work. 913 says they are not going to wait for 'liberation' by the government, the nation will liberate itself.
2. 913 says he wants to discuss three things with them, namely:
   – The issue of the political 'lifers'
   – The issue of a meeting between the ANC and the Government
   – The meeting with the SP [State President]
3. 913 gives a document to one of the visitors (possibly Ramaphosa) to give to Alfred Nzo. This is apparently the document that 913 gave to the SP and 913's summary of the 'response' (SP).
4. 913 says the SP will bring changes – he is serious. The Government is modernising apartheid without breaking it down. He (913) must deal with this. Apartheid will not be abolished in a few days, but a reasonable period must be stipulated.
5. 913 says if the Government agrees to meet the conditions imposed by the ANC, then they (ANC) can decide to negotiate. I (913) want to report this.
6. 913 says the SP has initiatives, the release of political prisoners and other initiatives, but the ANC is asking for violence to be stepped up. He (SP) says his people are saying, what have his initiatives brought

163

him [*wat het dit hom in die sak gebring*]. 913 says he will discuss this with the National Executive.
7. A visitor says they are receiving many applications from TV people to interview 913. 913 says he doesn't want to do this now, not before his release. 913 says it will be a mistake to make statements from prison.
8. A visitor says Peter Soal of the DP [Democratic Party] wants to see him. 913 says he must submit an application.

As it turns out, these cryptic notes constitute a vital link in the story told by the Coetsee archive. Firstly, they cast light on a document that features prominently in further communications between Mandela and Lusaka. Secondly, they convey Mandela's perception that De Klerk is serious about reform. Thirdly, they convey Mandela's belief that, should the government agree to meet the conditions laid down by the ANC (effectively the Harare Declaration), the ANC should negotiate. He adds that he wants to convey this to Lusaka.

Fourthly, they provide an extraordinary insight into the gist of the conversation between Mandela and De Klerk. Effectively, Mandela tells his visitors, De Klerk argued that continued calls by the ANC to step up the armed struggle were weakening his credibility and undermining his reform programme. Mandela seems to share this view, and expresses his intention to discuss this with the ANC's National Executive Committee.

16

A long-distance phone call

'I can come to Lusaka to see you and our comrades . . . you could come here, that is, whatever representative you might appoint for that purpose . . . we could meet you at a mutual spot . . . or we could use a go-between, an intermediary . . .'

LATER THE SAME DAY, on 19 December, Mandela spoke by phone to Alfred Nzo and Thabo Mbeki in Lusaka. It was the first direct contact between him and the ANC in exile; the first time he had spoken to Nzo in almost thirty years; and perhaps the first time he had ever spoken to Mbeki. It was the first of three telephone conversations between Mandela and key figures in Lusaka in the increasingly intense period leading up to early February 1990. A seemingly accurate transcript of the conversation appears in the Coetsee archive. Highlights of this historic call appear below.

913: Oh, hallo Alfi . . .

Nzo: Madiba . . .

913: How are you? [Laughter at both ends.]

Nzo: Very well indeed. How are you?

913: All right. How is Regina [Mrs Nzo]?

Nzo: She is fine, thank you.

913: Oh, very good. How are the children?

Nzo: No, they are fine.

913: No, that is very good.

913: Man . . . let me not delay very much. How is Oliver [Tambo]?

Nzo: He is slightly better, Madiba. We are expecting today that he might come out of the clinic. And in the next few days he will be getting to Sweden. For further management, you see.

913: Oh, that's good . . . That is very good. . . . I am happy about that.

Mandela expresses concern about Oliver Tambo, then in a clinic in Sweden after his stroke, and they discuss the possibility that his wife, Adelaide, would come to live with him when he returns to Harare.

Mandela then tells Nzo he has been trying to get in touch with him for several days. As Nzo is aware, he met F.W. de Klerk the previous Wednesday. At the end of the meeting, he told the President it would be necessary for him to get in touch with Nzo, to find out how to report on a proposal that came out of the meeting. This time, he thought it was worth reporting to the National Executive Committee. De Klerk delegated this matter to Coetsee, who authorised the call to Lusaka. Mandela goes on to say that Cyril Ramaphosa and four others visited him earlier the same day, and that he briefed Ramaphosa about the proposal.

> Of course, I did not discuss the report itself. I merely discussed with him the importance of me getting in touch with you, and more or less the importance of what I was to discuss with you.
>
> Now, I don't know how you want me to do it? . . . I have merely informed him so that when you consider with your colleagues how we should arrange the report . . . you should know just what it is, in the sense of the nature of the proposal that came out.
>
> Now, I can come to Lusaka to see you and your comrades, our comrades. The advantage of coming to Lusaka would be that I would see as many people as you want me to see. The other alternative is that you could come here, that is, whatever representative you might appoint for that purpose . . . or alternatively we could meet you at a mutual spot . . . or we could use a go-between, an intermediary . . . or I could send a written report, whichever you prefer. That is the position.
>
> Nzo: Yes . . . I see . . .

Mandela goes on to say that on 4 December he was visited by the new Commissioner of Police, Major-General Johan van der Merwe, together with General Smit, the national head of security. The next day, he was visited by the team of government officials with whom he was engaged in discussions.

> You have got the particulars of their names. Dr Niël Barnard has been phased out, you know, I have not met him since Mr De Klerk took over. But the other three are still there. And they visited me on the 5th, and then on the 12th . . . And the following day I saw the State President . . . that would indicate to you the importance of the matter . . .
>
> But Cyril will give you a further briefing. I would suggest that you should in the first place get a report from him. And then when you have got the report and considered it, you can come back to me . . . There is an element of urgency about the matter. Because eventually I will have to report back to the State President . . .

Mandela gives Nzo a code and telephone number, and tells him to ask for a Major Marais. Marais would come to call him (Mandela), who lived four kilometres away from the prison. They would then phone Nzo back.

> Nzo: I see . . . so then, Madiba, the scenario is that we should try to get Cyril.
> 913: Yes . . . I am sure he will get you before you do. Perhaps he will phone you first thing in the morning, or he may be trying to phone you now – we don't know.
> Nzo: He phoned earlier and spoke to Thabo. He told us to be here at this time (in Xhosa).
> 913: Oh, I see.
> Nzo: Thabo said they must phone tomorrow (in Xhosa).
> 913: Where is Thabo?
> Nzo: He is here (in Xhosa).
> 913: Let me just say hello to him, man!
> Nzo: O.K., all right, Madiba.
> 913: Hallo, Thabo, how are you? How are you?
> Mbeki: Fine, thanks, and how are you?
> 913: When are you coming to fetch me?

Mbeki: I am ready to come in the morning. [Laughter] . . . Can I come in the morning?

913: Man, you can, I want you to come now.

Mbeki: I am ready to move. [Laughter]

913: Very good.

Mbeki: But you are well.

913: No, I am quite well, Thabo.

Mbeki: Ja, that's good, and everybody has been reporting that . . .

////

The phone conversation contains some new information, first touched on in Mandela's conversations with Chikane and the delegation from COSATU. Firstly, Mandela confirms that a 'proposal' emerged from the meeting between him and De Klerk. He then envisages a discussion with the ANC, and sets out a startling array of options for doing so, including his travelling to Lusaka, the ANC sending a representative to visit him in South Africa, or a meeting at a mutually agreed location – all with the anticipated cooperation of the South African authorities.

The conversation does not give any indication of the nature of the proposals. It also implies that at least some have not been put in writing. All this will be explored later.

More generally, this and later conversations with Lusaka reveal that Mandela expected he would report back to De Klerk at least once, and that he might even have expected a series of meetings with De Klerk in which they would refine a combined strategy for dealing with the political transition. In the event, he never saw De Klerk again before 9 February, only to be abruptly informed – to Mandela's intense discomfort – that he would be released two days later. Again, though, a lot of water was first going to flow under the bridge.

17

The ANC takes stock

*'Whether the potential for a political settlement
is transformed into reality remains the urgent responsibility
of the Pretoria regime . . .'*

JUST MORE THAN a week later, on 8 January, the ANC released its traditional annual statement commemorating the founding of the organisation. While largely couched in the usual militant rhetoric, there was more to the statement than met the eye. Given that publishing ANC statements in South Africa was illegal at that time, it was not publicly available, and many people remained unaware of its contents. For these and other reasons that will become clear later on, it is worth recalling.

The statement acknowledged that change was in the offing. Yet the moment harboured the potential for change as well as the danger of a 'bloodbath'. The outcome would depend on the 'balance of forces', the steadfastness of the democratic movement, and the 'wisdom of all the people of our country'.

The NP had also spoken of a commitment to end apartheid. 'However, its leaders should understand if we remain unconvinced and sceptical, and demand that they translate their words into actions.'

Democratic forces had put forward a proposal for the political resolution of the conflict in the form of the Harare Declaration. So far, Pretoria's response to this historic proposal had amounted to nothing more than political gamesmanship, and it remained for the Pretoria regime to create a climate conducive to negotiations.

'In putting forward this universally accepted demand, we are not asking for special favours. We are asking that all those who should participate in any process of negotiations should enjoy equal political opportunities.'

Whether the potential for a political settlement was transformed into reality remained the urgent responsibility of the Pretoria regime. For its part, the ANC was committed to seizing any real opportunity to seek a political agreement for a speedy end of the apartheid system.

In the meantime, the conditions that had obliged the ANC to take up arms remained unchanged. The ANC remained an illegal organisation. Membership of the ANC was a treasonable offence. The state of emergency continued, and a series of repressive laws remained on the statute books. It had no constitutional means to change the government of the day.

'These observations are important in the context of the undertaking we have made, as reflected in the Harare Declaration, that we are ready to enter into an agreement with the Pretoria regime for a mutual suspension of hostilities as soon as a climate conducive to negotiations is created. Given our history and the practical situation in our country, we cannot be expected to surrender our weapons until an agreement to end apartheid has been arrived at.

'In this respect, we must make it clear that the Harare Declaration is not and was not meant to be a substitute for other forms of struggle, including our armed offensive . . . The armed struggle continues to be a critical and decisive component of our strategy. . . .'[1]

While reaffirming the ANC's formal commitment to the armed struggle, the statement also displayed a new emphasis on negotiations and adopted a more conciliatory and moderate tone – for instance, by appealing to whites and blacks alike to work together to end apartheid. Also significant was a reference to Mandela as a 'disciplined and committed member and leader of the ANC'. This seemed to be a deliberate effort to legitimise Mandela's position and quell uncertainty and disquiet about his status and actions in the organisation.

////

Winnie Mandela visited 'Prisoner 913' on the same day. A handwritten summary of the conversation appears on the standard form for monitoring conversations. A translation from the Afrikaans appears below.

1. Winnie says they have spoken to *Time* Magazine. They are preparing for 913's release. Winnie hands him a document from *Time* Magazine.
2. 913 tells Winnie about an impending visit from a group of prisoners from Johannesburg. Winnie expresses her surprise.
3. 913 talks about the daughter of a school friend who wants her brother to return to SA as well as to the organisation.
4. Winnie says the MDM wants to handle the Stompie [Seipei] question with her behind closed doors, but SAYCO [the South African Youth Congress] says no. A fight is now going on between the leaders as a result of the release of the so-called leaders. Winnie says she is not emotionally ready to handle this situation.

A note on the form reads:

1. They go outside. A stereo recording of this part of the conversation has been made. Contact has been made with NI [National Intelligence] to get the transcript as soon as possible.

18

Things hot up in Lusaka

> 'Well, you see I have put the matter to them very clearly that
> I do want to come out. Not next year, but I want to come out today,
> that is what I have said to them. That is what I said to the SP
> when I met him because he asked me the question pointedly.
> I told him that I wanted to be released immediately. . . .'

A WEEK LATER, Govan and Epainette Mbeki, Walter and Albertina Sisulu, Kathy Kathrada, Elias Motsoaledi and other political prisoners released in October flew to Lusaka. It was the first time the ANC's old and new leadership were united in almost thirty years. They were accompanied by an MDM contingent which included Chris Dlamini and Cyril Ramaphosa. The group attended a welcoming meeting in the Mulungushi Hall and a state reception given by President Kenneth Kaunda.[1] Following reunions and talks with ANC leaders, they were due to attend an extended meeting of the National Executive Committee (NEC) stretching over three days, from 19 to 21 January. Clearly, it was a vital gathering that would have a major bearing on the ANC's fortunes going forward. Lusaka was jam-packed with journalists.

////

Two days after their arrival, on Wednesday, 17 January, Thabo Mbeki phoned Mandela from Lusaka. The conversation was recorded, and a typed transcript stamped 'GEHEIM/SECRET' appears in the Coetsee archive. Both Mandela and Mbeki seemed aware that the conversation was being taped; at one point Mbeki tried to evade the monitors by speaking in Xhosa. These passages were translated into English. Extracts from the transcript appear below.

913: Hallo?

Mbeki: Hallo, Uncle Nel.

913: Oh, hallo, Thabo, how are you?

Mbeki: I am fine, thanks, and how are you?

913: O.K. You chaps must be very busy, hey?

Mbeki: Somebody took the car . . .

913: That's all right, you don't have to explain. It is an accomplishment that you are able to get free and to phone down here. So don't worry about that.

Mbeki: O.K., sir. I phoned yesterday in connection with the newspapers. They speculate that you are coming out either today or some time this week. (Note in the transcript: *Xhosa vertaal na Engels [Xhosa translated into English]*)

913: Oh?

Mbeki: The NEC said I should check on that.

913: No, it is not correct at all. I have been given no date. It is difficult to discuss these things over the telephone. I do think that it is imminent, but it is going to depend on a lot of things, like our reaction to the . . . hallo, hallo . . . I say it is going to depend on a lot of things which I could explain if we were speaking under conditions of confidentiality. The speculation that I am going out either today or in a week's time is very wild. I don't think it is going to come within the next month or so.

Mbeki: What I was then asked to convey to you was that everybody is here now.

913: Yes . . .

Mbeki: . . . and that it would be a very good thing if you could be here too.

913: I see. Yes.

Mbeki: Then the problem is . . . the view is that it would be better . . .

913: Hallo?

Mbeki: Hallo?

913: Hallo, yes?

Mbeki: Yes, it would be a very good thing if you could be here now, seeing that everybody is here.

913: Yes . . .

Mbeki: . . . But that would mean that you would not return to prison.

913: [Laughs] I see!

Mbeki: That would not be right, if you came from prison and went back to prison from here.

913: Yes, quite, I agree with that. I agree with that, it certainly would not be proper. I would have been very keen to have been there, when others are there. In fact, right from the beginning when the Ministers came to tell me that they were going to be released, I then raised the question of them going to Lusaka to report. Then of course the questions of their passports, we went into it and I am very happy that everything went smoothly. I felt I was there when I saw them leaving Jan Smuts [airport], and the welcome that side. I really felt that I am in prison . . . I really felt that I should have been there too.

It will not be possible because there is no question of my release now for reasons which have perhaps been conveyed to you by Govan and Walter and others because they are more or less aware of the position. I will be able to fill up the latest developments in regard to release. You can take it that it is not in the coming week or the next couple of weeks. They are still going to take some time, I think. Now . . . hallo? Hallo?

Mbeki: [something like]: They can't do it now?

913: Well, you see, I have put the matter to them very clearly that I do want to come out. Not next year, but I want to come out today, that is what I have said to them. That is what I said to the SP when I met him because he asked me the question pointedly. I told him that I wanted to be released immediately.

I did of course spell out the problems. I said that if I am released I will go to Lusaka to report and I will tell Lusaka that I am coming out with empty hands, they have put nothing in my hands, I said that there would be problems about that and I spelled them out. I said nevertheless that I want to come out, the ball is in their court.

I think they are now going into the question of making it easy for me to come out. It would have been very useful if we could meet, but I don't know how we can do it. It would be very good if we could meet so that I could brief you on the latest position, [but] there is no question of coming over there because I will come back to prison. The other alternative would be that a representative group could come down here, but that also has serious problems.

Mbeki: That is right.

913: It would be very difficult even to keep it quiet because you will have to have safe conduct, you have to have a visa, and a clerk could blurt it out. Hallo, hallo?

Mbeki: Yes, I agree.

913: Then there could be a go-between. The other alternative is to write a full report and send it to you. There is an element of urgency because I think the SP wants to make some announcement relating to this question on the 2nd of February. Already I think they are expecting that I would have some feedback from you before that. I don't know just how we will do it, you know, what would suit you.

Mbeki: Well, Uncle, I don't know if you have seen the January statement . . .

913: Yes, yes, I have seen it.

Mbeki: You have seen it?

913: Yes, they gave it to me. I asked for it and I was given [the statement].

Mbeki: Oh, I see. We tried to address a very serious issue, a lot of the questions we understand, we understand that they were expressing their concern. Questions like . . . you know, giving them something . . . like not claiming victory . . .

913: Yes, quite! Yes.

Mbeki: So we didn't, and recognised the advances that have been made.

913: Yes . . .

Mbeki: . . . and restated the point about a commitment to a negotiated solution . . .

913: Yes. I think that the statement is a very good one, but what is the position about the proposal that emerged from the meeting with the SP of a simultaneous declaration?

Mbeki: Yes, I . . .

913: I think if that could be done, they could comply fully with all our conditions.

Mbeki: Yes. We are discussing that because we think that all of the other people from home ought to be here so we are all of us discussing that question tomorrow.

913: You see, I think that if we agreed on a simultaneous declaration, I think all the conditions we have set up would be complied with. It would then not be necessary for us to meet, except to work out the procedures to be adopted to make sure that that declaration is done to the satisfaction of all the parties. I don't think it will be necessary at all, and I think then the way will be cleared. I could be able to say that I am on the verge of being released. We could then discuss other matters after I am released.

Mbeki: No, then that is clear.

913: You see, the question of . . . on the prisoners was the only one which was more or less a hitch. The definition of the concept of a political prisoner. I then suggested that this matter should be discussed directly with the ANC. All the others, I don't think there is going to be any problems at all. We are also addressing the question of those on death row, we are addressing that question. It does not appear to me that there is any urgency about us meeting if we are agreeable to a simultaneous declaration, that the Government must make a declaration to meet all the conditions, and we make a declaration committing ourselves to a peaceful solution at the same time.

Mbeki: O.K. Yes. No, that is clear.

913: It would certainly be no problem.

Mbeki: All right, so then, so we should not push for your release next week?

913: No, no, no. It is just out of the question. It is just out of the question. Thabo?

Mbeki: Yes, Uncle Nel?

913: There is a statement, I don't know if you saw it, that I no longer believe in nationalisation of industries and in state control of industry and business. Have you seen that statement?

Mbeki: No, I saw a headline in the local press here yesterday, but I did not read the article.

913: It is absolutely nothing of the sort! [Note: *skerp* (sharply)] In fact, I sent a message yesterday to Cyril Ramaphosa and also to Dullah Omar and suggesting how the matter should be handled. There is just no truth in that at all.

Mbeki: I will speak to Dullah, and Cyril is here.

913: Oh, is he there?

Mbeki: He is here, yes.

913: Oh, that is good. What about Sydney Mufamadi?

Mbeki: He is also here.

913: Oh I see. Then I don't know, but I sent a message to them and you can speak to them and then speak to Dullah.

Mbeki: O.K. Fine.

913: Yes. Well, otherwise, Thabo, man, I am very happy to hear your voice and I am very happy that you were able to meet all the old chaps. It must be a very great moment for all of you.

Mbeki: Yes, it is. They are all in very good shape.

913: Yes, man! They look very well, they look very, very well.

Mbeki: Yes, Uncle Nel, if there are any developments I will try and phone you again.

913: Very good. It is very good that you phoned because I was intending contacting you on Sunday night because I thought that by then the pressure will be a little reduced. I will be very happy if you phone me back when of course you have taken a decision, because if there is that simultaneous declaration, then I think everything will be very clear.

Mbeki: O.K.

913: Yes.

Mbeki: I will certainly call you back.

913: No, very good. Thabo, regards to everybody.

Mbeki: I will do that.

913: Tell the family to look after you, hey? [Laughs] O.K., Thabo.

Mbeki: Good. Very good to hear your voice.

913: It is very good to hear your voice too . . .

They go on to discuss O.R. Tambo, who suffered a stroke while working on the Harare Declaration the previous year, and was by then recuperating in a clinic in Sweden.

////

This conversation is another vital link in the chain of events revealed by the Coetsee archive. It emerges that, while Mandela believed his release was 'imminent', he was still uncertain about when he would be released, and under what conditions. This would depend on complex and sensitive negotiations, also involving the ANC in exile. This was urgent, because he thought De Klerk wanted to make 'some announcement' on 2 February. Before then, feedback was required from Lusaka.

Startlingly, it appears that a proposal had emerged from his meeting with De Klerk for a 'simultaneous declaration' by the NP government and the ANC. While the proposed terms were not fully spelled out, they appeared to involve the government committing itself to meeting the ANC's preconditions for constitutional negotiations as spelled out in the Harare Declaration, and Mandela and the ANC committing themselves to a 'peaceful solution'. Whether this was meant to include a formal suspension of the armed struggle is unclear.

Some kind of proposal to that effect had been sent to Lusaka. Mandela expected the NEC to make a decision about it and provide him with a reply by that Sunday, 21 October – presumably after the extended meeting of the NEC.

Mandela appeared to believe that there were no major obstacles to a simultaneous declaration. In his view, the only remaining hitch was an issue surrounding the release of 'political prisoners' – in other words, the looming issue of amnesty. He also seemed to believe he could effectively control the entire process surrounding his release – including the outcome of the NEC meeting – from Victor Verster Prison. In turn, Mbeki revealed that the ANC had moderated its traditional January 8 statement in response to the NP government's proposals.

////

In the event, Mbeki was less than frank with Mandela about what was happening in Lusaka. Specifically, Mandela's seemingly rosy notion of a happy reunion between the Robben Island veterans and the ANC in exile in Lusaka as well as a series of collegial discussions was materially misguided. Instead, the ANC was in crisis, and this spilled over to the visit by the released prisoners as well. In what follows, we largely follow an excellent account by the historian Thula Simpson.[2]

The crisis was largely triggered by the tripartite agreement between the governments of Angola, Cuba and South Africa signed in New York in December 1988, which provided for Namibian independence and the withdrawal of South African and Cuban forces from Angola.[3] While – at the time – the implications were not widely known or understood, the parties also agreed that they would no longer allow their territories to be used for 'acts of violence' against other countries in the region. In practice, this obliged the Angolan government to terminate its military support for the ANC. In concrete terms, this meant the ANC had to shut down its military camps in Angola.

Accordingly, in January 1989, Tambo announced that MK cadres in military camps in Angola would be relocated to Uganda, Tanzania and Ethiopia. In practice, however, many cadres were moved to Zambia, where the ANC was allowed to maintain 'transit' residences for MK operatives headed for South Africa.

179

At the time of the 1989 influx, Simpson writes, morale among MK members in Zambia was very low. Cadres expected to stay for a few weeks before proceeding to South Africa. However, they ended up staying much longer – in some cases, as long as two or three years. The ANC in Lusaka was divided into two categories. 'Regular' residents lived in middle-class areas, in houses with electricity, fridges, stoves and television sets. But members of MK lived in poor townships, in accommodation without electricity and often with no mattresses.

Regular ANC residents were provided with incomes which enabled them to buy their own goods. However, MK members only received 'underground supplies' of meat and vegetables provided by the regional military command. Marooned in Lusaka, with little prospect of being sent home, MK operatives became hostile towards their superiors. Despite frequent complaints, nothing was done to improve their situation. By 1989, representatives of the military command could not enter some MK locations for fear of being abused or even assaulted.

MK cadres in Lusaka were still better off than those sent into South Africa. By 1989, as Bill Anderson, an ANC Military Intelligence officer, later recounted, MK was in a state of 'absolute chaos', with cadres deployed without briefings, without proper documents, and even without proper clothing. Because the number of MK operations was perceived to be declining, intelligence staffers were told there was 'one objective and one alone', namely to 'make the graph of actions go up, irrespective of what actions were undertaken, irrespective of losing cadres, and so on'. Of about 240 MK cadres deployed from Zambia in 1989, a third had defected, a third were captured or killed, and a third were 'somehow in place, whether active or drifting'. In most cases, no proper communications were established, so nobody was too sure of the status of the last-named group.

From late 1986 onwards, MK suffered an 'almost 100 percent casualty rate' among those it sent into South Africa from Zimbabwe, defined in terms of people killed or arrested within 24 hours.⁴ Faced with the prospect of certain death in these 'ill-prepared, ill-planned missions', many MK cadres in Zimbabwe either deserted or defected. Moreover, the MK structures in neighbouring states were heavily infiltrated by double agents, making it hazardous for MK to operate in those territories.

Under these circumstances, there was widespread criticism of MK's commander, Joe Modise. In 1989, MK's record came under withering fire at a meeting of the Politico-Military Council, the organ responsible for pursuing the ANC's revolutionary struggle. Modise offered to resign, but this was turned down, and the discussion was abruptly terminated.

Poor conditions led to growing tensions within Zambia. Following several incidents of violence involving Zambian citizens, ANC security, in cooperation with Zambian security forces, disarmed MK guerrillas in Lusaka. Next a series of bomb attacks took place on ANC houses. At first it was assumed that the attacks had been carried out by South African agents, but the perpetrators turned out to be four ANC dissidents who had applied for refugee status with the United Nations High Commissioner for Refugees (UNHCR) in Zambia, and who were waiting to be resettled. Their arrest by the ANC infuriated the Zambian government as well as the UNHCR, which claimed they had been abducted, and demanded their release.

A relative of the four men claimed that 32 South African exiles in Zambia had been arrested and beaten by ANC security personnel, and that the dissidents' aim was to highlight the lack of democracy and poor conditions within the ANC in exile. At the same time, 12 defectors from the ANC fighting deportation from Sweden made similar charges of abuse within the movement.

According to a British newspaper, Kaunda then gave the ANC an ultimatum to leave Zambia, telling it that only a diplomatic mission would be allowed to remain. However, both parties realised they could not afford to fall out at that particular time. Among other things, African leaders were due to meet at an OAU summit in Harare on 21–22 August to discuss the ANC's preconditions for engaging in negotiations with the South African government (which turned into the Harare Declaration). On the basis of their common interest, the two parties acted to defuse the crisis.

The four men detained by the ANC in connection with the bombings were handed to the Zambian authorities, and the ANC and Zambian government acted to discredit the reports of an ANC expulsion, dismissing them as 'utter rubbish' and a 'malicious ploy to try and drive a wedge between the ANC and the Zambian government'. The ANC and Zambia succeeded in getting their line established that the withdrawal of MK soldiers was being undertaken by mutual consent, in place of the damaging reports of an irate Zambia kicking MK out of the country.

Despite this, an exodus of MK guerrillas from Zambia was taking place. This had huge implications for the armed struggle, because while Zambia could still be used as a 'transit route' to South Africa, the infiltration of large numbers of guerrillas was no longer a feasible option. In the aftermath of the expulsions from Angola, and the Nkomati Accord of 1984 in which the Mozambican government agreed to deny the ANC the use of its territory as a transit route, MK military camps in Tanzania and Uganda faced a 'swathe of territory stretching from the Atlantic to the Indian oceans'. Under these circumstances, Simpson concludes, 'it was impossible for the ANC to intensify its armed struggle within South Africa'.

This was the setting in which the eight veteran Robben Islanders and others from South Africa arrived in Lusaka.

////

A mass meeting was called to celebrate their arrival. The ANC leadership tried to prevent MK cadres from attending, declaring that a separate event would be arranged for them. However, this attempt failed, and the meeting ended up being controlled by MK cadres who used the opportunity to air their grievances. Their criticisms were acclaimed by the audience as a whole.

When Raymond Mhlaba – who had briefly served as MK commander in 1973 – went up on stage, everyone cheered and referred to him as 'Commander'. Someone in the audience stood up and asked him to resume his post, because 'MK had no leader'. Others rose and asked the existing leadership to account for MK's high casualty rate. Eventually one cadre stood up, pointed to the ANC leaders on the platform, and declared that if they truly wanted to represent the rank and file, they should all resign. The hall 'erupted in cheers of approval'.[5]

This did not prevent the ANC from maintaining its public rhetoric about the armed struggle. When, earlier the same day, the eight Robben Islanders arrived in Lusaka, Chris Hani, MK chief of staff, waited to receive them on the airport tarmac. He told assembled reporters that all forms of struggle had to be escalated, and there was a need for a lot more military pressure. 'Not even the release of Nelson Mandela,' he proclaimed, 'would spare the government MK's wrath.'

A different picture emerged when the extended NEC meeting started on 19 January, two days after Mandela's conversation with Mbeki. The ANC's secretary-general, Alfred Nzo, who had been serving as acting president since Tambo's stroke, made what analysts described as 'an extraordinary gaffe'.

At the opening ceremony, which was open to the public, he mistakenly delivered a speech intended for a closed session of the meeting. In front of an audience that included the international press corps as well as Kaunda, he asked whether the ANC should 'call it a day' as far as the armed struggle was concerned in the event of the organisation being unbanned, and operate 'solely as a legal movement', or whether it should continue to maintain 'some underground units' in South Africa.

He then said the armed struggle should continue, but added: 'Looking at our situation realistically, we must admit that we do not have the capacity . . . to intensify the armed struggle in any meaningful way . . .'⁶

The NEC continued its deliberations behind closed doors, and issued a statement on 21 January. Mandela and Mbeki spoke again the following day.

19

A tale of two statements

'Thabo, is there anything to say? . . .'

ON Monday, 22 January – the day after the conclusion of the extended NEC meeting in Lusaka – Mandela and Thabo Mbeki spoke again on the phone. As agreed in their conversation a few days earlier, Mandela wanted to know whether the NEC had adopted his proposals, and whether this was reflected in the statement released after the meeting. Again, a typed transcript of the call resides in the Coetsee archive.

Mandela enquires after the 'old chaps' (Sisulu and his colleagues). Mbeki explains that they are attending a summit of the Frontline States in Lusaka. From there, they would go to Tanzania, and from then to visit O.R. Tambo in Sweden. They would then return home.

Mandela then asks Mbeki: 'Is there anything to say?' Mbeki responds, but the line is bad and the conversation is unclear. Mandela eventually rings off and phones back. Mbeki then reads him two passages from the statement issued after the meeting. This is a laborious process. At one point, Mandela says: 'Man, Thabo, I can't hear you. I can just hear the first word. Speak louder, just shout . . .' He then repeats everything read out to him, and also writes it down.

The first passage states that the meeting reaffirmed the ANC's preference for a settlement arrived at by political means. 'The ANC has held this position from its very foundation. It has, throughout the 78 years of its existence, done everything it could to prevail on successive white minority regimes to adopt the same position, to no avail.

'The meeting reaffirmed that our commitment to these positions is not in doubt. It is fundamental to the nature of the ANC as a movement which seeks democracy, peace and justice for all. At the same time, the process of ending apartheid through negotiations requires that the Pretoria regime should itself also demonstrate its commitment to a political solution by taking the necessary actions which would make such a solution possible.

'The meeting warned that no solution can be arrived at while the apartheid regime seeks to impose its will on the majority of our people and their representatives. A negotiated settlement must address the fundamental aspirations of all the people of our country, with those aspirations having been expressed by the people themselves in open political activity and debate. The Nationalist Party and its government therefore need to take a decisive step forward by meeting the conditions for the creation of a climate conducive to negotiations, and recognise the central importance of the genuine representatives of the people of our country.'

Mbeki then reads Mandela another, earlier passage, which states that the meeting reaffirmed the significance of the Harare and UN declarations as the basis for a political settlement. In keeping with those declarations, no negotiations could take place until the necessary climate had been created. The meeting reaffirmed the importance of the immediate and unconditional release of Nelson Mandela and other political prisoners. It also paid tribute to 'our dear comrade and fellow leader, Comrade Nelson Mandela', and expressed its full support for his continuing actions even from within prison, which were fully in keeping with the policies and objectives of the movement.

Mbeki indicates that the first passage was considered to be a response to Mandela's proposal. The conversation then proceeds as follows:

913: Yes. Man, Thabo, I think the executive has handled the matter very well. Give them my congratulations. I have no doubt that by taking this resolution, we have not only complied with the actual proposal itself, but we have really opened the way forward. It is not easy to discuss these matters over the telephone, but my own impression is that there is going to be full compliance by the Government with the condition that we have put. I have no doubt about that, although it is a risky thing to say. From the discussion I have had with them, it seems clear that there is going to be full compliance . . .

Mandela asks Mbeki whether he has listened to statements by Adriaan Vlok (then Minister of Police) and generals Van der Merwe and Smit, which came over the news that morning. Mbeki says he hasn't, but will get them immediately.

> 913: It is clear that they are opening the way for the statement the State President wants to make when he opens parliament. I am happy that we have responded so constructively and so positively. I am looking forward to meeting the SP again. I have a very powerful instruction to put forward, which I am happy to do. I think that we have done very well.
>
> Mbeki: Thank you.
>
> 913: I must congratulate you and other members of the executive for the excellent way in which you are handling matters.
>
> Mbeki: I will go back to them now and report to them.
>
> 913: Yes, give them my regards and compliments to Alfred [Nzo] and Joe [Modise] and to the whole executive and also my colleagues from the country, Walter and the others, and tell them I am happy to receive this report. I am sure everybody in the country will be happy when it is released.
>
> Mbeki: O.K., thanks a lot. I will do that immediately.

The passages Mbeki read out to Mandela were accurate, and conformed with the formal statement issued after the meeting.[1] Mandela laboriously wrote out a fair copy of the two passages read to him, a copy of which also appears in the Coetsee archive. A handwritten note on the document, seemingly made and signed by General Willemse and dated 27 January 1990, states: 'Document which 913 undertook to make available to the Minister.'

What Mbeki did not tell Mandela was that the NEC had also declared that the armed struggle should continue and be intensified. 'Having carefully assessed the situation within the country,' the statement said, 'the meeting reaffirmed that the conditions which forced the ANC to resort to armed struggle have not changed. This situation continues to make the struggle a key component of our strategy.

'. . . All necessary measures must be taken to strengthen our army within its theatre of operations so that it can carry out its noble tasks with even greater effectiveness.' It went on to say, though, that the meeting had reiterated the commitment of the ANC to 'negotiate and agree to a mutual suspension of hostilities as provided for in the Harare Declaration'.

Whether inadvertent or deliberate, the omission of this passage had significant consequences, as did the statement itself. As previously agreed, Mandela sent his handwritten version of the statement to Coetsee and Viljoen. However, they found it did not correspond with the media reports, and confronted Mandela about this during a meeting on Thursday, 1 February – the day before De Klerk's historic speech in parliament.

According to Thula Simpson, De Klerk was 'enraged' by the public statements made by ANC spokesmen in Zambia during the visit. 'He was looking for a clear indication that the movement was committed to achieving peaceful solutions. Instead, a torrent of belligerence spewed forth. Reports in the media quoted official sources as saying that an unhappy De Klerk was having second thoughts about unbanning the ANC.'[2]

On Friday, 26 January, the *New York Times* reported: 'After a cabinet meeting on Wednesday, the President and fellow ministers were said to have deferred a final decision on Mr Mandela's release, apparently because of dissatisfaction with a weekend statement by an ANC meeting in Lusaka that reaffirmed the commitment to armed struggle.'[3]

And on 2 February – the day of De Klerk's address in parliament – the *Christian Science Monitor* reported: 'On the eve of a major policy speech, President F.W. de Klerk was yesterday due to hold a last-minute meeting with jailed ANC leader Nelson Mandela.' The government did not release details of the meeting, but official sources said its primary purpose was to discuss sticking points that had arisen in plans for Mr Mandela's release.

A senior government source said the meeting could have a 'significant impact' on the final draft of De Klerk's speech. 'Government officials have indicated that the ANC has not gone far enough in committing itself to a peaceful negotiating process. And a renewed wave of defiance and protest by anti-apartheid groups appears to have further weakened De Klerk's hand in the cabinet.'

Earlier in the week, the *Financial Mail* reported that the cabinet had rejected two earlier proposals from some of its members to release Mandela – first before Christmas, and again four days earlier. However, other official sources said he was likely to be released on 9 February.[4]

In the event, Mandela did not see De Klerk on 1 February. This emerges from two accounts by Mandela of this chain of events which appear in the Coetsee archive. The first is a transcript of a visit by Winnie Mandela on Sunday, 4 February – two days after De Klerk's address in parliament.

Mandela first tells Winnie that the planned visit to F.W. de Klerk did not take place, because news leaked out, and the press followed the convoy from Victor Verster Prison. Instead of Tuynhuys, they went to the house of the Commissioner of Prisons at Pollsmoor, and Coetsee and Viljoen visited him there. They told him what De Klerk would say the next day.

Mandela then tells her that Thabo Mbeki had made a mistake. 'The ministers said the NEC should respond. I said they had already responded. They said, no, the ANC had again declared that the armed struggle should continue. The ministers got this [the NEC statement] from Sapa Reuters, and showed it to me.' He goes on to say: 'We should be careful about what we say in the press. Thabo should have read the whole statement to me.' Winnie agrees, saying: 'It was a mistake on Thabo's side.'

On Friday, 9 February – just two days before Mandela's release – he also told a UDF delegation about this incident in the course of reporting back about his activities. Following his meeting with De Klerk in December, he says, he told Coetsee and Viljoen that he would need to report back to the ANC, and then spoke with Alfred Nzo and Thabo Mbeki. The latter phoned back and said they had accepted the 'compromise' (an apparent reference to the proposals he had sent to the ANC).

Viljoen told him that they had not, and had announced that they were stepping up the armed struggle. He [Mandela] disputed this, saying, 'Thabo had never said it.' He looked again at the statement that night (presumably his record of the statement Mbeki had read to him over the phone), and could not find it. He then asked Viljoen to send him a copy. While the transcript does not state this explicitly, Mandela implied that he was forced to concede that Viljoen was right. He then restated his own position.

20

Things go south

> 'It is proper that all who read this document recall that it was written by a courageous man while still a prisoner . . .'

ON 26 JANUARY 1990, the Cape community newspaper *South* published extracts from Mandela's memorandum to P.W. Botha, written in early 1989. It attracted widespread interest; as the *Washington Post* pointed out in an editorial on 28 January, it was the first substantive public statement by Mandela in 25 years. Various overseas newspapers – including the *New York Times* – published lengthy summaries of the document on the same day.[1]

It also created a lot of confusion, and caused a stir within the ANC. Most members of the ANC and the broader liberation movement still had no inkling that Mandela had been talking to the South African government, which the memorandum openly reveals. In the febrile situation in mid- to late January 1990, it added to fears and suspicions in the resistance movement both internally and abroad about Mandela's rumoured interactions with Pretoria.

The political process had also moved on in style and substance since Mandela and his colleagues had written the memorandum. Notably, his proposals for a two-stage approach to negotiations had been superseded by the Harare Declaration. Effectively, the memorandum had been overtaken, but it was difficult to convey this to the public as well as to the rank and file of the ANC.

According to a report in the *New York Times*, Ismail Ayob, one of the Mandela family's lawyers, said the document had been given to *South* two months previously. With Mandela's release apparently imminent, lawyers who visited him in prison the previous day – on Wednesday, 24 January – conveyed an appeal from the newspaper for the document's release. According to Ayob, Mandela responded by saying that he had 'reservations', but that he would not prohibit publication.

Reflecting the document's impact at that time, the report stated: 'For many South Africans long accustomed to what appeared to be an endless cycle of violence and repression, this emphatic declaration in favour of a peaceful solution was the core of the declaration, and the guarantee, as some saw it, that the document would eventually come to be seen as one of South Africa's most historic texts.

In going as far as he has – meeting with Mr Botha, a man widely hated among blacks, and repeating this gesture with Mr De Klerk, who succeeded to the presidency in September – Mr Mandela has already strained the tolerance of many of the country's younger black leaders, some of whom believed that black emancipation could only be won through armed revolution. In the immediate future, the release of the document seems likely to complicate the delicate manoeuvres required before Mandela was released from Victor Verster Prison.[2]

Two public statements on this issue appear in the Coetsee archive – one by Mandela, and the other by Coetsee. They were probably meant to be released together, but whether this ever happened is uncertain today.

Mandela's statement reads as follow:

> The material now published by *South* (25 January 1990) is an accurate version of a document I handed to a team of government officials during the first half of 1989. However, this document was definitely not handed by me either to the retired State President P.W. Botha or State President F.W. de Klerk or Minister H.J. Coetsee.
>
> As is customary, I kept the leadership of the ANC informed of the document. However, as I have previously stated, at this early stage statements to the press as a means of conducting possible future discussions are not the appropriate course of action to promote peaceful development.
>
> Signed: N. Mandela, 26 January 1990

Marked as a 'draft', Coetsee's statement reads as follows:

> I have ascertained that the document being referred to in the media as a so-called 'non-paper' was handed to a team of officials who studied it and handled it in a responsible manner.
>
> The officials concerned concluded that the document could not serve as a meaningful point of departure for a political discussion aimed at promoting peaceful negotiations.
>
> The team informed Mr N Mandela accordingly and provided him with their viewpoints in this respect, whereafter the document and its contents received no further attention.
>
> In fact, the only document that is at present considered to be in the system is a document drafted by Mr Mandela entitled 'A document to create a climate for discussion' [effectively Mandela's letter to F.W. de Klerk], dated 12 December 1989. This, however, is a confidential document.

Clearly, the two statements were meant to distance Mandela from the contents of the memorandum and indicate that it was no longer relevant. One can only surmise that, at that stage of the process, Coetsee believed it was also in the government's interests to do so and to forestall further confusion, particularly about Mandela's proposals for negotiations.

Coetsee's formulations about a 'non-paper' and documents 'in the system' resonate with Niël Barnard's remarks in his 2015 memoirs, quoted in chapter 7. On the other hand, Mandela's remarks about whom he gave the document to and whom he did not are revealing and partly puzzling. It confirms that he did not hand a copy of the document directly to P.W. Botha when they met in August, and it stands to reason that he did not hand it to F.W. de Klerk. However, why he should deny so emphatically that he handed the document to Coetsee – effectively drawing a distinction between a 'team of officials' and the ministers involved in the working group – is unclear. This also conflicts with Barnard's assertion that Mandela handed the document to Coetsee.

////

In the meantime, the ANC undertook its own damage control. It hastily released the full text of the memorandum to Botha in a pamphlet that also contained a long introduction, clearly aimed at placing the matter in some kind of context, warding off criticism of Mandela and bolstering his legitimacy. The cover featured a full-page photograph of a smiling Mandela, taken before his imprisonment. Besides the title, *The Mandela Document*, it also carried the following bulleted strapline: 'In a document presented to P.W. Botha in July 1989, Nelson Mandela states his views on armed struggle, relations with the SACP, and majority rule.'

The introduction recalls Mandela's political history at some length, and quotes his remarks on the armed struggle during his famous statement from the dock in the Rivonia Trial. It then goes on to say:

> It is a matter of record that over the last three years, Comrade Nelson Mandela has been engaged in a series of meetings involving himself and a team of representatives of the Pretoria regime. The exchange that took place ranged over a number of issues, finally focusing on finding a way out of the deadlock occasioned by the regime's insistence that the ANC meet two principal conditions: a renunciation of armed struggle as the means of bringing about change; and the renunciation of its alliance with the South African Communist Party.
>
> When it became clear that P.W. Botha himself would meet with Comrade Mandela, during mid-1989, Mandela prepared a written statement which would be transmitted to Botha in preparation for such a meeting.
>
> We are publishing that statement to make it more widely accessible to the ANC membership, the South African people and the international community, who have made so impressive a contribution to the fight for his release from prison. It is a testament of his political faith and beliefs after more than a quarter of a century in the dungeons of the Pretoria regime. We are certain that, like his speech from the dock during the Rivonia trial, this statement from prison will be remembered as one of the most outstanding.

Throughout his discussions with the representatives of his jailers, Comrade Mandela made it clear that he was not engaged in negotiations. Such a course could only be undertaken by the elected leadership of the African National Congress or its accredited representatives. His role, he made clear, was to act as a facilitator, exploring the difficult terrain together with the state's representatives, by explaining the ANC's policy on a number of thorny issues. It is our considered view that there could not be a better exposition of those policies than this statement.

The introduction concludes:

It is proper that all who read this document recall that it was written by a courageous man while still a prisoner. Imprisonment has not diminished Nelson Mandela. His is a voice that deserves to be heard consistently and clearly regarding the future of South Africa . . .

A note at the end of the pamphlet reads:

The last part of the document containing the idea that there could be an exchange between the regime and the ANC on the question of what steps each side could take to create conditions for talks was considered by the National Executive Committee. The National Executive Committee was able to convey its thinking to Comrade Mandela on this question; he fully accepted the organisation's insistence that before talks could take place the preconditions contained in the Harare Declaration had to be met by the government.

Today, a copy of the pamphlet appears on South African History Online,[3] and the text appears elsewhere on the internet – all without explanation. Where and how it was distributed is unknown. While this would require further research, it might well be the only – or the most explicit – public comment by the ANC leadership at that time on Mandela's role as facilitator while still in prison.

On 30 January, in what was clearly intended as another corrective exercise, *South* also published extracts from Mandela's letter to F.W. de Klerk. By then, however, as expectations of Mandela's release were mounting to fever pitch, it made much less of an impact.

On 4 February 1990, Mandela told Winnie during a visit to Victor Verster that publishing the document in *South* was a 'mistake'.

21

Two notable memorandums . . .

> 'Politically, lifting the prohibition on the
> ANC and PAC is unavoidable for the Government's
> constitutional initiatives to succeed . . .'

TWO related government documents written in late January 1990 appear in the Coetsee archive. The first is a memorandum produced by a working group reporting to a ministerial committee comprising Coetsee, Viljoen and a third, unknown member. It contains a comprehensive analysis of the state of play, as well as recommendations for '2 February' – the date of F.W. de Klerk's widely anticipated speech at the start of the no-confidence debate in parliament.

The second is a report in which the ministerial committee itself made a series of recommendations based on those in the memorandum, presumably to the cabinet or De Klerk himself, and again directed at '2 February'. It recommended the unbanning of the ANC, PAC, and SACP as well as the military wings Umkhonto we Sizwe and Poqo; a statement of intent about the state of emergency; and an announcement about the release of Mandela.

These documents provide new insight into the genesis of De Klerk's epochal address in parliament on 2 February 1990, a mere five days away. They also cast light on the government's internal assessment of its interactions with Mandela as well as the latter's efforts to influence the course of events. As such, they are among the most significant documents in the archive and, indeed, the entire canon of material about Mandela's incarceration and release.

Stamped 'TOP SECRET', the main memorandum is titled '2 February 1990: Some considerations of particular interest [*Enkele oor-*

weginge van besondere belang]'. It is made up of four sections, namely 'Background', 'Motivation' [*beredenering*], 'Scenarios', and 'Recommendations in respect of time frame'. The background section deals with the ANC, the internal security situation, the 'release of the eight', Nelson Mandela, and constitutional [*staatkundige*] considerations.

The section on the ANC is devoted to a trenchant and partly pessimistic analysis of its January 8 statement, notably the passages about the Harare Declaration. It concludes that the ANC is still intent on the 'transfer' of political power to the majority of the people, after which apartheid would be destroyed by 'people's power'. However, the ANC warns that the changed political situation in the RSA requires a new tactical flexibility in the unfolding of the 'struggle': 'In this respect, the ANC emphasises the political aspect of its "struggle" rather than the armed struggle. This argument is probably an effort to convince supporters of the violence option that the ANC is merely making some tactical adjustments and embarking on a strategic change of course.'

According to the memorandum, the message displays a 'cautious optimism' about the potential for political change in the RSA, as well as a concern about deficiencies in the functioning of the 'democratic movement' and the unsatisfactory state of mass organisations. However, it emphasises mass mobilisation, while the other three pillars of the ANC's strategy (violence, international isolation, and underground structures) are mentioned only in passing.

As could be expected, the issue of negotiations is dealt with in the context of the Harare Declaration. 'The ANC seeks to project a moderate image of an organisation favouring a peaceful solution. By contrast, an accusatory finger is pointed at the government as the party that needs to take the initiative in meeting certain conditions laid down by the ANC. However, it is clear that the ANC is not prepared at this stage to make any reciprocal commitment, and that it regards the Harare Declaration as sufficient proof of its commitment to negotiations.'

Measured against visible incidents of unrest, the internal security situation has stabilised significantly, while internal resistance politics have begun to assume a more sophisticated political and less violent dimension. 'The ANC is focusing on the political dimensions of its strategy rather than on violence. By contrast, information indicates that the organisation is planning to strengthen its internal underground (military) structures for application should the negotiation option not result in a takeover of political power by the ANC.'

The MDM, the memorandum says, was founded at the instruction of the ANC. MDM leaders and members of the ANC's National Executive Committee are in constant contact, and the ANC has begun to relocate its 'Political Military Committees', which coordinate military activities from the Frontline States, to the Republic.

The memorandum then states: 'The heightened unrest around the September [1989 parliamentary] elections and its abatement thereafter demonstrate that radical groups have the capacity to exploit situations in order to radicalise the masses. Recent events have also shown that peaceful protests could degenerate into violence. Should the capacity to mobilise the masses be fully exploited, events such as those in Eastern Europe and China would not be far-fetched. An unusually large contingent of journalists and television teams have applied for visas to enter South Africa. Such a high-profile media presence could encourage mass action, and perpetuate it once it has broken out.'

The central theme during talks in Lusaka between MDM representatives and the ANC NEC on 21 to 23 November 1989 was that the 'struggle' in the Republic had to be intensified. It was stated that supporters had to become part of a revolutionary army to fight the police and soldiers in the streets, support members of Umkhonto we Sizwe, and arm themselves with home-made and confiscated weapons. A call was also made for the strengthening of underground structures. The memorandum notes: 'The SA Police reports that a number of recently established arms caches have been found.'

This section of the memorandum closes with a reference to the resolutions passed at the Conference for a Democratic Future held in Johannesburg on 9 and 10 December 1989. Several resolutions were adopted to the effect that, during 1990, mass resistance by means of marches, boycotts and so on should be intensified. Planning in this regard encompassed the spheres of labour, education, and sport, as well as local government. It also included a comprehensive campaign for the dismantling of the 'independent' homelands and self-governing territories. 'The ANC has also appropriated these resolutions.' (This is an oddly prescient passage, which reminds today's reader of the infamous incident at Bisho, then capital of the 'homeland' of Ciskei in the Eastern Cape, in September 1992 when Ciskei soldiers opened fire on an ANC–MDM contingent – including Chris Hani, Ronnie Kasrils and Cyril Ramaphosa – who tried to invade the Ciskeian city of Bisho, killing 28 people and wounding 200 more.)

The memorandum goes on to say that the released eight, and particularly the seven ANC members, were 'immediately appropriated by radical organisations'. While they initially tried to maintain a low profile, as agreed with Mandela, pressures to exploit them as symbols of the 'struggle' rapidly gained the upper hand. 'The released prisoners are therefore domestic actors in a play directed by a dynamic young leadership.'

////

The memorandum then turns to Mandela. Firstly, it provides a remarkably frank account of Mandela's incarceration, clearly informed by Kobie Coetsee. During the first decade, it notes, Mandela was detained under strict and in some respects uncompromising [*ongenaakbare*] conditions, with the focus on discipline, labour, and the earning of privileges according to strict criteria. Contact with the outside world was limited to close family, a doctor, a minister, and a legal representative. Relations between personnel and prisoners were initially tense, with personnel mostly

Afrikaans and prisoners anti-status quo, anti-white and explicitly provocative. 'However,' the memorandum notes, 'Mandela always acted with dignity and integrity, although he took a strong stand on the rights and demands of prisoners as well as their conditions and handling.'

From 1972, a 'more enlightened' regime held sway with a focus on living out the 'spirit of the policy for the management and treatment of prisoners' – in respect of this category of prisoners as well, but with a 'thorough appreciation of their potential to present a national threat'. The memorandum confirms that Mandela and other members of the Rivonia group were moved to Pollsmoor Prison to quell increasing militancy on Robben Island and its growing role as a 'university' for the anti-apartheid struggle.

The memo then moves to an equally remarkable and highly revealing account of the interaction between Coetsee and Mandela, as well as the latter's efforts to act as facilitator between the government and the ANC. Mandela's admission to the Volks Hospital in Cape Town, it says, created an 'opportunity for the start of the process of interaction between him and Minister Coetsee, later assisted by a team of senior officials'. After his discharge, he was separated from the Rivonia group and, with his cooperation, placed in accommodation in the prison hospital at Pollsmoor.

His separate detention in relatively comfortable conditions created a situation in which his colleagues (both inside and outside prison) became irritable and even distrustful towards him, especially when it became known that he was holding discussions with ministers and senior officials. This situation was 'subtly exploited' in his treatment. However, Mandela sought throughout to prevent a wedge being driven between him and his organisation, or even that such perceptions should develop and take root.

The contact and interaction with Mandela began as a 'mere exploration of possibilities', but gradually developed until he committed himself to a process of peaceful development in South Africa (in contrast to an earlier checkmate situation of refusing to renounce violence) until his statement that he was prepared to act as 'facilitator' between the government and the ANC.

After his first visit to P.W. Botha, Mandela came under 'tremendous pressure' owing to uncertainty within his organisation about his role, and sought 'desperately' to convey to the broadest possible spectrum of his organisation what he was trying to achieve. Via his 'ability', he also kept his organisation in Lusaka informed, and was eventually sanctioned to continue his discussions, but told that his approach should be that no conversation between the Government and the ANC could take place before the Government complied with the ANC's 'preconditions'.[1]

Further interaction between him and the minister or team led to him accepting a role as facilitator, and it became increasingly clear that, despite other rhetoric, he was not eager to be released without a 'deal' in his pocket which he could take to his organisation. 'He argued that, if he was released with "empty hands", he would soon be back in prison.'

Startlingly, the memorandum then discloses that, during his first meeting with F.W. de Klerk, Mandela was invited to serve as personal adviser to the State President, as a member of a 'group of wise men'. He asked whether he could consult the ANC, and was authorised to discuss this telephonically with Alfred Nzo. However, in a conversation with Nzo on 19 December 1989, he merely stated that he had a 'proposal' which he urgently needed to discuss with the ANC's NEC or its representatives. He could travel to Lusaka; they could visit him in Victor Verster; they could meet at a neutral venue; they could make use of an intermediary; or he could put it in writing. He did not mention the nature of the so-called 'proposal'.

On 17 January 1990, he received a call from Thabo Mbeki, who wanted to establish whether he was about to be released, following rumours to this effect on the eve of the NEC meeting. He denied these rumours. However, he asked Mbeki: 'What is the position about the proposal that emerged from the meeting with the State President of a simultaneous declaration?'

The memorandum continues: 'This was a new angle, seemingly formulated due to the exchange of ideas during his visit to the State President, but not in line with the proposal made to him. He seemed to believe that the original "proposal" would not be acceptable to his organisation, and would discredit him or raise suspicions about him within the ANC. He indicated that if the idea of a "simultaneous declaration" should be acceptable to the ANC, a discussion between him and the NEC would no longer be necessary.'

In a telephone conversation between Mbeki and Mandela on 22 January, the former conveyed the decision of the NEC to Mandela, namely that the government should first create a climate for negotiations; a reaffirmation of the Harare and UN declarations; a demand for the release of Mandela and other political prisoners; a sanctioning of Mandela's role while in prison; and confirmation that the ANC still gave preference to a political solution. Mandela expressed his satisfaction with this, and said he was under the impression that the government would fully conform to the ANC's conditions: 'I have a very powerful instruction to put forward, which I am happy to do. I am looking forward to meeting the SP again.' (At this point, this passage in the memorandum stops abruptly, leaving several major issues hanging.)

Moving on to 'constitutional considerations', the memorandum embarks on a sophisticated, realpolitikal rationale for unbanning the ANC and other organisations. The government, it says, is 'striving towards a new system that could be negotiated and accepted by all significant political entities'. On the other hand, most political groupings refuse to participate in negotiations unless the ANC and its leaders are also able to participate freely. 'The ideal (also for the Government) is that the ANC should not only be able to participate freely in negotiations, but should actually do so.'

The ANC–SACP alliance is still intent upon a forcible seizure of power (especially via mobilised street violence). However, the government's current initiatives are 'aimed at creating circumstances in which it would be possible for the ANC not only to participate freely in negotiations, but in which it would lose its credibility should it continue to cling to the violence option and not enter into peaceful negotiations'.

The memo goes on to say: 'The only thing distinguishing the ANC (and the SACP and PAC) from other political groupings in respect of freedom of participation in the political process and therefore also negotiations is the fact that it is a prohibited organisation, and that some of its leaders are serving prison terms or are in exile. Should the prohibition be rescinded, those prisoners who were sentenced for offences related to the prohibition be released, and the only remaining leader who is still serving a prison sentence due to non-technical offences (Mr Nelson Mandela) also be released, the ANC will be able to participate just as freely as any other political party in the political process and the negotiations.'

In the section entitled 'Motivation', the memorandum begins to argue explicitly for the unbanning of the ANC, SACP and PAC; a relaxation of the state of emergency; and the release of 913 (who has now become 'Mr Mandela') – amounting to an (unacknowledged) convergence with the Harare Declaration.

It asserts that the ANC, SACP and PAC remain committed to the use of armed violence. However, lifting the restrictions on any of these organisations will not amount to legalising their use of violence. Violent offences (*geweldsoortredings*) remain punishable, but after rescinding the prohibitions, these organisations would be able to practise politics in the same way as any other political party. The South African Police believes that lifting the prohibition on any of these organisations will not have a meaningful effect on its ability to curb their terrorist activities.

In the interests of the government's constitutional initiative, the memorandum says, it is necessary to make it possible for the ANC and PAC in particular to freely practise politics. In light of the previous paragraph, it is therefore possible to rescind the prohibition on these two organisations as well as the SACP without worsening the danger of terrorism.

In a landmark sentence, it states: 'Politically, lifting the prohibition on the ANC and PAC is unavoidable for the Government's constitutional initiatives to succeed.' It goes on to say that 'no one is really asking for the lifting of the prohibition on the SACP', and that, given events in Eastern Europe [with the collapse of Communist regimes], this might be more difficult to justify. On the other hand, it 'would perhaps be good to wipe the whole slate clean in one go'. Simultaneously lifting the prohibition on all three organisations (including the SACP) would also compel all three to state and defend their viewpoints in public, and to justify their alliances. This would also prevent the ANC from hiding behind the prohibition on the SACP to stay away from the negotiating table, or the SACP to justify concealing itself within the ranks of the ANC. 'Each ship would have to sail under its own flag.'

Terminating the current state of emergency, it says, is being touted 'in numerous quarters' as a condition for entering a negotiation process. Calls to do so are also emanating from the international community. 'Therefore, this matter has to be considered, and addressed on 2 February.' However, the memo goes on to develop a significant argument against lifting the state of emergency on that day.

States of emergency, it says, are only declared when a state of emergency has already developed that cannot be ended by means of the ordinary laws of the country. The democratic ideal requires that as soon as the state of emergency ends in practice, the proclamation should also be repealed. Therefore, the only correct approach to this matter is for the government to ask itself whether a state of emergency still exists, and if not, whether it could develop again in the future. 'Therefore, requiring that the state of emergency be lifted as a precondition for entering negotiations is a violation of the legal principles in question.'

The same is true of the retention or lifting of the state of emergency as a manoeuvre to get the negotiation process going. 'The

ANC argues that it should be placed in the same position as the National Party to practise its politics. However, the current state of emergency applies to everyone. Retaining or lifting it would not put the ANC in a better or worse position than the NP. Therefore, the question simply remains: Does a state of emergency still exist? If presented in this way, the Government will retain the moral high ground.'

The document then turns to 'Mr Nelson Mandela – release'. Unlike the release of the eight security prisoners, it says, which caught the MDM slightly unawares, 'the scene for Mr Mandela, from an internal and international organisational viewpoint, is well suited to a comprehensive reception by the NRC' [National Reception Committee].

Whereas the MDM leadership, the released leaders and the Lusaka leadership first had to find one another and develop communications and coordinating mechanisms, Mr Mandela would walk out into a well-organised collective leadership structure, and it is already clear that he will allow himself to be led by this leadership – also in respect of his own position in the party hierarchy.

This would result in him being expected to lead as a symbolic 'Messiah', and to give substance to the optimism of 'walking the last mile'. He would find it difficult to exercise any control over the spirit of the times and the momentum of the moment, although he is probably the only black leader with the stature to exercise significant influence over the momentum and content of the 'struggle'. However, he is unlikely to act against the wishes of his organisation, should he not be able to persuade them to adopt his particular views.

It may be expected that, given that he is 'national property', he will attend countrywide welcoming gatherings, and that attendance will be significantly larger than previously, given the mystical image he has built up around him over the years. The NRC hopes that he will become the 'Natal peacemaker' in the conflict between supporters of Buthelezi's Inkatha Freedom Party and the UDF/MDM.

In a total lapse of judgement, the document goes on to say: 'Due to their age, neither he nor Sisulu has any use [or] value for the ANC in the longer term, but both are indispensable in the shorter term for the organisation in terms of their symbolic and unifying role.'

In a section on 'other political prisoners', the memorandum goes on to state that there are 383 security prisoners in detention in the following categories: political violence offences, 353; political technical offences, 26; and other (largely common law), 134. Should the prohibition on the ANC be lifted, the continued detention of prisoners whose sentences are related to the status of the ANC as a prohibited organisation, and activities emanating from this status, would be at issue. 'There will definitely be serious agitation on this score for their release.'

Prisoners whose sentences are merely related to membership of the ANC as a prohibited organisation and other related technical offences will need to be released when the prohibition is lifted. Offences accompanied by violence in which people were killed or injured or property was damaged, or which had the potential to do so, would need to be handled differently. Amnesty for prisoners could only start receiving attention at the negotiating table.

Dealing with the sensitive issue of exiles (the first document in the Coetsee archive to do so), the memorandum says there are people in exile who cannot return to South Africa because they would be charged with one or other offence related to their own political aspirations or those of their organisations. In most cases, the relevant offences are probably political/technical offences related to the prohibition on certain organisations, or the way in which they left the country. In other cases, offences involving violence and terrorism are at stake.

It would only be necessary to make it possible for people who committed political/technical offences to return. This could happen together with the lifting of the prohibition on the organisation to which they are connected, and by granting amnesty for offences related to leaving the country. Announcing the annulment of offences related to leaving the country would even advance the government's initiative. (This, it says, would be in line with the Western ideal of freedom of movement, which is currently being prioritised or emphasised in Europe.)

As regards those accused of violent offences, this is a matter that could be addressed in the course of the negotiations. 'There are probably not many people who would argue seriously that they should receive amnesty at present.'

In the section titled 'Scenarios', the document sets out 'pro' and 'con' analyses for four elements: lifting the prohibition on the ANC and PAC; lifting the prohibition on the SACP; general lifting of the state of emergency; and the release of Prisoner 913.

In the last section, titled 'Recommendation in respect of time frame', the memorandum says all these matters would have to be addressed in the President's address on 2 February. The actual release, lifting of the prohibition and repeal of the state of emergency (or adaption of the regulations) would not necessarily have to happen at the same time. Various combinations are possible. The working group recommends the following combinations:

a) Release of Mandela

It is proposed that Mandela's release on a later date that would suit everyone be announced on 2 February. If the announcement could be made in more or less the same wording as in the document submitted separately (which demonstrates consultation and collaboration with Mandela), this would greatly benefit him as well as the government, and clear the way to properly planning his release. Release before or on 2 February would shift the focus away from the speech and the following week's debate to Mandela and the ANC. The possibility of uncontrolled reaction would then be greater because proper planning would not be possible;

too many things would need to happen at once; the world media would then focus on a series of events that could be presented as revolutionary, and the prohibition on the ANC would not yet have been rescinded.

b) Lifting of the prohibition on the ANC (with or without the SAP and PAC)

It is proposed that the lifting of the prohibition on all three organisations be announced on 2 February, and it should, for logistical reasons, be promulgated in the *Government Gazette* the next day. It is also proposed that any announcement about the retention, repeal or scaling down of the state of emergency should occur on 2 February, and that the formal steps should also be published later on the same day.

////

We now turn to the covering memorandum. Stamped 'TOP SECRET', and simply titled 'Report', it is anonymous and undated. However, it emerges from the document itself that it was written on 29 January 1990 by a working group reporting to a Three-Minister Committee [*Drie Ministerskomitee*] – clearly Coetsee and Viljoen and a third, unknown minister. A translation of the entire document follows.

> REPORT:
>
> Today (29/1/1990) the Three-Ministers Committee gave instructions that a working group should reconsider the existing report to Minister Coetsee about the ANC, the State of Emergency and Mandela in the light of the most recent available information. The group was tasked with making recommendations with reference to the following aspects:
>
> (a) The ban on the ANC and PAC
> (b) The ban on the SACP
> (c) The State of Emergency

(d) The release of Mr Nelson Mandela
(e) The latest security profile
(f) The importance of negotiations
(g) Umkontho [sic] we Sizwe and Poqo [the PAC's armed wing]

The working group reviewed the existing report, which is attached hereto, and is of the opinion that the security situation as well as the importance of negotiations have been fully argued. The Commissioner of Police called for a security update and then confirmed that there was nothing new to add to the report as it stood.

Against this background, and after internal discussions and analyses of all the relevant circumstances, the working group makes the following recommendations:

A. The ANC and PAC

It is recommended that the unbanning of the ANC and PAC should be announced on 2 February 1990. This should be presented as a way of normalising the practice of politics as a means of setting the negotiation table. It should also be stated that the unbanning would not affect violent and other offences that are unrelated to the banning of those organisations Similarly, as regards amnesty, this will only involve those people who committed offences related to the banning of those organisations.

B. The SACP

It is proposed that the unbanning of the SACP should be announced at the same time. The arguments/motivations in the report refer, but added to this it will be difficult to explain why the ANC and PAC no longer constitute a danger to state security, but the SACP does.

C. Umkontho we Sizwe and Poqo

The same argument holds for Umkontho and Poqo. Added to this, these two organisations are merely extensions of the ANC and PAC and it is not possible to separate them from their parent organisations. To maintain the ban on these organisations would cause awkward technical problems in terms of enforcement.

The lifting of the bans on Umkontho and Poqo would certainly cause pain among own supporters [an apparent reference to supporters of the NP government]. Therefore, it [is] proposed that the ban on the ANC, PAC, SACP and other similar or subordinate organisations should be rescinded. The proclamation could then refer to Umkontho, Poqo and a number of other organisations (which are no longer functioning). Emphasis could also be placed on the fact that violent and other misdemeanours would remain punishable.

D. State of Emergency

It is recommended that a scaling down of the State of Emergency should be announced on 2 February 1990, and that the formal steps should also be published on the same or the following day. It is further recommended that the complete lifting of the State of Emergency should be presented as ideal, but that this would depend upon the orderly progression of events after the organisations had been unbanned and Mandela had been released.

E. Release of Mandela

It is suggested that the release of Mandela at a later time that will suit everyone's needs should be announced on 2 February 1990. If the announcement could be made more or less as formulated in the document that is being submitted separately (and which demonstrates consultation and collaboration with Mandela), it will be to his and the government's advantage, and open the way to the proper planning of his eventual release. Release before or on 2 February would shift the focus away from the speech and the subsequent debate and towards Mandela and the ANC. The possibility of uncontrolled reaction is then also bigger because planning could not be optimised, too many things would be happening at once, and the world media would be focused on a series of events (which could be presented as revolutionary) and because the ban on the ANC would not yet have been lifted.

////

By now, the significance of these documents will be fully apparent. Firstly, they cast vital light on the government's perceptions of the secret process of 'engagement' with Mandela. In the course of doing so, the main memorandum discloses that, during their meeting, Mandela was invited to serve as a personal adviser to the State President, as a member of a 'group of wise men'. Clearly, this proposal was linked to the fatal misjudgement that, after playing symbolic roles in the short term, both Mandela and Sisulu would be sidelined.

One notable feature is that the memorandum defends Mandela as a man of 'dignity and integrity', who, among other things, stood up for his fellow prisoners. Another is that the memo seeks to credit Coetsee for Mandela's gradual conversion towards 'peaceful development' and persuading him to act as facilitator between the government and the ANC. This is not borne out by other material, including the transcript of Mandela's meeting with the EPG, and Coetsee's own notes of his first meeting with Mandela.

The two documents also build arguments for legitimising the measures announced in De Klerk's speech in parliament, for presumed use in motivating final cabinet decisions, and quelling last-minute resistance from the security establishment[2]. The extent to which De Klerk utilised these arguments and followed these recommendations will be addressed below.

In the meantime, two issues remain. The first is why, in an otherwise quite detailed and accurate narrative about Mandela's activities, the main memorandum says nothing about the problems surrounding the statement issued by the ANC's NEC the week before. Coetsee and Viljoen must have known about this by then, but for some reason this is not mentioned. The second will be explored in the following chapter.

22

. . . and an enduring mystery

"Mandela made it quite clear that he fully expects President F.W. de Klerk to make several major announcements . . .

AS NOTED in the introduction, the full story of the process surrounding Mandela's release will probably never be told. Among numerous other considerations, the Coetsee archive is too incomplete to allow the development of anything resembling a continuous and comprehensive narrative. However, the existing material does point to a central mystery, namely the nature of the proposals Mandela sent to Lusaka.

In its summary of Mandela's interaction with F.W. de Klerk and his subsequent telephone conversations with Alfred Nzo and Thabo Mbeki, the government memorandum of 29 January effectively acknowledges that this remains a puzzling issue, but this passage stops abruptly without offering an explanation. So the question remains: what did Mandela say to Lusaka which was so sensitive that nothing about it has emerged then or since?

There are some clues besides those in the Coetsee archive. On 19 January 1990, the *Mail & Guardian* reported that Mandela had sent a ten-point proposal on negotiations to the ANC for consideration at the crucial NEC meeting due to start on the same day. Mandela told the ANC he would phone them on Sunday, 22 January, to hear their response.[1]

The report continued: 'The document, which was brought to Lusaka some weeks ago, was the same one he presented to State President F.W. de Klerk during their meeting last year. It deals with a number of issues, but centres around a proposal of how negotiations should be handled.

'It emerged yesterday that Mandela is in regular contact with the ANC. Acting ANC president Alfred Nzo indicated in a speech that he had communicated with Mandela as recently as Wednesday. Nzo said this weekend's meeting of the National Executive Committee would discuss and decide on Mandela's proposals.

'ANC leaders were not giving away any details of the contents. However, one NEC member indicated that the document showed that Mandela was "right on the mark", and any speculation that his position differed from that of the ANC or the UDF was ludicrous.'

The report added that the extended NEC meeting would play a crucial role in determining attitudes towards the prospect of negotiations with Pretoria, the future of the armed struggle, sorting out leadership structures following the release of prisoners and Oliver Tambo's illness, and charting a course for the rest of the year.

The reporter was well informed, and the assertion that Mandela had sent a document containing his proposals for negotiations squares with other evidence. But the remarks about the contents seem less plausible. For one, it seems unlikely that Mandela would simply have sent his letter to F.W. de Klerk to Lusaka. Moreover, the letter did not contain a ten-point plan. Added to this, there is nothing in the letter that would have merited Mandela's caution in talking about it to Nzo and Mbeki.

More recently, another strand of evidence has emerged, courtesy of none other than Julian Assange, founder of the controversial website WikiLeaks. On Wednesday, 17 January 1990, the American Consulate in Cape Town sent a confidential cable to the US secretary of state in Washington, copied to the American embassies in Pretoria, Lusaka, Harare, London and Paris, and the American consulates in Johannesburg and Durban.

Blandly titled 'Essa Moosa talks about Mandela and other topics', it conveyed the gist of a discussion between a consulate official and Essa Moosa, then a UDF lawyer based in Cape Town, who had visited Mandela at Victor Verster Prison the previous week. The cable remained buried for more than twenty years, but came to light in November 2010 when it formed part of a cache of classified US diplomatic cables released by the controversial non-profit organisation WikiLeaks to five major global newspapers, including the British newspaper *The Guardian*.

On 28 November 2010, *The Guardian* carried a report on the cable entitled 'Embassy cables reveal Mandela release plan', with the following subhead: 'Leaked dispatch shows South African president F.W. de Klerk gave African National Congress leader set of release proposals for negotiation'.[2] The introductory paragraph went on to read: "F.W. de Klerk's historic announcement that Nelson Mandela would be released stunned the world, but came as no surprise to Mandela himself.'

The article was replicated in the South African *Mail & Guardian* a day later. However, it did not gain much traction. South Africa was grappling with an escalating series of crises triggered by the presidency of Jacob Zuma, who had risen to power two years before. Added to this, the seemingly far-reaching allegations in the cable did not tally with any other public evidence. Another decade later, the Coetsee archive has finally corroborated its contents.

The cable itself appears in *The Guardian*'s WikiLeaks database.[3] The main portion reads as follows (paragraph numbering has been omitted):

> In a half hour conversation with Poleconoff [the Politics and Economics officer], Essa Moosa, the Western Cape UDF's lawyer and one of the attorneys who met with Mandela last week, made the following remarks:
>
> **Mandela release will be announced February 2 in parliament**
> Mandela made it quite clear that he fully expects President F.W. de Klerk to make several major announcements in his February 2 speech at the opening of parliament. De Klerk will announce:
> - the unbanning of the ANC, PAC and other political organisations;
> - the end of the state of emergency;
> - the return of political exiles to South Africa;
> - the release of a number of political prisoners, including Nelson Mandela.

These announcements will not necessarily mean that all the items listed will take effect as of the time of the speech, but firm plans and a commitment to carry them out swiftly will be part of the announcement.

Where will Mandela be released?

Moosa sidestepped a question about where Mandela's home base would be upon his release. He only remarked that Mandela can tell the SAG [the South African Government] where he wants to be released and where his first public appearance would thus take place. Sentimentally, said Moosa, Paarl (where Mandela is now in prison) seemed to appeal to Mandela. (Comment in the cable: but politically and practically this makes little sense. Johannesburg seems by far the most suitable venue.)

De Klerk–ANC communication through Mandela

When he met several weeks ago with Mandela, De Klerk provided a set of proposals and asked for the ANC's response. Mandela has not discussed those proposals in any detail with people here (at least he did not do so with the lawyers' group of which Moosa was a member), but he did transmit them to Alfred Nzo and Thabo Mbeki. Moosa believes (piecing together stray remarks here and there) that the proposals related principally to the need to allay white fears. Specifically, he thinks one issue was the relationship of the ANC to the SACP (South African Communist Party) and another was the definition of one man, one vote.

Aside from being an effort to seize the moral high ground by publicly demonstrating flexibility, the ANC's recent announcement that it is prepared to negotiate even while apartheid laws remain in place may be part of the organisation's reply to De Klerk.

Moosa understands Mandela to have worked out a game plan for 'next steps' in a negotiation with De Klerk so as to ensure that he is not released from prison into a vacuum.

Mandela has told various visitors that he has a good opinion of De Klerk as a sincere individual even though he regards him as still the leader of the National Party and not more than that.

Commitment on SAG and MDM side to reduce confrontation

Moosa agreed that the atmosphere is much less tense than even six months ago. For example, last year the return to school resulted in the usual accusations and physical confrontations between the Department of Education and Training (DET), aided by the police, and students supported by parents, teachers and the MDM. This year there is an even worse crisis due to lack of space in black schools and the failure of over 100,000 students to pass their 'matric exams'. Yet there is a new spirit of dialogue at the DET and activists are therefore able to channel student frustrations in a constructive manner.

The SAG's new 'tactic' of allowing dissent and engaging in dialogue instead of stonewalling 'is working for them', Moosa said. He acknowledged, however, that it could also, if dealt with positively, work for the MDM and ANC. Though an absence of direct confrontation is 'demobilizing for the masses', fewer raw nerves among activists could make them more amenable to the ANC's increasingly pragmatic strategy for dealing with the SAG. That strategy, Moosa said, is not understood by many activists, especially youth, who fear a sell-out of their cause. There remains a lot to do to explain the virtues of flexibility to them.

PAC and BC – a thorn in the side

Moosa described the conference on a democratic future [held in December 1989] as 'not a positive experience in cooperation'. He opined that the PAC and BC [Black Consciousness movement] could turn out to be a real problem. He expects them to remain aloof, sniping at the ANC's positions from the sidelines and stirring up young people in particular.

Jesse Jackson visit

Moosa inquired about the dates for [the US civil rights activist] Jesse Jackson's visit and expressed concern that Jackson had met with the press at South African Ambassador [Piet] Koornhof's residence [in Washington]. Moosa feared that the SAG was doing too good a job of cultivating Jackson and that he might return to the US and announce that sanctions should be lifted. Moosa appeared to have greater confidence in Koornhof's persuasive ability than in that of the SACC [South African Council of Churches] leadership which is hosting the Jackson visit.

(The Jesse Jackson visit to South Africa went ahead. The *Guardian* report on the cable goes on to note that, when Mandela addressed an unruly crowd on the Cape Town Parade on 11 February 1990, 'Jackson had to be restrained from muscling his way on to the balcony to join him'.)

In contrast to the *Mail & Guardian*, Moosa's version suggests that De Klerk himself provided Mandela with a set of proposals, and asked for the ANC to respond. Mandela then sent those proposals to Nzo and Mbeki. (This squares with the account in the government memorandum reflected in chapter 21.) It also suggests, though, that Mandela worked out a game plan for 'next steps' which he might not have shared with his interlocutors.

The document Mandela sent to Lusaka is not in the Coetsee archive, and has never surfaced elsewhere. Until it does, this vital aspect of the process will remain unclear. Given the available evidence, the following is plausible:

Prior to their meeting, Mandela wrote De Klerk a letter in which he set out the ANC's updated preconditions for negotiation – effectively those in the Harare Declaration. They discussed these during their meeting on 13 December and reached some tentative agreements. Mandela drew up a document comprising his letter, De Klerk's 'response' and some additional proposals, and handed it to Ramaphosa to send on to Lusaka.

Besides this, De Klerk and his team also asked Mandela to serve in a 'committee of wise men', tasked with providing De Klerk with personal advice during the remainder of the envisaged transition. Mandela agreed to discuss this with Lusaka, but later decided (wisely) that the idea would not fly. He then conceived the idea of a 'simultaneous declaration' by Pretoria and Lusaka, in which the former would presumably announce its willingness to meet some or all of the preconditions, and the latter a new commitment to 'peaceful' negotiations, even stretching to a suspension of the armed struggle.

Mandela proposed this to the ANC and asked for a response. Perhaps this reflected his expectation that he would report back to De Klerk, as part of an ongoing process in which they would continue to discuss the unfolding transition. However, things didn't work out that way, and he did not see De Klerk again until 9 February, when he was summarily told that he would be released two days later.

But even if all this is correct, why he regarded the single paragraph in the NEC statement read out to him by Mbeki as an adequate response, and did not press him further on the issue of the simultaneous declaration, remains a tantalising mystery.

23

At the last minute

> 'After two substantial meetings between myself and Mr Mandela,
> we have agreed that he will, after his release,
> from time to time give me the benefit of his advice in order to
> get negotiations between all relevant parties going . . .'

IN *The Last Trek*, F.W. de Klerk writes that he spent much of his three-week holiday at the end of 1989 in 'deep thought and reflection', reaching the insight that, rather than a step-by-step approach, he needed to make a paradigm shift that would convince other role players of the government's bona fides in respect of negotiations and a unified South Africa.[1]

Armed with this certainty, and working with a few key ministers, he then began to put together the package he announced on 2 February. The entire package was presented to the cabinet on 31 January, just two days before he was due to deliver his speech. (Some historical sources say it was presented to a 'shocked' NP caucus at six o'clock the next morning.)

De Klerk continues: 'These decisions set the framework for my speech of 2 February. It was now up to me to package them. I cut myself off, and started to write. I passed my first draft formulations on particular matters to the responsible ministers to obtain their comments and suggestions. When I had received these, I completed the first full draft during the morning of 1 February. I called together a few key ministers, and worked through the speech with them.

'With the benefit of our discussion and their contributions, I returned to my desk. I began the speech from the start again. I weighed every word, and where necessary, reformulated and added passages. As I completed each page, my secretary, Pets van Niekerk, typed it and gave it to Chris Rencken (an adviser in my office who had previously been a journalist and a member of parliament) for translation into English. At about 6 pm on the evening of 1 February, I was more or less satisfied . . .'

A set of documents appears in the Coetsee archive that casts more light on this process. Classified as 'Secret' and 'Top Secret', they are anonymous and undated, but were clearly generated just before De Klerk's speech on 2 February. The first is a one-page typed document headed 'Organisations'. It reads as follows:

> The Cabinet resolves that the prohibition on the ANC, PAC and SACP and similar or subsidiary organisations such as Umkonto [sic] We Sizwe and Poqo, as well as their publications, should be rescinded.
>
> A proclamation signed by the Minister of Justice to give effect to this decision must be submitted to the State President for signature on 1 February 1990.
>
> The Proclamation, together with the notices of rescission signed by the Minister of Justice, must be published in the Government Gazette on 3 February.

It therefore appears to record a decision taken at the cabinet meeting on 31 January. However, it is more likely to have been a draft resolution submitted to the meeting for approval – probably prepared by Coetsee or his team of officials. This chimes with handwritten notes that appear on the same document. Written in a flowing hand, they read: 'Get Slovo in respect of *Africa Confidential*. Slovo said this in respect of Socialism.' (This was obviously a reference to a recent paper by Joe Slovo entitled 'Has Socialism Failed?', in which he said that 'the future of socialism is indeed bleak'.) And then:

1. Wipe the slate clean.
2. Concentrate on crime. Information about funding.
3. Security forces.

Whether these notes were made by Coetsee or someone else – and at what point – remains unknown. However, the most likely explanation is that they were made just before or during the cabinet meeting at which the resolution was tabled. The first point recalls the passage in the 29 January memorandum about unbanning the SACP, which starts off by saying that 'no one is asking for the unbanning of the SACP', but goes on to argue that it 'might perhaps be good to wipe the whole slate clean in one go'.

Therefore, the phrase might well have been used in the course of the cabinet meeting, and noted down to confirm the decision. (The phrase gradually became ingrained in accounts of the transition to democracy, and particularly in the treatment of the negotiations around the issue of amnesty.) The other notes seem to refer to issues or recommendations that might have been raised by the security establishment.

The next document is entitled 'State of Emergency'. It says the cabinet recommends to the State President that the state of emergency should not be rescinded. It then recommends a series of relaxations in wording that differs substantially from those in De Klerk's eventual address. (Clearly, the wording was refined in the interim.) It also goes on to say that the necessary proclamations signed by the Minister of Justice should be submitted to the State President on 1 February, and published in the *Government Gazette* on 3 February. Again, this seems to be a template for a cabinet decision probably drawn up before the meeting.

This is followed by a 'top secret' document containing drafts of various proposed passages in De Klerk's address. They are largely written in Afrikaans. For the most part, they comprise different ways of motivating and justifying the unbanning of the ANC, PAC and SACP, in wording which De Klerk did not adopt. However, a first-class surprise emerges in a draft passage about Mandela's release. It reads as follows:

Given that Mr Mandela's release affects him personally, and the Government feels he has played an honourable and sensible role over the past few years, I met with him on 1 February to personally convey to him what the Government has decided in respect of his release as well as its thoughts about his future role.

The decision conveyed to him is that the Government of the RSA has decided to release him unconditionally in the foreseeable future. Therefore, from the side of the Government, there is no further constraint on Mr Mandela's release. However, a date will depend on official, practical, personal and security considerations. For his own sake as well, Mr Mandela's release should take place in an orderly manner.

Moreover, the Government's expectations generated by Mr Mandela's own utterances were conveyed to him, namely that he should play a positive and constructive role [a handwritten addition reads: '... and which he himself described as a facilitating role'] in terms of a peaceful process of negotiation, and that he will help, via moderating and realistic leadership, to find a solution to the South African problem [*problematiek*]. The fact that the ANC is being unbanned resonates with previous arguments that Mr Mandela would find himself in a political vacuum.

After two substantial meetings between myself and Mr Mandela, we have agreed that he will, after his release, from time to time give me the benefit of his advice in order to get negotiations between all relevant parties going. We share the perspective of a peaceful, prosperous country where people will live in circumstances characterised by equality, justice and dignity.

We entertain different views on how to achieve this vision, but share a determination that our differences should be resolved by means of negotiation and democratic processes.

In order to prepare thoroughly and efficiently for the negotiation stage, I shall approach various other prominent South Africans, representative of the broad spectrum of political opinion, on an individual basis to avail me of their advice on the same basis as Mr Mandela will be doing.

The Government is in deadly earnest about the process with which it is engaged. The end result should be a democratic community, in the best sense of the word, and a country where freedom and order are in equilibrium with each other.

Sooner or later, a leader confronts the situation that he has to grasp the courage of his convictions by *leading* [emphasis in the original] and not merely allowing himself to be manipulated by his followers. In difficult times, when decisions have to be taken, a leader must be prepared to take risks. Surely, Mr Mandela is the best known black leader in the history of South Africa. For this reason, I once again wish to make an effort to utilise his release as the start of a process of reconciliation instead of provoking radicalisation and confrontation. I have always believed that Mr Mandela, since the conversations with him began, shares this approach.

I therefore commit myself to continue creating the space and opportunity for Mr Mandela to play a facilitating role, because his history and talents make him eminently suited to build bridges over the chasms that divide our society.

REMARK: (Not part of speech unless agreed):
Therefore, SP would like to announce that 913 declares himself willing to advise SP on a bilateral basis in order to facilitate negotiations. This means that 913 will not be limited to a committee which could inhibit his room to move [*beweegruimte*], but that his role will symbolise the emphasis that will need to be placed on reconciliation instead of confrontation.

Astoundingly, this passage discloses that the notion of Mandela serving as a personal adviser to F.W. de Klerk (in tandem with other 'elder statesmen') – and continuing to serve as 'facilitator' between the NP government and the ANC, presumably at some distance to the latter – was still alive just before 2 February. This revelation and its implications deserve closer analysis.

The proposal was made to Mandela some six weeks previously, at his first (and only) meeting with De Klerk. According to the 29 January memorandum, Mandela then asked whether he could consult the ANC. Taken together, the memorandum and this passage indicate that, by end January, he had not yet provided the government with a response.

The passage says De Klerk 'met Mandela on 1 February', and refers to 'two substantial meetings' between them, but, as Mandela would reveal in a conversation with Winnie a few days later, this meeting never happened. Instead, Coetsee and Viljoen met with Mandela, supposedly on De Klerk's behalf, at Pollsmoor Prison. Therefore, this passage must have been written just before 1 February, based on the simple presumption that the meeting would take place.

Similarly, the passage states that De Klerk and Mandela had agreed – presumably at their 'second substantial meeting' – that the latter would provide the former with the 'benefit of his advice', and the final paragraph envisages an announcement that Mandela had declared himself willing to advise De Klerk 'on a bilateral basis, in order to facilitate negotiations'. However, the extraordinary 'remark' preceding this paragraph reveals that this was also a presumption, and Mandela had not yet provided his agreement.

As we now know, this whole set of proposed announcements was entirely absent from De Klerk's speech on 2 February. The question, then, is why. One obvious possibility is that Coetsee and Viljoen renewed the proposal to Mandela on 1 February, and that he finally told them he did not agree. If this is what happened, it's unclear why Mandela never mentioned it to anyone, including Winnie, in their otherwise frank conversation a few days later. (That transcript does record that Mandela spoke 'softly and inaudibly' when he told Winnie what he had discussed with the ministers about his release, but still does not suggest that he spoke about this offer.) Mandela also did not say anything about it when he met with the National Executive Committee of the UDF at Victor Verster Prison, seven days after De Klerk's speech. If this is what happened, he might have agreed not to discuss this proposal with anyone, or took this decision himself.

The second possibility centres on the other party to the proposed agreement, namely F.W. de Klerk. It is clear that the draft passage was written by Coetsee, and/or Viljoen, and/or their team of officials, and intended as input into De Klerk's developing speech. As such, it reflected a particular, paternalistic, set of ideas developed over months and based on a range of misguided assumptions. Among others, it reflected the entirely erroneous view, expressed in the memorandum written a few days previously, that, following his release, Mandela's celebrity would be short-lived and he would soon be sidelined. It also seemed to envisage a lengthy and orderly transitional process controlled by the government, and populated by a neatly balanced spectrum of leaders and parties besides the ANC.[2] The other explanation, then, would be that De Klerk himself had realised that this whole idea was unviable, and had simply decided to let it slide.

Either way, it was a fateful conjuncture that, like a fish glimpsed in a dark pool, rose to just below the surface, and then disappeared. If the offer had stood, and Mandela had accepted it, the impact on South African political history is hard to imagine.

////

The systematic confusion about De Klerk's intended meeting with Mandela circled out still further.

No. 229 Minute from Mr Powell (No. 10) to the Prime Minister, 1 February 1990 – Confidential (PREM 19/3171)

Robin Renwick [the British ambassador] has just called me from South Africa. De Klerk had telephoned him a few minutes ago to say that he had spent several hours with Mandela today. Mandela does not want to be released immediately: he still has problems to resolve with the ANC as well as personal problems (presumably Mrs Mandela!). De Klerk will therefore announce tomorrow that Mandela will be released, without giving a date. He also intends to announce other major steps which he thinks will satisfy you. He was very anxious for you to know that tonight.

Robin thinks we should warmly welcome the steps when they are announced tomorrow. This will require a more positive statement than the one in your box. I will draft it first thing tomorrow morning.

C.D. POWELL[3]

The statement that De Klerk met Mandela in person was obviously incorrect. This might have been a simple misunderstanding. However, the minute does add to Mandela's version of the substance of the meeting. Among other things, it indicates that his own preferences played a role in the eventual delays in his release.

24

'Reform in a stable climate . . .'

F.W. de Klerk's speech in parliament on 2 February 1990

ON 2 February 1990, Mandela writes in *Long Walk to Freedom*, F.W. de Klerk stood before parliament to make the traditional opening speech and did something no other South African head of state had ever done: 'he truly began to dismantle the apartheid system, and lay the groundwork for a democratic South Africa'.

In dramatic fashion, De Klerk announced the lifting of the bans on the ANC, the PAC, the SACP and 31 other illegal organisations; the freeing of political prisoners incarcerated for non-violent activities; the suspension of capital punishment; and the lifting of various restrictions imposed by the state of emergency. 'It was a breathtaking moment, for in one sweeping action he had virtually normalised the situation in South Africa . . .'[1]

Since then, De Klerk's address has been enshrined in local and global political history.[2] While it did achieve all the things Mandela described, it was also more complex than either his account or its sanctified global status suggests. It is worth revisiting, with the hindsight provided by the intervening years, because of the added insights into its genesis provided by the Coetsee archive, and because it provides a window on De Klerk's mindset and his conception of the process to follow. It is also interesting to trace how it relates to the concerns expressed by the secret working group during their months of talks with Mandela. Lastly, it also resonates in numerous ways – sometimes disconcertingly – with South Africa's post-transition fortunes.

De Klerk did not simply make the series of announcements

referred to above. Instead, he systematically made the case for a negotiated settlement, and set out a framework for achieving this and reaping the benefits. The country, he said, was on the road to drastic change, and only a negotiated understanding among representative leaders would ensure lasting peace. The alternative was growing violence and conflict, which was in no one's interest. For its part, the government would give the process of negotiation the highest priority. He then proceeded to deal with various policy and governance challenges in the context of this new framework.

On foreign relations, he said the world at large had a major role to play in realising the country's national interests. Dynamic developments in international politics had created new opportunities for South Africa as well. While the expiry of 'Stalinist Communism' would have unpredictable consequences in Europe, it would be vital to Africa. The collapse of the economic system in Eastern Europe was a warning to those who wanted to persist with this in Africa, and those who sought to force this failed system on South Africa should 'totally revise their point of view'.

The southern African region had a historical opportunity to set aside its conflicts and ideological differences and draw up a joint programme of reconstruction.

The government accepted the recognition and protection of fundamental individual rights. However, a system for the protection of the rights of individuals, minorities and national entities had to form a balanced whole. The formal recognition of individual rights did not mean that the problems of a heterogeneous population would simply disappear. Any new constitution which disregarded this would be 'inappropriate and even harmful'.

A changed dispensation implied far more than political and constitutional issues. Poverty, unemployment, housing shortages, inadequate education and training, illiteracy, health needs and numerous other problems still stood in the way of progress and prosperity. To this end, the Separate Amenities Act would be abolished, and various other initiatives would be announced soon.

A new South Africa was only possible if it was bolstered by a sound and growing economy, with particular emphasis on job creation. To this end, South Africa needed to make structural changes to its economy. The government would reduce the role of the public sector in the economy and give the private sector maximum opportunity for optimal performance. Market forces and a sound competitive structure would be allowed to bring about the necessary adjustments. At the same time, sound fiscal and monetary policy would be maintained.

The role of the state in the economy would be reduced by restricting expenditure on parastatal institutions, privatisation, and deregulation, and by curtailing government expenditure. This did not mean the state would forsake its development role, especially in South Africa's 'particular circumstances', and suitable priorities would be determined.

Efforts to curb state expenditure had begun to succeed. Government expenditure was under control, and it would close the year with a surplus. The government was serious, especially in this particular period of South Africa's history, to promote a dynamic economy that would make it possible for increasing numbers of people to be employed and share in rising standards of living.

Finally, De Klerk turned to 'negotiation'. Practically every leader, he said, agreed that negotiation was the key to reconciliation and a new and just dispensation. However, numerous excuses for refusing to take part were being advanced. Some were valid, and others were merely part of a political chess game. While the game proceeded, valuable time was being lost.

During his inauguration address, he had committed the government to giving active attention to the most important obstacles in the way of negotiation. He was now able to announce far-reaching decisions to this end. They would shape a new phase marked by a movement away from measures that had been seized upon as a justification for confrontation and violence. 'The emphasis has to move . . . to a debate and discussion of political and economic points of view as part of the process of negotiation.

'I wish to urge every political and community leader, in and outside parliament, to approach the new opportunities which are being created, constructively. There is no time left for advancing all manner of new conditions that will delay the negotiating process.'

He then announced the following:

- The prohibition on the ANC, PAC, SACP and a number of subsidiary organisations would be rescinded.
- People serving prison sentences merely because they were members of one of these organisations, or because they had committed offences which merely existed because these organisations were prohibited, would be identified and released. Prisoners sentenced for other offences such as murder, terrorism or arson would not be affected.
- Media emergency regulations as well as the education emergency regulations would be abolished.
- The security emergency regulations would be amended to allow effective control over visual material pertaining to scenes of unrest.
- Restrictions under the emergency regulations on 33 organisations – including the UDF, COSATU, and the Blanke Bevrydingsbeweging van Suid-Afrika – would be rescinded.
- Conditions imposed under security emergency regulations on 374 people following their release would be rescinded, and the regulations would be abolished.
- Detention under the security emergency regulations would be limited to six months. Detainees would also gain the right to legal representation and medical practitioners of their own choice.

These decisions, he said, corresponded with the government's declared intention to normalise the political process without jeopardising the maintenance of good order. They were preceded by thorough and unanimous advice by a group of officials which included members of the security community. Important facets included the following:

- Events in the Soviet Union and Eastern Europe had weakened the capability of organisations which were previously supported from those quarters.
- Activities of the organisations that would now be unbanned did not threaten internal security to the extent that had made it necessary to ban them.
- There were important shifts of emphasis in the statements and points of view of the most important organisations, which indicated a new approach and a preference for peaceful solutions.
- The South African Police believed it was able, in the present circumstances, to combat violence and other crimes also perpetrated by members of these organisations and to bring offenders to justice without prohibitions on the organisations.

The lifting of the prohibition on these organisations did not signify the approval or condonation of terrorism or crimes of violence, and should not be interpreted as a deviation from the government's rejection of their economic policies and aspects of their constitutional policy. However, this would be dealt with in the course of debate and negotiation. The maintenance of law and order would also not be jeopardised.

De Klerk had been advised that an emergency situation still existed. He intended to terminate the state of emergency as soon as possible, but those responsible for unrest had to bear the blame for its continuation. In the meantime, it would only inhibit those using 'chaos and disorder' as political instruments. Otherwise the rules of the game under the state of emergency were the same for everybody.

At last, De Klerk turned to Mandela. The government, he said, had proved its good faith, and the table was laid for sensible leaders to begin talking about a new dispensation. In this connection, Mr Nelson Mandela could play an important part. The government noted that he had declared himself willing to make a constructive contribution to the peaceful political process in South Africa.

'I wish to put it plainly that the government has taken a firm decision to release Mr Mandela unconditionally. I am serious about bringing this matter to finality without delay. The government will take a decision soon on the date of his release. Unfortunately, a further short passage of time is unavoidable.

'Normally there is a certain passage of time between the decision to release and the actual release because of logistical and administrative requirements. In the case of Mr Mandela there are factors in the way of his immediate release, of which his personal circumstances and safety are not the least. He has not been an ordinary prisoner for quite some time. Because of that, his case requires particular circumspection.'

He went on to say: 'Today's announcements in particular go to the heart of what black leaders – also Mr Mandela – have been advancing over the years as their reason for having resorted to violence. The allegation has been that the government did not wish to talk to them and that they were deprived of their right to normal political activity by the prohibition on their organisations.

'Without conceding that violence has ever been justified, I wish to say today to those who argued in this manner that the government wishes to talk to all leaders who seek peace; the lifting of the prohibitions on various organisations places everyone in a position to pursue politics freely; and the justification for violence . . . no longer exists.

'These facts place everybody in South Africa before a fait accompli . . . There is no longer any reasonable excuse for the continuation of violence . . . Therefore, I repeat my invitation with greater conviction than ever: Walk through the open door, take your place at the negotiating table together with the government and other leaders who have important power bases inside and outside of parliament. Henceforth, everybody's political points of view will be tested against their realism, their workability and their fairness. The time for negotiation has arrived . . .'

////

To what extent did the address conform with the 29 January memorandums? Again, this is not entirely straightforward. The first issue is the lifting of prohibitions on the ANC, PAC and SACP. Despite the residual reservations in the memorandums, to the point of saying that 'no one had asked for the SACP to be unbanned', De Klerk clearly opted for 'wiping the slate clean'.

The second is the lifting of the state of emergency. While it left a decision open, the main memorandum introduced a line of argument about lifting or retaining the state of emergency, which it said would enable the government to 'retain the moral high ground'. The ministerial committee then went on to recommend that the state of emergency should be scaled down, and presented lifting it as ideal, but that this would depend upon the 'orderly progression of events'. De Klerk followed these recommendations almost to the letter.

The third is the release of political prisoners. This effectively raises the question of indemnity and amnesty, which later became two of the most complex and bitterly contested issues in the course of negotiations.

The terms 'indemnity' (being granted immunity against prosecution) and 'amnesty' (being granted immunity from prosecution or official pardons specifically for political offences) do not appear in the Harare Declaration, presumably because these would need to be granted by the South African state, which the ANC and the declaration did not recognise. However, they are implied by several of its preconditions for entering negotiations, namely releasing all political prisoners and detainees; lifting all bans and restrictions on proscribed and restricted organisations and persons; and ceasing all political trials and political executions.

The underlying idea, as expressed in the declaration and the ANC's January 8 statement, was that all members of the ANC and other previously proscribed organisations, including those in prison and in exile, should enjoy the same freedom to engage in political activity as members of the NP. This implied that ANC members in prison should be pardoned and released, and that all members of the ANC in exile who faced charges in South Africa for politically related offences should be granted indemnity against prosecution, thus allowing them to return to South Africa.

This later became controversial because it was reciprocal; the notion of 'amnesty' for political offences applied not only to members of banned organisations, but to members of right-wing organisations and the South African security forces as well, thus protecting them against possible prosecution for human rights violations in the course of acting against banned people and organisations and defending the apartheid state.

In this regard, the main memorandum of 29 January began to develop a significant distinction between 'technical' offences, namely those 'merely' related to membership of a prohibited organisation, and 'violent' offences, namely those related to people being killed or injured, or property being damaged. While 'security prisoners' jailed for 'technical' offences would need to be released when the prohibitions on their organisations were lifted, amnesty for 'violent' offences could only start receiving attention in the course of a negotiation process. For some reason, the covering memorandum containing the recommendations of the Ministerial Committee did not refer to this issue at all.

De Klerk again adopted this argument, announcing that people serving prison sentences merely because they were members of prohibited organisations, or because a prohibition on one of the organisations was in force, would be released. Prisoners sentenced for offences such as 'murder, terrorism or arson' would not be affected.

As noted previously, the memorandum developed the same distinction with respect to exiles. However, De Klerk did not refer to the issue of exiles at all. Given the importance this issue would assume in the coming months and years – with the continued involvement of Kobie Coetsee – this was a notable omission. Indeed, De Klerk would later write that the question of amnesty was probably the government team's 'greatest failure' during the constitutional negotiations.[3]

All this helps to underline that De Klerk's speech was more complex than was generally realised, either then or since. Taken together, his speech and the memorandums underline that it was more of a group effort, drawing on consultations and a series of cabinet mandates and decisions, than a purely personal one – again, partially working against the 'personal epiphany' explanation living on in popular memory.

Indeed, in the speech itself, he stated: 'These decisions by the Cabinet are in accordance with the government's declared intention to normalise the political process in South Africa without jeopardising the maintenance of good order . . . They were preceded by thorough and unanimous advice by a group of officials, which included members of the security community . . .' This seems to refer to the Ministerial Committee and the working group that produced the 29 January memorandums. At the same time, as De Klerk suggests, the draft passages in the archive reveal that he put his own stamp on the speech, in style as well as substance.

The speech demonstrates that, at that stage, De Klerk still believed in the protection of 'collective, minority and national rights'; and that negotiations should take place, non-negotiably, in a context of the 'maintenance of law and order'. But it also contains other themes and lines of argument that have gained significance over time.

To the extent that De Klerk's remarks about the economy can be taken to constitute a template for post-apartheid economic development, it is sobering to juxtapose this with the extent to which South Africa's post-apartheid governments have failed progressively to achieve these objectives, and are stumbling over aspects – such as the prudent fiscal management of state economic enterprises, and limiting state expenditure as well as levels of national debt – that De Klerk believed his government was in the process of addressing. If a sound economy was a baton De Klerk thought he would pass to the next government in the 'new South Africa', he has grounds for believing that it has been comprehensively dropped since then.

Lastly, the address underlines that the Harare Declaration played a far more important role in shaping the government's actions at that stage than has generally been acknowledged. It was perhaps understandable that De Klerk did not refer to the declaration; he could hardly be seen as acknowledging that the government was responding to terms dictated to it by the ANC and the United Nations. However, a close reading, against the background of the secret memorandums, reveals the extent to which the declaration had come to dominate government strategy at that time and, eventually, De Klerk's renowned address.

The proceedings in parliament on 2 February, then, were dominated by two absent figures: Prisoner 913, who was watching them on a TV set in his cottage at Victor Verster Prison; and Oliver Tambo, who was recovering from his stroke in a clinic in Sweden.

25

A visit from Winnie

*'I warned our people that De Klerk meant what he said.
They should have prepared themselves for this . . .'*

WINNIE MANDELA visited Prisoner 913 on Sunday, 4 February 1990 – just two days after De Klerk's speech in parliament. A handwritten transcript of the conversation – written in Afrikaans – resides in the Coetzee archive. Translated extracts appear below.

> 9Mandela tells Winnie he is glad to see her. He then asks: 'How is Johannesburg?'
> Winnie replies: 'People are excited . . .
> However, they do not seem overtly excited themselves.

They spend some time discussing Zindzi and her response to the death in detention of Clayton (Twala) Sithole, her former partner and father of her child, the previous week. (Sithole and four other men were arrested in Soweto on Friday, 26 January, on suspicion of belonging to an 'ANC cell' responsible for killing numerous people, including two policemen, during the previous two years. On Thursday, 1 February, police announced that he had been found hanging from a shower pipe at police headquarters in Johannesburg. F.W. de Klerk announced a judicial commission of inquiry into his death on the same day. It found later that Sithole had committed suicide.)

They discuss problems around Zindzi getting a passport. Mandela calls the person writing the transcript, and asks him to take up the issue with the Director-General of Justice, S.S. van der Merwe. Winnie wants to leave at 2.20 pm, but 913 asks her to leave later.

They continue to discuss Zindzi, as well as a UDF mass meeting in Alexandra. 913 mentions a visit the next day from Joseph Balizulu, as well as impending visits from the clerics Desmond Tutu and Allan Boesak. 913 then tells Winnie that a planned visit to F.W. de Klerk the previous Thursday had not taken place.

> Winnie: Would it really have happened?
> 913: Yes, but news of the visit leaked out.
> Winnie: It must have been [leaked by] themselves . . .
> 913: We left at 09h30, and the press were on us. It wasn't just our people; N.I. [National Intelligence] also took part in the exercise. We were at the Commissioner's house at Pollsmoor the whole day. I then heard it on the seven o'clock news . . . Then Minister Coetsee and Dr Viljoen came to the Commissioner's house . . .
> Winnie: Good God.
> 913: That is what happened. I then saw the two ministers . . . They informed me about what F.W. was going to say. F.W. wanted to tell me himself, but I did not see him. [A note in the transcript reads: Speaking softly and inaudibly, he tells Winnie what he discussed with the ministers about his release . . .] You must say nothing to the press . . . I am sure we will soon hear about the release of the political prisoners. I warned our people that De Klerk meant what he said. They should have prepared themselves for this.

Winnie talks about a statement by an ANC or UDF figure that 913 could not simply leave prison and take over the leadership of the ANC. She says it was handled in a very clumsy way.

> 913: He just didn't choose the right words.
> Winnie: I think we underestimated him [probably De Klerk].
> 913: Yes.
> Winnie: Thabo [Mbeki] was very diplomatic . . .
> 913: By the way, the press will ask you about my reaction to Friday's announcements. Tell them the press has provided good coverage and

that there is no room for my opinion. Tell them I will issue a statement later. We have to be careful . . .
[Mandela tells Winnie about the groups of people he has already seen.]
They have asked me to keep 14 days open. I might still see him. [Note in the transcript: This seems to be F.W. !!]

They discuss issues surrounding Mandela's lawyer, Ismail Ayob. Referring to his conversation with Thabo Mbeki on 22 January, Mandela then says:

Thabo made a mistake. The ministers said the ANC should respond. I said they had already responded. They said, no, the ANC still declared that the armed struggle should continue. This is what the ministers got from Sapa Reuters. [Note in the transcript: He shows the report to Winnie.]
Winnie: Nzo's statement about the armed struggle put us in a difficult position . . . This has caused many problems among the youth. They wanted to know how the organisation could give up the struggle . . .
913: We must be careful what we say in the press. Thabo should have read the whole statement to me.
Winnie: It was a mistake on Thabo's side . . .
913: We say the armed struggle is purely defensive. We should reach a settlement about how the RSA should be governed, then we can stop the armed struggle. We should follow Namibia's example.
Winnie: What about the defence force . . . on our side and the government side?
913: We don't accept that we should disband our defence force. We will never do this.
Winnie: While F.W. spoke, the shooting in the townships continued. By the time the defence force and the police leave the townships, it will be 1995.
913: This is why I am writing the letter. We will not disband our army before there is certainty about how the RSA will be governed. This is the position. I have stated this clearly. [They have lunch, and talk about the heat in Paarl.]

913: It was a mistake to publish the document in *South*.

Winnie: Maybe, in the end, it was a good thing . . .

An argument develops about Winnie's conduct in public. At one point, Winnie says: 'I'm trying, I'm trying . . .' And later: 'You don't know the other side of the story . . .'

At this point, the author of the transcript records: 'I go outside. Members report that the press have climbed in a tree to try to take pictures of 913 and Winnie in the garden. The tree is about 1 kilometre from the house. I don't think they can see them from where they are . . .' The transcript continues:

> 913 talks about the RMC [Release Mandela Campaign] and that there are no prominent people serving on the committee. Winnie laughs.
>
> Winnie: People throughout the country are celebrating the legalisation of the ANC . . .
>
> 913: The whole story about whether I am a leader or not . . . We must handle this carefully. I have never said anything of this nature. I have never said I should have things easy when I go out.
>
> Winnie: No one else has said this either . . .

At the end of the visit, Mandela goes to his study and writes Zindzi a note about the death of Sithole. A copy of the note is appended to the transcript. It reads:

> 4.2.90
>
> Darling,
>
> What has happened has happened and no useful purpose can be served by torturing yourself over it. Pull yourself up, darling, and remember that we love you very dearly. Let's forget what . . . cannot be changed . . . I love you.
>
> Tata

26

Pressures in Paarl

'Of course, they can release me like a "jailer" towards a prisoner, but then I will be of no use to them. Also, I will then have no obligation towards them at all . . .'

On 5 February, Mandela's first visit was from the Reverend Anthony Simons. A handwritten account of the conversation appears in the archive. A translation of parts of the conversation appears below.

08h30: General greetings.
913: It looks like you had traffic problems.
Simons: Yes. Terrible.
913: I am expecting another visitor at nine. The pressure is extreme . . . (Mandela talks about the heat, and asks about Simons's daughter and her studies at the University of Cape Town.)
Simons: How do you cope with the pressure?
913: Just go and have a look at my table. It's terrible.
Simons: Are people coming after two?
913: Oh yes. Dr Stock is coming after you, and then a person from Robben Island. He is the son of my paramount chief in the Transkei.
Simons: There was jubilation in the streets of Cape Town, and the ANC flag flew after Friday's announcement. There is huge anticipation.
913: Yes. The government said they wanted to release me in an atmosphere in which I could participate, and they told me what they would do. I said the state of emergency must first be lifted before I could go. Of course, they can release me like a 'jailer' towards a prisoner, but then I will be of no use to them. Also, I will then have no obligation towards them at all.
Simons: Your wife says you don't want to (go out).

913: That is not so. I have my conditions. That is the position. Well, let us continue with the purpose of the visit.

Simons: Starts with spiritual ministration. Prayer and end of visit.

////

The anticipated visit from Joseph Balizulu took place in the afternoon. A transcript of this meeting also appears in the archive. Again, it records that Balizulu is the son of Mandela's area chief in Qunu in the Transkei.

Balizulu tells Mandela about his trip from the Island, and how he was summoned and only informed at the last minute that he would be taken to see him. Mandela asks him about his arrest. Balizulu explains that he was arrested in November 1987 while on his way into exile via Botswana. He was sentenced to twelve years, but was told he would only serve eight years. Colleagues were being arrested in the Transkei, where they had hidden firearms.

Previously, he had worked in Salt River, Elsies River, Koeberg and Stellenbosch, but had then returned to the Transkei. Mandela shows him the house and garden. They talk at length about people and places in the Transkei, as well as Transkeian politics.

Mandela tells Balizulu that he had seen P.W. Botha in July the previous year, and F.W. de Klerk in December. They had spoken about preconditions. (The transcript notes that Mandela is whispering, and a noisy fan is running.) He was again due to see De Klerk the previous Thursday, but the press ruined this, and he then spoke to Minister Coetsee. They spoke about political prisoners and the state of emergency, and that he did not want to leave prison and leave his comrades behind.

913: They must first go. All the prisoners must be out before I leave, and the state of emergency must be ended. That is what I said. If they want to, they can simply release me, but then I will go straight back to MK. This is what I said. If all the conditions are met, I can still make a contribution.

> Balizulu: On the Island they are saying that everyone should leave, or otherwise everyone will stay. But there are others who say they don't agree with us. (Conversation very soft and unclear.)
> 913: If they want me to cooperate, they have to release all the political prisoners, and all our conditions must be met. I will leave when all my comrades have left. If they release me in any other way, I will go straight to MK.
> Balizulu: I will report this on Robben Island. What about your safety?
> 913: That is our affair.

They move to Mandela's study, where he shows his visitor some documents and correspondence. The transcription notes: 'The conversation is very faint, but the Revox machine is on. The tapes will be given to Mr Van den Heever.')

Mandela and Balizulu then have lunch. Mandela switches on a radio and tunes in to a station playing Indian music. They discuss people and places in the Transkei, as well as people and conditions on Robben Island.

Mandela asks Balizulu to convey his greetings to everyone on the Island. 'Tell them I am working hard, and I want them all out. Foreign pressure about this is very high . . .'

27

Snacks, drinks and lunch for 22

*'I have no date . . . They still want me, so they
must first normalise the situation. Minister Viljoen said yesterday
it will happen within weeks . . .'*

MANDELA MET the National Executive Committee of the UDF on 9 February. A group of 22 people, they came in the morning and stayed for lunch. Both Mandela and his visitors had no idea that he would be released two days later. The meeting was taped by both the Prisons Service and the NIS. The Coetsee archive contains a summary based on the first set of recordings, and selected pages from the record compiled by the NIS. It starts with a long peroration by Mandela.[1]

913: I am glad for the opportunity to see the entire NEC. I don't know whether you have an agenda, but I first want to explain the situation about my release. It is difficult to convey this in the press. I have discussed this intensively with the Government. From 1986, I have addressed two questions: first, the release of political prisoners, and second, a meeting between the government and the ANC.

I will not abide by any restrictions. If they want me to cooperate, they must first meet all the demands. I met Minister Coetsee in Cape Town on 25 January, we talked about the preconditions. He said the ANC would be unbanned, I would be released, and would I continue to talk to them. I said when I am free, the ANC will decide about my fate and not me. [Note in the transcript: He explains the two options for his release.] We spoke for three hours, but could not agree.

On 1 February I was meant to see the SP, but this was wrecked by the press. We then went to Pollsmoor, and it was surrounded. Minister

Coetsee and Minister Viljoen were sent to me to tell me what the SP would have said. I said it wasn't enough. As long as the state of emergency remained in force and political prisoners remained in prison, it was not acceptable. They said they had met two thirds [of the preconditions] and the ANC should now meet its side of the bargain. I said they should talk to the ANC, it still wasn't enough.

When I saw the SP in December, he asked me how I would define a political prisoner. Given the complexity of this question, I said they should talk to the ANC. I said I would have to report back to the ANC, and I then spoke with Nzo and Mbeki. Thabo phoned back and accepted the 'compromise'. Viljoen said no, they did not, they are stepping up their onslaught. I looked at it again that night, and could not find it. I asked them [Minister Viljoen] to send me a complete statement. I then clarified my position.

I also spoke about how I want to be released. I want to be released here. They said, no, it isn't safe. I said, the NRC [National Reception Committee] will see to it, and the government must talk to them. This is what they did with 916 [Sisulu], and they were satisfied.

They are scared of crowds. They are coming again today at two, so we have to finish before then. I want to ask the Major whether we can continue until we are finished or until they arrive. They are often late.

They also spoke about security – threats against my life. I said this might come from right-wingers, but not from my own people. No leader [in this position] would accept the government's 'protection'. We have our own trained people. I want peace in the way in which the ANC wants it.

Mandela reads some letters handed to him by Colonel Gordon, apparently containing requests for meetings and interviews.

913: The team has already asked whether I would address the South African press. I said this was in the hands of the NRC. Talk to them. I don't want to make distinctions – everybody supported our struggle. The NRC must decide.

Mandela and others talk about people who have submitted applications or requests to see him in prison. They also talk about providing Walter Sisulu with a secretary, as he is falling behind in his work. Tea and snacks are served. A delegate hands Mandela a copy of a document on the NEC's resolutions and the state of the UDF.

> There is one aspect which is not reflected in the media, namely the feeling underground, and we hope it will help you. You are now a free man. We must just mobilise our forces. Fifty thousand, 80 000 are just figures to you, but there are many people . . . The people are moving, and they are just waiting for your leadership. [General laughter]

The same speaker then briefs Mandela on the genesis and current state of the UDF. He says the UDF and other organisations are trying to establish a national organisation, and the UDF is due to discuss mass mobilisation with COSATU the next month. Seemingly trying to brief Mandela on the state of play in the government (which was rather like carrying coals to Newcastle), he continues:

> Fighting in the cabinet continues. President De Klerk is honest and flexible. He is assisted by Minister Coetsee and Minister Viljoen. The three of them want change. I told the ANC our policy should be based on harsh realities. We must be led by this.
>
> I am glad about the ANC's comments thus far. They are now going to sit and debate this. Their response thus far has not been identical. They expect us to respond in a day or two. From this distance, it is difficult to understand everything. We said an election for the government should be held separately. A ceasefire is something between the government and the ANC.
>
> The government has also seen homeland leaders, and they must treat the ANC in the same way. There must be voting about who should sit down [in negotiations], otherwise we will be in a minority. To forestall this, we have to vote. We are on the way to negotiations, and if we vote we

will be able to say who will sit down and who not. I am glad the UDF and ANC are talking with one voice. We want victory in our lifetime, and if we don't get it, our followers will have it. [Applause]

913: The violence in Natal is a subject of discussion between myself and the government. I wrote to Gatsha [Buthelezi], and the government objected to certain passages, and I had to rewrite it. I told the team the government should talk to the ANC, and those problems would disappear.

I am sorry that the UDF and Inkatha have stopped talking. We mustn't destroy what we have built over seventy years. Inkatha's power is waning. He [Buthelezi] is making mistakes, and that is encouraging . . . We have to neutralise Inkatha . . . but forces outside Inkatha are helping them to fight . . .

The ANC said he [Buthelezi] should go to Lusaka, but then the NEC wouldn't see him. He is angry because he believes we have lowered his status. We are meeting people like P.W., so why not him? He should meet with O.R. [Tambo] – it will help a lot.

Visitor: There are almost 5 000 journalists in South Africa. We are going to ask the government to advise us in advance when you will be released, so that we can address this problem. We want the NRC to come here on Monday to discuss these problems.

913: Although we are not under supervision, don't believe that we are alone. Nothing has been said that cannot be disseminated, but please be careful . . . [Note in the transcript: Silence. Somebody whispers, and there is laughter. Silence. People talk to one another in whispers.]

913: I think the release will be here, but they are scared of crowds. I hope to convince them. It will be the task of the NRC to take me away. I have no date. [He again talks about the two options for his release.] They still want me, so they must first normalise the situation. Minister Viljoen said yesterday it will happen within weeks.

Delegate: Did you ask the government to see the NRC?

913: Yes. This is about the release. I am not going to grant interviews inside prison. We will have to have a prepared statement when I go, and a press conference could follow. They are worried about prisoners coming out, and groups uniting outside. This must be addressed.

They talk about the house in Soweto Mandela would return to. He says if they can't get house number 8114, he would be satisfied with 8115. A delegate remarks that he would have to get a more spacious place.

> 913: I think I have dealt with everything.
> Visitor: We hear what 913 says. He does not want any interviews before his release.
> 913: I will be grateful if the NRC could manage everything.
> Visitor: We must convey to the press that we are going to work through one channel.
> [They adjourn for lunch.]

Delegates talk about the release. One suggests that diplomats should be present – including the Swedish delegation. So should Sisulu and the other recently released prisoners. They talk about sanctions, and someone says the pressure should not be lifted.

> 913: I am satisfied with your decisions outside. I am seeing almost everyone – from right to left. I also have to say, I am on the point of going out and am not familiar with life outside. I am going to meet officials and others, and I have to be prepared.

A delegate says the UDF will undertake political briefings, and the NRC will deal with the reception. Another delegate talks about the Commonwealth Group, and wants a set of proposals from 913.

> 913: Let us first leave that matter there. Let me know later. Dullah [Omar], what about a response to President De Klerk's speech?
> Omar: When Winnie was here last, she said you were preparing a statement.

249

913: I am ready with it. But I must first talk to them this afternoon. When they want to make a statement, they first show it to me.
(He goes on to defend Winnie): You must handle this. The media will probe. What everybody should be concerned about is what I have said to the government, not what other people are saying.

A delegate talks about the preconditions for negotiations. He says he agrees that there must be a vote to decide who will sit at the table and negotiate.

913: We must think about tactics. What we want is an economic climate that will suit everybody. We should not say we have a socialist or capitalist system. You immediately divide people. There must be a vote on who will sit down. We must say we want a constituent assembly.

Mandela is informed that the 'team' has arrived. A visitor praises 913 for his good work, and says his interaction with the government will be reported back to every region. Everyone applauds. Mandela thanks them for their support for the movement and the struggle, and the opportunity to exchange ideas. He says he will report back to the NRC. The visitors applaud again, and sing 'Nkosi Sikelel' iAfrika', followed by chants of 'Amandla! Awethu!' The meeting ends at 2.21 pm.

At that point, Mandela was entirely unaware that the 'team' would take him to Tuynhuys, where De Klerk would tell him that he would be released in Johannesburg in two days' time.

28

Panic stations

'I have no plans, except to walk out of here . . .'

In *Long Walk to Freedom*, Mandela writes that he and the 'team' arrived at Tuynhuys at six o'clock in the evening, to be met by a smiling De Klerk. 'As we shook hands, he informed me that he was going to release me from prison the following day.' Although his release seemed imminent, this came as a surprise. 'I had not been told that the reason De Klerk wanted to see me was to tell me that he was making me a free man . . .'[1]

Mandela felt a 'conflict between his blood and his brain'. He wanted to leave prison as soon as he could, but to do so at such short notice would be unwise. He thanked De Klerk, but said that, at the risk of appearing ungrateful, he would prefer a week's notice so that his family and organisation could prepare for his release.

Taken aback, De Klerk continued to talk about releasing him in Johannesburg the next day. However, Mandela told him he wanted to walk out of the gates of Victor Verster, to thank those who had looked after him and to greet the people of Cape Town, which had been his home for nearly three decades. Once he was free, he would look after himself. De Klerk initially said it was too late to change the plans. After a 'short standoff' during which De Klerk left the room twice to consult with others, he agreed to a compromise, namely that Mandela would be released from Victor Verster the next day.

Mandela writes that he did not get back to his cottage until shortly before midnight. He immediately sent word to his colleagues in

Cape Town that he would be released the following day. He managed to get a message to Winnie, and telephoned Walter Sisulu in Johannesburg. They would all fly down in a chartered plane. The same evening, members of the NRC came to the cottage to draft a statement he would make the next day. They left in the early hours of the morning, and he had no trouble falling asleep.

Throughout this passage, *Long Walk to Freedom* reflects an elementary error. It suggests that Mandela would be released 'the next day', on Saturday, 10 February. Instead, other sources confirm that De Klerk told him from the outset that he would be released two days later, on Sunday, 11 February, and this date never changed. Members of the NRC visited him on the Saturday evening.

////

Dullah Omar and five other members of the National Reception Committee arrived at Mandela's cottage in the late afternoon. The group also included Bulelani Ngcuka, UDF leader in the Western Cape. A handwritten record of the visit resides in the Coetsee archive. After greeting Mandela, they call for whisky.

A visitor says they were due to have a conference with General Willemse that morning, but it was cancelled. They then met with him in the H.F. Verwoerd Building, next to the Houses of Parliament. Afterwards they talked to Brigadier Griebenouw, the officer in charge of the South African Police. The next morning, access to certain areas would be restricted. Brigadier Griebenouw wants to hear about the NRC's plans after the release. 'We phoned London and Lusaka, but we could not raise Lusaka, and in London we had to leave a message on a machine.' They ask for more brandy and whisky. Omar proposes a toast to 913's leadership.

913: I was so glad to get the news yesterday evening . . . They took me there after you left.

Omar says thousands of people are gathering. Another visitor says there are already ANC flags at the gate.

> 913: We took some photographs last night. [He talks about the convoys when he leaves the prison; about the press undermining some excursions; and photographs that should not be published.]

A visitor reads a fax from Willemse. Another says they are planning a rally for 4.30 pm. Mandela asks them when the news leaked out.

> Visitor: I heard it from the press at about 13:00. But I think we should look at actions. What are your thoughts?
> Mandela: I have no plans, except to walk out of here.
> Visitor: We spoke today with KVG [Willemse]. With their help we will bring Winnie down. We decided that the NRC would arrange everything. The first venue we considered was Dal Josafat Stadium in Paarl, but too many people from Cape Town would come. We have thought about a press conference at the Cape Sun [a hotel in central Cape Town] at 16:30. We could ask the mayor for some streets to be closed off. We could then get the Mayor's Balcony at the City Hall. The mayor will co-operate. Transport has already been laid on for you and the NRC.
> Another visitor: We also need to consider security. The City Council will provide an escort of traffic officers on motorcycles, complete with ANC flags. We also think you should stay with Archbishop Tutu in Bishopscourt tomorrow evening.
> 913: Have you contacted him yet?
> Visitor: No.
> 913: I don't think the government would like this. [Note in the transcript: This could also be the ANC.]

A visitor explains the advantages. Security is very good. They are also worried that the press will harass Mandela. They could also place marshals at strategic points. Mandela again harks back to his meeting with De Klerk:

913: When the SP told me about the release, I pointed out to him that this was on very short notice. I said the NRC will have problems. [He explains the arrangements that had been made, and which the SP passed on to him, and says it was done for security reasons.]

I also said I was surprised by the lengths they had gone to. They wanted to release me in an orderly way. I could not accept it because I want to be released here. They talked again about the security considerations. I referred to the orderly protest march [in Cape Town] the previous year, and said the NRC could handle the situation. I also told them that my stay in Cape Town – probably a day or two – would depend on the NRC. The government is afraid of crowds. I was at Tuynhuys from 18:00 until midnight.

Visitor: So they accepted Plan A.

913: Yes.

Omar: I'm not very impressed with Bishopscourt. I think we should look at Gugulethu [a black township of Cape Town]. The people there will come up with a solution.

Visitor: I don't agree. It is important for the people to hear what their leader thinks as quickly as possible.

Visitor: This is a difficult situation, and we have to be careful. It comes back to safety and security.

Visitor: We will get the regional committee of the NRC to see to the local situation.

Visitor: The first choice remains that the people's feelings are also taken into consideration.

913: That is so. I'm in your hands.

Omar: I still think the Grand Parade is the most important.

Visitor: The idea of going into the townships is problematic, because you would have to go in unseen.

Visitor: Let us leave it there for the moment. Bulelani [Ngcuka] and I will see to the security arrangements.

913: As regards the speech, I can do it, but I will leave the form and layout to you.

Visitor: This is still quite unreal.

> 913: My reaction is also still one of . . . [illegible]. When they told me yesterday evening, I got a shock. The SP called me to inform me about the release. Ministers Coetsee and Viljoen were also present. I told them what when I am free, the discussions will be different, because then I would fall under the banner of the NEC of the ANC.
>
> [Committee members ask him about the meeting.]
>
> 913: As regards the state of emergency, they said there are developments. The issue of political prisoners should form part of the negotiation process. I also explained that due to political changes, people in prison should no longer serve political sentences. They said I should meet them halfway, because they are under tremendous pressure. I also said I want to be released immediately.

Mandela leaves the room. Committee members discuss the situation surrounding Jesse Jackson, who has arrived in Cape Town. They differ about whether he should be involved in the proceedings. One committee member says Jackson should rather not be involved. Another says he told Jackson he was needed. He is the first person who has come out to South Africa after the State President's speech. Therefore, he has to be accommodated. They discuss the size of the balcony at the City Hall. Mandela says he is glad about the decision that Jackson should be involved.

> 913: If tomorrow the people are told, there is the South African Defence Force, the crowd would attack them with their bare hands.

He goes on to suggest that a press release should be issued after the rally. An official press conference could be held a few days later.

> Visitor: The questions that could be asked at a press conference could be problematic – especially when someone has been in prison for such a long time. I still think a press conference should be held tomorrow, and I'm convinced the press knows what to expect and could handle this in terms of questions.

Mandela suggests that the rally should be held on Monday evening instead of the next evening. They discuss this option for a while. Omar says the press conference could be held at the University of the Western Cape in Bellville. Another committee member says it would still develop into a rally. However, they decide on a press conference at UWC at 3 pm. [This never took place.]

> 913: I have no idea what to say.
> Visitor: We will first make a broad statement, and then call for questions.
> 913: Good. They will ask about the leadership of the ANC, and the press does not understand this. I will have to explain the concept of the leadership of the ANC and how they are elected. We must clarify this at the first opportunity. But we must not expand on this – we must simply say we are loyal members of the ANC.
> Visitor: We must not create the impression that you have abandoned the struggle, because the government has not yet touched apartheid. At this point, we should rather intensify it.
> Another visitor: The speech must fit with the press release. In our view we should stick to the fundamental things we believe in. We have strong organisation, and we must keep up the pressure. We should also bear the international community in mind.
> Omar: In your speech, I don't think you should get involved with the issue of negotiations. Our opponents are suddenly also negotiating with other organisations.
> Visitor: The press will also ask you a lot of questions about the organisation. Have you agreed with the State President about certain things? What will your role be in the organisation? What will you now offer the government? What is your view about sanctions? And the involvement of exiles in the negotiations? [Mandela offers them coffee.]

Omar says they will work out some questions and answers, and get them to Mandela the next day. At the press conference, they will tell the journalists they will not allow too many questions. Questions must have international impact, otherwise they will not be answered.

> 913: I will leave the first meeting to you. When I am out and address a rally in Johannesburg, it will be different.

A visitor says he is worried about the next day.

> 913: You can decide what you want and don't want in the press releases. There is a rally, so there must be a media conference tomorrow as well about the intensification of the struggle. The document states clearly what the ANC's viewpoints are. I also conveyed this to the government and team. They can't expect us not to rely on the intensification of the struggle. Negotiations have not begun, and we are still trying to normalise the situation. The ANC is still banned, its leaders are still outside, and the government still has the initiative. We can now talk to the ANC to get a mandate. The people will also ask, the SP has made his moves, so what are you (the ANC) going to do now?
>
> Omar: I need to raise another problem. There are differences in the ranks of the MDM. I think we should call on everyone to collaborate. Winnie has discussed certain things about this. The UDF and NRC wanted to approach the people involved, but this did not happen.
>
> [Note in the transcript: it seems that Winnie is not happy about certain things.] I want you to be aware of this. I could not talk to Winnie, because she was at the funeral today. We will still contact her. Should the planning change, we will contact you.

Mandela says Winnie was supposed to visit him the next day. Omar says he thinks she is on the 7.30 am flight. Willemse said he would help if problems arose.

> 913: This is all good. There are certain things I want to discuss with Winnie – also things she should discuss with the ANC. My problem with Winnie is that when she leaves here, she discusses certain things with people and I don't always know who they are. It was very good to see you.
>
> Visitor: I came to Cape Town for a completely different reason, and now I'm involved in this . . .

913: What will happen about transport?

Omar: We will provide transport, but we will also discuss this with the government. How much stuff do you have?

913: Let me show you. [They go to the bedroom.] We can leave the goods here, they will look after it.

Omar: If some of it is essential, we will take it with us. We can't remove the goods tomorrow, in front of all the people.

913: This is fine. [He talks about Adjutant Swart, who also worked on the Island.]

Omar tells Mandela that Cyril Ramaphosa wants to see him about the house in Soweto. It seems as if problems have arisen. Mandela says Winnie has told him the neighbour doesn't want to sell. The meeting ends.

29

The last report

*'He says he will miss us a lot and
that we should not lose contact with him . . .'*

AN undated typed document stamped 'SECRET' appears in the Coetsee archive. It is written in Afrikaans. A complete translation appears below.

THE CHRONOLOGICAL EVENTS SURROUNDING MANDELA AFTER HIS RELEASE WAS MADE KNOWN TO HIM ARE AS FOLLOWS:
FRIDAY, 9 FEBRUARY 1990

00:30   Leaves Tuynhuys.

00:45   913 asks Brigadier Gillingham who the lady was who took the photographs and that he does not want them published without his prior permission. (Photographs of him with officials.)
 Brig G   Says it is a lady from NI [National Intelligence] and that the photographs will not be published. After all, there is an agreement between the Commissioner of Prisons and 913 in this regard.
 Note   913 sat and slept all the way from Paarl – he did not speak further.

01:15   Arrival at Victor Verster. 913 says he is tired and does not want to eat anything and goes straight to bed.

SATURDAY, 10 FEBRUARY 1990

06:50   913 and W/O J. Swart greet.
 913   Says he is very tired, came back late. Only wants something light to eat. He explained briefly how late he got home, and said that they

(Government) should not make decisions without consulting him first (private flight to Pretoria). Asks to see Warrant Officer Gregory, because he wants to see Winnie very urgently. (Sunday, 11 February 1990.)

W/O Gregory informs 913 that he cannot find Winnie – probably gone to Twala's funeral.

913   Oh, thank you very much.

10:00

913   Can you find me some cardboard boxes?

Jack [Swart]   Yes.

11:30

Jack to town for boxes.

13:30

913   Please put the boxes in my room and I will start packing tonight.

15:00   Lieutenant Koekemoer arrives and hands documents to 913. (Letter in which Commissioner informs him that State President after consideration of further aspects has decided that he may be released from Victor Verster, but that date of release cannot be postponed. A copy of the S.P.'s media release is appended for his prior information.)

15:30

913   Hands a note to Lieutenant Koekemoer for the Commissioner of Prisons. (About the issue of photographs of him and certain officials that were taken – requests that photographs not be published without consultation, and also expresses wish to obtain copies of previous photographs taken of him.)

Commissioner informs 913 that photographs he is concerned about have not yet been processed and are in good hands. This will be handled in a way that will accommodate his request.

As regards the previous photographs, making these available will first have to be cleared with other involved parties.

15:35

Jack: 913 says the documents are in order, but he will not leave the prison without his wife. Asks Warrant Officer Swart to help him pack.

17:00   Advocate Omar & 5 other persons from the NRC arrive for a visit. Contents of visit are briefly as follows:

Heard at 13h00 about release from the press – only announced on the news at 17h00. NRC has spoken to Commissioner – with their help Winnie will be brought down – decision that the NRC will organise everything. Will talk to Mayor and request that streets be closed off and 'Mayor's Balcony' made available – he will cooperate.

Perhaps 913 should sleep over with Tutu – safety reasons.

913 tells about President De Klerk informing him of his release and the arrangements made for his safety – cannot accept this because he wants to be released from Victor Verster. Government is scared of crowds.

NRC asks what 913 possibly expects – 913 leaves all of this to the NRC – regional committee will be tasked to see to security aspects – the feelings of the people must be taken into consideration.

913 says as far as the speech is concerned, 913 can do this but he leaves the form and layout in the hands of the NRC.

Being informed of release has shocked 913 – discussions with Government will be different after release because he will then be under the banner of the ANC NEC.

913 – Government says there are developments around the state of emergency, and the release of political prisoners forms part of the negotiation process.

Government has asked that 913 must be amenable [*tegemoetkomend*] – Government under pressure.

913 must be informed of the sentiment of people on the ground – [Jesse] Jackson must not be involved, he will get a later opportunity to talk to 913 – Jackson has his own world and ideas and this remains 913's day. 913 is glad that Jackson is involved in some way – the global impact is important.

913 says that the crowd will tackle the SADF with bare hands if this is said so tomorrow.

913 says a statement should be given to the press after the 'rally'. The press does not have to be told what has been discussed – as in the Sisulu case – only hold an official press conference a few days later – TV will be informed accordingly. Press conference can be held at UWC – announce this 3 hours before the time – 913 has no idea what to say – NRC suggests a broad statement first and press can then ask questions – leadership of the ANC will be a question that will have to be clarified – issue of democratic elections – secondly the issue of cooperation – refer in particular to released prisoners – the organisation's policy explained.

The contents of the release are discussed – stick to the fundamental things the ANC believes in – pressure must be maintained – international community must be kept in mind – negotiations could possibly be ruled out in speech – opponents are also suddenly busy with negotiations with other parties – questions must be about what international impact [the release] will have otherwise they will not be answered.

913 leaves this to the NRC.

21:30   Advocate Omar and others leave.

SUNDAY, 11 FEBRUARY 1990

06:45   913 is very quiet – seems tense and only eats a light breakfast. Asks whether we have made contact with his wife.

Major Marais says they are still trying to get hold of her.

07:30   Brigadier Keulder visits 913 and concludes documentation related to his release. Hands 913 a wallet on behalf of Commanding Officer and Staff. A month's medical supplies are also handed to him. (913 emotional)

Note: 913 walks around the house in his pyjamas the whole morning and asks every now and then whether there is any news of Winnie.

09:00   Omar and 2 others visit and bring 913 a typed version of speech.

10:00   913 showers and puts on suit (shirt and trousers).
Still asks whether Winnie is on her way. (We don't know.) He says he will miss us a lot and that we should not lose contact with him.

11:00   Asks after Winnie once again. Lies down on bed in spare room for a 'nap'. Does not really want to talk – seems very tense.

14:00   913 gets up – asks for something light to eat. Again asks after Winnie, inform him that she landed at 14h00 and that she is on her way. (Seems relieved.)

15:15   Winnie and 30 people with vehicles arrive (4 helicopters circle the house). Winnie first enters the house alone – no product (recording) could be made due to the noise. The other people enter the house. Short speeches by various people. 913 again goes through his speech.

15:35   Commanding Officer Victor Verster receives telephonic report from SAP (SB – Security Branch) that a London media office received an unconfirmed report that 913 would be shot by a member of the Prisons Service in the course of release. The Commanding Officer takes necessary precautionary steps and under instructions of Commissioner informs Mr Trevor Manuel (NRC) (who at that stage assumes the lead of the group that has come to collect 913) about information and about precautionary measures.

16:15   Persons leave with 913. (When he greeted us, he and Winnie were very emotional – both say we must stay in contact with them.)

A note about the references

We have described the documents in the Coetsee collection that we refer to and draw on as comprehensively as possible. At the time when our research was conducted, it was not possible to provide meaningful archival references.

Endnotes

My journey with the Coetsee archive
1. Willie Esterhuyse in collaboration with Gerhard van Niekerk, *Die Tronkgesprekke: Nelson Mandela en Kobie Coetsee se Voorpuntdiplomasie*, Tafelberg, 2019.

Eavesdropping on Mandela
1. Niël Barnard, with Tobie Wiese, *Secret Revolution: Memoirs of a Spy Boss*, Tafelberg, 2015, pp. 163-4.
2. Michelle Jones, 'The long walk to recovery from apartheid', *Cape Times*, 19 July 2012.
3. Jones, 'The long walk to recovery from apartheid'.

Who was Kobie Coetsee?
1. The Convention for a Democratic South Africa (CODESA) was the forum for South Africa's formal constitutional negotiations which began in December 1991.
2. Peroshni Govender, 'Nat minister hailed as "reformer" on death', IOL News, 29 July 2000, at https://www.iol.co.za/.
3. *The Telegraph*, 'Kobie Coetsee', Obituary, 31 July 2000, at https://www.telegraph.co.uk/news/obituaries/.
4. *The Guardian*, 'Kobie Coetsee: Afrikaner leader who foresaw the collapse of apartheid and met Mandela in jail', 5 August 2000, at https://www.theguardian.com/.
5. *The Telegraph*, 'Kobie Coetsee'.
6. John Carlin, *Knowing Mandela*, Atlantic Books, London, 2013.
7. Frontline, 'The Long Walk to Freedom: an intimate portrait of one of the 20th century's greatest leaders', interviews by John Carlin, PBS, at https://www.pbs.org/.
8. Carlin, *Knowing Mandela*, p. 87.
9. Carlin, *Knowing Mandela*, p. 85.
10. Nelson Mandela, *Long Walk to Freedom*, Abacus, London, 1995.
11. Nelson Mandela, *Conversations with Myself*, Macmillan, London, 2010, p. 252.

12. F.W. de Klerk, *The Last Trek: A New Beginning – The Autobiography*, Macmillan, London, 1998, p. 116.
13. De Klerk, *The Last Trek*, p. 117.
14. De Klerk, *The Last Trek*, p. 109.
15. De Klerk, *The Last Trek*, p. 174.
16. De Klerk, *The Last Trek*, p. 252.
17. De Klerk, *The Last Trek*, p. 288.
18. John Carlin, interview with F.W. de Klerk, 'The Long Walk to Freedom: an intimate portrait of one of the 20th century's greatest leaders', PBS, at https://www.pbs.org/.
19. Comprising key documents, timelines, biographies, and other material besides the interviews, the O'Malley Archive is an important source for students of the South African transition. O'Malley: The Heart of Hope [online], at https://omalley.nelsonmandela.org/.
20. Padraig O'Malley, interview with F.W. de Klerk, 24 July 1998.
21. John Carlin, interview with Dr Niël Barnard, 'The Long Walk to Freedom: an intimate portrait of one of the 20th century's greatest leaders', PBS, at https://www.pbs.org/.
22. Barnard, *Secret Revolution*, pp. 135-6.
23. Dr Niël Barnard, interview with Padraig O'Malley, 8 November 1999.
24. Tony Leon, *On the Contrary: Leading the Opposition in a Democratic South Africa*, Jonathan Ball, Johannesburg and Cape Town, 2008, pp. 221ff.
25. Leon, *On the Contrary*, p. 486.
26. Drawn from Patti Waldmeir, *Anatomy of a Miracle: The End of Apartheid and the Birth of the New South Africa*, Rutgers University Press, New Brunswick, NJ, 1998.

1. Let the games begin . . .
1. Also, Kobie Coetsee was not the first cabinet minister to visit Mandela in prison. In 1976, Jimmy Kruger, a previous Minister of Correctional Services, visited him twice on Robben Island with an offer to 'drastically' reduce his sentence if he agreed to move to the Transkei. Mandela, *Long Walk to Freedom*, pp. 573-4.
2. Mandela, *Long Walk to Freedom*, pp 611-12.
3. Soon after, Mandela was also visited by Prof. Samuel Dash, a law professor at Georgetown University, Washington DC. Dash was attending a NICRO conference in South Africa when, after making a critical statement about Mandela's imprisonment, he was invited by Kobie Coetsee, with the approval of the cabinet, to visit and interview Mandela in prison. Several months later, Dash wrote an article about his visit in the *New York Times* magazine ('A Rare Talk with Nelson Mandela', 7 July 1985), which was widely read internationally. Given that Mandela could not be quoted in South Africa, it received no local coverage.

4. Hansard, House of Assembly, Thursday, 31 January 1985, cols. 309-311.
5. Mandela, *Long Walk to Freedom*, pp. 621-3.

2. The missing letter to P.W. Botha
1. Mandela, *Long Walk to Freedom*, p. 621.
2. The letter itself did not surface publicly for 38 years. A copy finally appeared in *The Prison Letters of Nelson Mandela*, edited by Sahm Venter, which was released during the Mandela centenary celebrations in July 2018. Like many others, it was probably drawn from Mandela's own records of letters written in prison, including letters he was not allowed to send or distribute, which gradually became available to archivists in one way or another over the years. (According to an introduction to *The Prison Letters*, Mandela meticulously wrote handwritten copies of all these letters and kept them in files.) It was reproduced without analysis or comment.

3. Tardy ministers and the State Security Council
1. Mandela, *Long Walk to Freedom*, pp. 624ff.

4. Brothers in arms
1. Mandela, *Long Walk to Freedom*, pp. 628ff.

5. The birth of an idea
1. The full group comprised seven members, namely Malcolm Fraser, former prime minister of Australia; General Olusegun Obasanjo, former Nigerian head of state; Lord Barber, a former British cabinet minister; Dame Nita Barrow, a president of the World Council of Churches; John Malecela, former foreign minister of Tanzania; Sardar Swaran Singh, former Indian cabinet minister; and Archbishop Edward Scott of the Anglican Church of Canada. Dame Nita Barrow was not present at the meeting with Mandela.
2. This was a chamber for representatives of the Indian community, forming part of the newly introduced tricameral parliamentary system with separate representation for coloured and Indian minorities, implemented by Botha but largely devised by Heunis's father.
3. A reference to Oliver Tambo, Alfred Nzo and Thomas Nkobi – president, secretary-general and treasurer of the ANC respectively.

6. A meeting with Coetsee
1. In 2012, Pik Botha told an interviewer from the Institute of Commonwealth Studies that this request had never been conveyed to him. He clearly still felt bitter about this. 'Perhaps they decided not to inform me of Mandela's request in the light of my media statement in February

1986 to the effect that we could one day have a black president.' Sue Onslow, interview with Mr R.F. 'Pik' Botha, Akasia, Pretoria, South Africa, 13 December 2012, Institute of Commonwealth Studies [online], at https://commonwealthoralhistories.org/.
2. Mandela, *Long Walk to Freedom*, pp. 631ff.
3. Mandela, *Long Walk to Freedom*, pp. 633ff.

7. Mandela's 'political testament'
1. Mandela, *Long Walk to Freedom*, pp. 644.
2. Mandela, *Long Walk to Freedom*, pp. 646ff.
3. Barnard, *Secret Revolution*, p. 213.
4. Surprisingly, no copy of the memorandum appears in the Coetsee archive. While the wording of all known versions is similar, they vary in length, and an original title does not appear to be on record. A widely utilised source, the O'Malley Archives, now hosted by the Nelson Mandela Foundation, carries an abbreviated version titled 'Notes Prepared by Nelson Mandela for His Meeting with P.W. Botha, 5 July 1989'. Barnard, who reproduces the unabridged text in an appendix – the only document to receive this treatment in his book – does so under the title 'Nelson Mandela's Memorandum to P.W. Botha (March 1989)'. A pamphlet also containing the complete text and issued by the ANC itself in January 1990 carries the (doubly inaccurate) title *The Mandela Document: The Full Text of the Document Presented by Nelson Mandela to P.W. Botha in July 1989*.

8. Botha crosses the Rubicon, and then tries to swim back
1. Mandela, *Long Walk to Freedom*, pp. 634ff.
2. Barnard, *Secret Revolution*, p. 220.
3. *Business Day*, 'Govt takes first step on long path to ANC talks', 14 July 1989, cited in Barnard, *Secret Revolution*, p. 221.
4. Barnard, *Secret Revolution*, pp. 236ff.
5. Reports in *Rapport*, *Sunday Times* and *Sowetan*, cited in Barnard, *Secret Revolution*, p. 238.
6. Reports in *Beeld* and *Business Day*, quoted in Barnard, *Secret Revolution*, p. 239.

9. 'A conjuncture of circumstances'
1. Declaration of the Organisation of African Unity (OAU) ad hoc Committee on Southern Africa on the question of South Africa, Harare, Zimbabwe, 21 August 1989, at https://www.justice.gov.za/.
2. In what follows, we partly draw on a useful account by Kgolane Alfred Rudolph Phala, written at the time of the 25th anniversary of the Harare Declaration in 2009. K.A.R. Phala, 'The Harare Declaration: Celebrating

and Commemorating Twenty Years of the Harare Declaration', 2009, South African History Online, at https://sahistory.org.za/.
3. For a useful exegesis of the progression of ANC policy, see chapter 5 of the ANC Statement to the Truth and Reconciliation Commission, 19 August 1996, at https://www.justice.gov.za/trc/.
4. L. Callinicos, *Oliver Tambo: Beyond the Engeli Mountains*, David Philip, 2004, pp. 576, 580, cited in Phala, 'The Harare Declaration'.
5. Statement of the National Executive Committee of the African National Congress of South Africa on the question of negotiations, 9 October 1987, South African History Online, https://sahistory.org.za/.
6. Phala, 'The Harare Declaration'.
7. William Claiborne, 'De Klerk rejects interim, multiracial rule', *Washington Post*, 26 November 1989.

12. The release of the 'eight'
1. Roger Omond, 'Release of Sisulu heralds freedom for protege Mandela', *The Guardian*, 11 October 1989, at https://www.theguardian.com/.
2. De Klerk, *The Last Trek*, p. 650.
3. Mandela, *Long Walk to Freedom*, pp. 661ff.
4. Patrick Salmon, 'Chapter III: From P.W. Botha to F.W. de Klerk, January–November 1989', in: *The Unwinding of Apartheid: UK–South African Relations, 1986–1990: Documents on British Policy Overseas*, Series III, vol. XI, Whitehall Histories: Foreign and Commonwealth Office Publications, Routledge, January 2019.
5. Peter Younghusband, 'Mandela uses prison as base for political moves', *Washington Times*, 17 October 1989.

13. 'You are to blame . . .'
1. Associated Press, 'ANC leaders plan to address rally in South Africa', *Baltimore Sun*, 22 October 1989.
2. Scott Craft, 'Apartheid foes stage huge rally: South Africa: 70 000 activists welcome freed leaders of the outlawed African National Congress', *Los Angeles Times*, 30 October 1989.
3. Thula Simpson, 'Toyi-toyi-ing to Freedom: The Endgame in the ANC's Armed Struggle, 1989–1990', Unpublished MA thesis, Department of Historical and Heritage Studies, University of Pretoria, undated, at https://repository.up.ac.za/.
4. Among others, see South African History Online, https://www.sahistory.org.za/archive/speech-comrade-walter-sisulu-national-welcome-back-rally. Significantly, it is titled 'Speech by Comrade Walter Sisulu at the national welcome back rally, Johannesburg, 29 October 1989'.
5. As noted by Colin Bundy in *Nelson Mandela: A Pocket Biography*, Jacana, Johannesburg, 2015, this famous 'autobiography' is not a straightforward

text. It began with text written on Robben Island in the mid-1970s, which was revised by Sisulu, Kathrada and others. In the version published in 1994, the earlier chapters were revised and edited by Richard Stengel, and the post-1970s material was largely written by Stengel, based on interviews with Mandela. Perhaps, at the time of his conversation with Coetsee (1989), Mandela himself was working on some of the material.

14. 'A grain of sand in an oyster . . .'
1. Mandela, *Long Walk to Freedom*, pp. 662ff.
2. In fact, when the two documents are compared, it becomes clear that, whatever Mandela's own role might have been, they were almost certainly written, partly written or edited by different people.
3. Nelson Mandela, 'A document to create a climate of understanding': Nelson Mandela to F.W. de Klerk, 12 September 1989, O'Malley: Heart of Hope, https://omalley.nelsonmandela.org.
4. De Klerk, *The Last Trek*, pp. 156ff.
5. An odd anomaly arises here. In *Memoirs of a Spy Boss* (2015), Barnard writes that he was in Russia when the first meeting between De Klerk and Mandela took place, but was present during a meeting between Mandela, De Klerk and Gerrit Viljoen some time later.
6. Mandela, *Long Walk to Freedom*, pp. 664-5.

17. The ANC takes stock
1. Statement of the National Executive Committee on the Occasion of the 78th Anniversary of the ANC, 8 January 1990, South African History Online, at https://sahistory.org.za/.

18. Things hot up in Lusaka
1. Michael Savage, 'A chronology of meetings between South Africans and the ANC in exile 1983–2000', South African History Online, https://www.sahistory.org.za/.
2. Simpson, 'Toyi-toyi-ing to Freedom'.
3. This account draws heavily on Simpson, 'Toyi-toyi-ing to Freedom'.
4. According to Garth Strachan, an ANC operative then based in Zimbabwe. Cited in Simpson, 'Toyi-toyi-ing to Freedom'.
5. Bill Anderson, interviewed by Howard Barrell, 8 April 1991, Historical Papers, University of the Witwatersrand, Karis-Gerhart Collection, Folder 1, Part 1. Cited in Simpson, 'Toyi-toyi-ing to Freedom'.
6. United Press International, 'ANC admits inability to intensify armed struggle', 18 January 1990; *The Guardian*, 'ANC prepares to take the initiative on negotiations', 19 January 1990; *The Times*, 'ANC admits limits of armed struggle in South Africa', 19 January 1990; all cited in Simpson, 'Toyi-toyi-ing to Freedom'.

19. A tale of two statements
1. *Sechaba*, 'Statement of the Extended Meeting of the National Executive Committee of the African National Congress, Lusaka, Zambia, 21 January 1990', March 1990.
2. Simpson, 'Toyi-Toyi-ing to Freedom'.
3. John F. Burns, 'Call to Pretoria for negotiations issued by Mandela', *New York Times*, 26 January 1990.
4. John Battersby, 'Expectations soar in South Africa', *Christian Science Monitor*, 2 February 1990.

20. Things go south
1. *New York Times*, Excerpts from essay by Mandela for Botha, *New York Times*, 26 January 1990, https://www.nytimes.com/.
2. Burns, 'Call to Pretoria for negotiations issued by Mandela'.
3. *The Mandela Document*, at https://www.sahistory.org.za/.

21. Two notable documents . . .
1. This passage seems to refer to a clandestine channel of communicaitons between Mandela and Lusaka, probably the conduit organised by the ANC intelligence operative Mac Maharaj between Mandela and Oliver Tambo. It also implied that the government knew about it, and was aware of the contents of the communications.
2. Indeed, In *the Last Trek*, De Klerk writes that he presented his 'package' to the cabinet on 31 January.

22. . . . And an enduring mystery
1. *Mail & Guardian*, 'Mandela sends ANC his plan for peace', 19 January 1990, at https://mg.co.za/.
2. David Smith, 'Embassy cables reveal Mandela release plan', *The Guardian*, 28 November 2018, at https://www.theguardian.com/.
3. The cable itself appears in *The Guardian*'s database. See 'US Embassy cables: Essa Moosa talks about Mandela and other topics', Wednesday 17 January 1990, at https://www.theguardian.com/.

23. At the last minute 152
1. De Klerk, *The Last Trek*, pp. 63ff.
2. In the same vein, the passage also refers to Mandela's release in the 'foreseeable future' and subject to a range of 'official, practical, personal and security considerations', suggesting that the drafters still thought this would and could take far longer than it eventually did. By contrast, in his eventual speech, De Klerk merely said there were some factors in the way of Mandela's 'immediate release'.
3. No. 229 Minute from Mr Powell (No. 10) to the Prime Minister, 1 February 1990, Confidential (PREM 19/3171). Chapter IV: The Release of Nelson

Mandela, December 1989–July 1990. In *The Unwinding of Apartheid: UK–South African Relations, 1986–1990*, Documents on British Policy Overseas, Series III, vol. XI, 1st edition, edited by Patrick Salmon, Whitehall History Publishing and Routledge, 2016.

24. 'Reform in a stable climate . . .'
1. Mandela, *Long Walk to Freedom*, p. 666.
2. It appears in the O'Malley archives. See O'Malley: Heart of Hope, 'F.W. de Klerk's speech at the opening of Parliament, 2 February 1990', at https://omalley.nelsonmandela.org/.
3. De Klerk, *The Last Trek*, p. 289.

27. Snacks, drinks and lunch for 22
1. The main summary is partly written in telegram style, and cannot be regarded as an entirely accurate record of the proceedings.

28. Panic stations
1. Mandela, *Long Walk to Freedom*, p. 666ff.

Index

Africa Confidential 221
African National Congress (ANC) xi, xii, 5, 11, 16, 22, 25-29, 34-36, 38-39, 43-45, 48, 51-52, 56, 58-63, 66-69, 71-72-75, 77, 79-81, 83-86, 88-96, 99, 101, 106-110, 113, 115, 118-120, 122, 126, 131, 134, 137-140, 142-144, 152, 154-158, 161-165, 168-170, 172, 176, 178-183, 185-195, 197-219, 221-225, 226-227, 230, 234-235, 238-240, 245-248, 253, 255-257, 261-262, 267-269
amnesty for political prisoners & crimes 11, 17-19, 160, 179, 207-208, 210, 222, 234-236
Anderson, Bill 180
Archive for Contemporary Affairs (ARCA) 1, 3, 27
Asmal, Kader 107
Assange, Julian 214
Aucamp, Inus 8
Ayob, Ismail 39-41, 91, 115-116, 191-192, 240

Babangida, Ibrahim 60, 64
Balizulu, Joseph 239, 243-244
Bam, Fikile 116
Banda, Kamuzu 100
Barber, Lord 57, 68-69, 71-73, 75, 267
Barnard, Niël xi, xiv, 17-20, 31-32, 89, 92, 98-99, 102-105, 114, 134, 154, 158, 167, 193, 268, 270
Benson, Mary 115
Bethell, Nicholas 35-36, 51, 54
Bill of Rights 11, 107-108
Black Consciousness movement 217

Boesak, Allan 116, 128, 239
Botha, Elize 103-104
Botha, Pik 41, 47, 71, 77, 80, 267-268
Botha, P.W. xiv, 8-13, 15-16, 18-19, 23, 25, 28, 30-31, 33, 35-47, 51, 53-55, 59, 72, 77-78, 80, 86-87, 89-93, 97-99, 102-107, 109, 113, 118, 122, 124, 127-129, 142, 146, 149, 154-155, 158-159, 191-194, 202, 243, 248
Breytenbach, Breyten 25-26, 50
Broederbond 63
Buthelezi, Mangosuthu 36, 46, 73, 130, 134, 207, 248

Carlin, John 12-13, 16, 18, 23
Chikane, Frank 115, 128, 148, 161, 168
Chissano, Joaquim 100
Christian Science Monitor 189
Coetsee, Helena (Ena, nèe Malan) 10
Coetsee, Jan 10
Coetsee, Josephine (Van Zyl) 10, 20
Coetsee, Kobie ix-xiv, 2-6, 8-27, 29-30, 35-36, 41, 44, 46-48, 50-51, 53-57, 59-64, 66-68, 77, 79-80, 86-89, 91-92, 98-99, 101-102, 104, 113-114, 117, 120, 123-132, 134-137, 139-154, 158-162, 164-166, 172, 178, 185, 187-190, 192-193, 197, 200-201, 207, 209, 212-213, 215, 218, 221-222, 225-227, 236, 239, 243, 245-247, 252, 255, 259, 264, 266
Commonwealth Eminent Persons Group (EPG) x, 42, 57-59, 64, 66, 73, 77-79, 83-84, 86, 212
Commonwealth of Nations 106, 110, 156

Conference for a Democratic Future 200, 217
Congress of South African Students (COSAS) 76
Congress of South African Trade Unions (COSATU) 97, 125-126, 138, 154, 163, 168, 231, 247
Constitutional Court 20-21
Convention for a Democratic South Africa (CODESA) 9, 17, 265

Dash, Samuel 53, 266
De Klerk, F.W. xi-xiii, 15-20, 22, 24, 26, 47, 103-106, 112-113, 122-123, 133-134, 138, 141-142, 149, 154-162, 164, 166-168, 178, 188-190, 192-193, 196-197, 202, 212-216, 218-222, 224-239, 243, 247, 249-253, 261
Delport, Tertius 22
Democratic Party 9, 164
Dlamini, Chris 126, 163, 172
Dlamini, Thumbumuzi (Muzi) 114-116

Ehlers, Ters 102-103
Esterhuyse, Willie 5
Ex-Political Prisoners' Association 32

Fassie, Brenda 115
Financial Mail 189
Fouché, Jim 10
Fraser, Malcolm 57, 69-72, 74, 76, 267
Freedom Charter 58, 75-76, 83, 94
Frontline States 109, 149, 156, 185, 199

Gillingham, Brigadier 77, 161, 259
Goldberg, Denis 32, 45
Gomomo, John 163
Gorbachev, Mikhail 159
Gordon, Colonel 246
Gregory, Warrant Officer 260
Griebenouw, Brigadier 252
Groote Schuur Minute 11
group rights 11, 157-159
Gumede, Archie 146-147
Gwala, Harry 130

Hani, Chris 183, 200
Harare Declaration 106-108, 110, 112-113, 139, 152, 155, 161, 164, 169-170, 178, 182, 186, 188, 191, 195, 198, 203, 204, 218, 234, 237, 268
Heunis, Chris 20, 66, 72-74, 76-77, 267
Houphouët-Boigny, Felix 100
Howe, Geoffrey 84-86

Indemnity Act 11
Information Scandal 10
Inkatha Freedom Party (IFP) 207, 248
Instituut vir Eietydse Geskiedenis (INEG) 1

Jack, Mkhuseli 74
Jackson, Jesse 217-218, 255, 261
Jordan, Pallo 109
Judicial Service Commission 21

Kasrils, Ronnie 200
Kathrada, Ahmed 34, 41, 45, 89, 122-123, 129, 172, 270
Kaunda, Kenneth 100, 110, 149, 172, 181, 183
Keulder, Brigadier 262
Knowing Mandela 18
Koekemoer, Lieutenant 260
Koornhof, Piet 217

Le Grange, Louis 36, 47
Leon, Tony 9, 20-22
Lombard, Huibré 1
Long Walk to Freedom xi, xiii-xiv, 13, 34, 39, 41, 79, 86, 123, 154-155, 161, 228, 251-252
Los Angeles Times 137
Louw, Mike 102, 154, 158

Mabandla, Brigitte 107
Madikizela-Mandela, Winnie xiv-xv, 2, 4, 6, 9, 12, 20, 28, 34, 39-42, 45, 55, 59, 84, 90, 115-116, 119, 150, 152, 162, 171, 189-190, 196, 225, 238-241, 249-250, 252-253, 257-258, 260-263
Maduna, Penuell 8-9, 107, 109
Magubane (Makobane) 116
Mahomed, Ismail 151, 153
Mail & Guardian 213, 215, 218

Mail on Sunday 35-36
Malan, DF 38
Malan, Magnus 10, 78
Malecela, John 57, 73, 267
Mandela, Nelson ix-xvi, 2-6, 8-14, 16-28, 30-58, 64-77, 79-93, 95-99, 102-104, 109, 113-152, 154-168, 170-172, 173-179, 183-198, 200-204, 206, 208-209, 211-216, 218-220, 222-227, 231-232, 236-251, 254-258, 263
   monitoring conversations of (*gespreksmonitering*) 5, 7-8, 10-12, 31-32, 114-115, 161, 171-172; on Robben Island i, 8-9, 34, 55, 66, 70, 83, 91-92, 116, 118, 123, 129, 136, 146, 157, 179, 182-183, 201, 241, 243, 265, 269; in Pollsmoor 8-9, 14, 17, 23, 31, 34-35, 38, 40-41, 51, 53, 55, 57, 65, 79-81, 83, 88, 91-92, 97, 118, 123, 136, 189, 201, 225, 238, 244; at Victor Verster Prison 8-12, 19, 23, 31, 55, 87, 91, 97, 118, 129, 134, 151, 162, 179, 189, 192, 202, 214, 236, 250, 259-260, 262; and renunciation of violence & armed struggle 35-38, 42-43, 51-54, 58, 62, 68-69, 72, 74-75, 81-83, 86-87, 89, 93-94, 97, 99, 101, 103, 107, 118, 159, 163, 179, 181, 192, 198-199, 201, 203-204, 207, 232, 247; and Tuynhuys meetings with President PW Botha and FW de Klerk 92, 97-100, 103, 154, 157-161, 189, 250-258
Mandela, Zenani (Zeni) 28, 34, 114-116
Mandela, Zindzi 38, 45, 114, 116, 149-150, 152, 238, 241
Mangope, Lucas 148
Manuel, Trevor 263
Marais, Charl 28, 97, 148-149, 167, 262
Marx, Gawie 88
Masemola, Jeff 122, 129, 146-147
Mass Democratic Movement (MDM) 97, 138, 152, 154, 171-172, 199-200, 206, 217, 257

Matanzima, Kaiser 33, 36-37, 46, 54, 64, 100
Matrimonial Property Act 11
Matthews, Frieda 77
Matthews, Z.K. 62, 77, 84
Mayekiso, Moses 163
Mbeki, Epainette 172
Mbeki, Govan 48-50, 53, 55, 122-123, 172, 174
Mbeki, Thabo 84, 109, 165, 167-168, 172-179, 183-190, 202-203, 213-214, 216, 218-219, 239-240, 246
Mdlalose, Elphas 129, 131, 136, 148, 157
Meer, Fatima 150, 152
Meyer, Roelf 22, 24
Meyiwa, Matthews 129, 131, 135-136, 157
Mhlaba, Raymond 34, 41, 89, 122-123, 183
Mkwayi, Wilton 115, 122
Mlangeni, Andrew 34, 41, 89, 122-123, 129
Mobuto Sese Seko 100
Modise, Joe 181, 187
Mokoena, Aubrey 116
Moosa, Essa 214-218
Morobe, Murphy 126, 140, 143, 151
Motsoaledi, Elias 115, 122, 172
Mpetha, Oscar 122, 129, 133
Mufamadi, Sydney 163, 177
Munro, FC 53, 57, 79
'My Father Says' speech 38-39, 41, 45

National Intelligence Service (NIS) xi, xiv, 10, 12, 18-19, 30-32, 89, 103-104, 171, 239, 245, 259
National Party (NP) xii-xiii, 1, 6, 8-11, 15-17, 20-21, 23-24, 35, 42-44, 72, 86, 90, 97, 100, 103, 107, 131, 157-159, 169, 178-179, 206, 211, 216, 220, 224, 235
National Reception Committee (NRC) 137, 140, 206, 246-250, 252-254, 257, 261-263
National Security Management System 154
National Statutory Council 15

National Union of Mineworkers 126
Nelson Mandela: Conversations with Myself 14
Nelson Mandela Foundation 38
Nene, John 157
Netshitenzhe, Joel 109
New Nation 140, 143-144
New York Times 188, 191, 266
Ngcuka, Bulelane 252, 254
Nkobi, Thomas 73, 267
Nkomati Accord 107, 182
Non-Aligned Movement 156
Nzo, Alfred 73, 83, 110, 162-163, 165-167, 183, 187, 190, 202, 213-214, 216, 218, 240, 246, 267
Nzo, Regina 165

Obasanjo, Olusegun 57, 59-66, 68, 71-75, 77, 267
O'Malley, Padraig 8, 17-19, 22-26, 50, 266, 268
Omar, Dullah 20, 177, 249, 252-254, 256-258, 261-263
On the Contrary: Leading the Opposition in a Democratic South Africa 20
Organisation of African Unity 95, 106, 109-110, 156, 182

Pan Africanist Congress (PAC) 69, 116, 122, 129, 197, 204, 208-210, 215, 217, 221-222, 228, 231, 234
Peirce, Mr 133
Politico-Military Council 181
Poqo 197, 210-211, 221
Powell, Charles 133, 226-227
Pretoria Minute 18
Prisoner 913 (see Mandela, Nelson)
Progressive Federal Party 25, 44
Protection of Information Act 102

Ramaphosa, Cyril 21, 24, 126, 137, 140, 143, 146, 151, 163, 166, 172, 177, 200, 218, 258
Ramatlhodi, Ngoako 109
Release Mandela Campaign, movement 5, 36, 116, 162, 241
Rencken, Chris 221
Renwick, Robin 226-227

Rivonia trial 29, 32, 45, 50, 83, 122, 124, 129, 194, 201
Rubicon speech (PW Botha) 55, 97-98
Rumpff, Chief Justice 83

Sachs, Albie 107
Saloojee, Cassim 126
Savimbi, Jonas 100
Secret Revolution: Memoirs of a Spy Boss xi, 18, 31, 92, 102
Seipei, Stompie 22, 150, 171
Separate Amenities Act 154, 229
Setsetse, Paul 8
Sharpeville massacre 76
Shultz, George 97
Simons, Anthony 242-243
Simons, Jack 107
Simpson, Thula 138, 179-180, 182, 188
Sisulu, Albertina 126, 141, 143, 146, 152, 172
Sisulu, Walter xi, 34, 41, 48, 50, 53, 89, 99, 101-102, 122-123, 126, 133-134, 137-138, 140-142, 144, 146, 152, 172, 174, 185, 207, 212, 224, 246-247, 249, 252, 262, 270
Sithole, Clayton (Twala) 238, 241
Skweyiya, Zola 107
Slabbert, Frederik van Zyl 25
Slovo, Joe 221
Smit, Basie 167, 187
Soal, Peter 164
South 191-192, 195-196, 240
South African Communist Party (SACP) 63, 73, 84, 89, 91, 93-94, 103, 107-108, 113, 137, 140, 144, 152, 194, 204-205, 208-211 216, 221-222, 228, 231, 234
South African Council of Churches 148, 161, 218
South African Youth Congress (SAYCO) 171
Statement on the Question of Negotiations (ANC NEC) 107-108
State of Emergency 15, 55, 78, 90 101, 108, 111, 160, 170, 197, 204-206, 208-209, 211, 215, 222, 228, 232, 234, 242-243, 246, 255, 261

State Security Council 10, 18, 26, 46-48, 50-51, 53, 99
Stengel, Richard 18-19, 41, 269
Steyn, M.T. 15, 100
Stock, Dr 242
Strijdom, J.G. 38
Sunday Star 150
Suzman, Helen 25, 37, 41, 44
Swart, C.R. 9-10
Swart, Jack 32, 91, 257-261

Tambo, Oliver 38, 56, 58, 63, 73-75, 83, 89-90, 97, 107, 109-110, 138, 165-166, 178-179, 183, 185, 214, 237, 248, 267, 271
Terre'Blanche, Eugène 148
Thatcher, Margaret xii, 36, 133, 135, 159, 226
The Guardian 9, 122, 215, 218
The Independent 12
The Last Trek: A New Beginning xi, 15, 122, 157, 159, 220, 271
The Mandela Document 194-196, 268
The Telegraph 9, 12-13
Three Ministers Committee 209
Time Magazine 171
Transvaal Indian Congress 126
Treason Trial 76
Truth and Reconciliation Commission (TRC) 22
Tshwete, Steve 109
Tucker, Raymond 116
Tutu, Desmond 38, 84, 116, 128, 148, 239, 253, 261

Umkhonto we Sizwe (MK) 11, 31, 138-139, 179-183, 197, 199, 210-211, 221, 243-244
United Democratic Front (UDF) 35, 38, 76, 97, 126, 146, 161, 162, 206, 214-215, 225, 231, 238-239, 245, 247-249, 252, 257
United Nations High Commissioner for Refugees (UNHCR) 181

Van den Heever, Mr 244
Van der Merwe, Johan 167, 187
Van der Merwe, S.S. (Fanie) 51, 53, 54, 89, 238
Van der Merwe, Tiaan 41, 45
Van der Walt, Piet 104
Van der Walt, Tjaart 76
Van Niekerk, Pets 221
Van Schalkwyk, Marthinus 8
Van Sittert, Major 51, 64
Verwoerd, H.F. 38
Viljoen, Gerrit 47, 120, 123-124, 126, 135, 158, 188-190, 197, 209, 212, 225-226, 239, 245-248, 255, 270
Vlok, Adriaan 187

Waldmeir, Patti 24, 26
Washington Post 112, 138, 191
Washington Times 135
Weekly Mail 142
WikiLeaks 214
Willemse, Willie xiv, 57, 79, 88, 97, 114-115, 123-125, 129, 134-135, 139, 145-151, 154, 158, 161, 188, 252-253, 257, 260

Xaba, Anthony 157

About the authors

RIAAN DE VILLIERS is a former journalist turned editor and contract publisher. In previous years he worked for *Die Burger*, the *Rand Daily Mail*, the *Cape Times*, *Die Suid-Afrikaan*, and *Leadership Magazine*. He holds an honours degree in political philosophy from Stellenbosch University. After many years spent in Johannesburg, he now lives in Cape Town.

JAN-AD STEMMET is a senior lecturer in history at the University of the Free State. He holds a PhD from the same university. Stemmet is the author of two books, namely *'n Lewe van Sy Eie: Die Biografie van Die Volksblad* (2004) and *On Wings of Wisdom*, a history of Jamie Uys, Boet Troskie and Mimosa Films International (2011), and has also published widely in accredited academic journals. He has conducted extensive research on the last phases of the National Party government and the transition to an inclusive democracy. He is married to Karlien, an economist. They live in Bloemfontein.

Kantoor van die Staatspresident
State President's Office

STAATSPRESIDENTSMINUUT NO:

Kragtens die bevoegdheid my verleen by artikel 69(1) van die Wet op Gevangenisse, 1959 (Wet no 8 van 1959) soos gewysig keur ek goed dat spesiale afslag van vonnis aan die ondergenoemde gevangene toegestaan word en dat hy op 11 Februarie 1990 vrygelaat is nadat ingevolge artikel 69(2) van genoemde Wet gehandel is:

NELSON ROLIHLAHLA MANDELA

STAATSPRESIDENT

Datum:

H.J. COETSEE

MINISTER VAN DIE KABINET

19.1025.DK

Note: Approval of 'special remission' of sentence of 'undermentioned prisoner' Nelson Rolihlahla Mandela, awaiting signature by the State President. Stamped by Minister H.J. (Kobie) Coetsee. Source: Coetsee Collection, ARCA.